T0205411

Advances in Information Security

Volume 84

Series editor
Sushil Jajodia, George Mason University, Fairfax, VA, USA

The purpose of the *Advances in Information Security* book series is to establish the state of the art and set the course for future research in information security. The scope of this series includes not only all aspects of computer, network security, and cryptography, but related areas, such as fault tolerance and software assurance. The series serves as a central source of reference for information security research and developments. The series aims to publish thorough and cohesive overviews on specific topics in Information Security, as well as works that are larger in scope than survey articles and that will contain more detailed background information. The series also provides a single point of coverage of advanced and timely topics and a forum for topics that may not have reached a level of maturity to warrant a comprehensive textbook.

More information about this series at http://www.springer.com/series/5576

Roberto Di Pietro • Simone Raponi
Maurantonio Caprolu • Stefano Cresci

New Dimensions of Information Warfare

 Springer

Roberto Di Pietro
Hamad Bin Khalifa University
College of Science & Engineering
Education City
Doha, Qatar

Simone Raponi
Hamad Bin Khalifa University
College of Science & Engineering
Education City
Doha, Qatar

Maurantonio Caprolu
Hamad Bin Khalifa University
College of Science & Engineering
Education City
Doha, Qatar

Stefano Cresci
National Research Council
Institute of Informatics and Telematics
Pisa, Italy

ISSN 1568-2633   ISSN 2512-2193   (electronic)
Advances in Information Security
ISBN 978-3-030-60620-6   ISBN 978-3-030-60618-3   (eBook)
https://doi.org/10.1007/978-3-030-60618-3

This Springer imprint is published by the registered company Springer Nature Switzerland AG
The registered company address is: Gewerbestrasse 11, 6330 Cham, Switzerland

Foreword

It would be difficult to imagine our daily life, our production systems and, in general, our society without the technology solutions we are immersed in and surrounded by. However, technology, and in particular information technology, is a double-edged sword.

The capillary diffusion and reach of social networks enable us to communicate our ideas to the world, but they could easily be used to spread fake news; the adoption of digitized industrial control systems is rewarded with a boost in cost reduction, efficiency and performance, but those very same controls can also make the controlled systems much more fragile; the advent of novel digital financial instruments and tools, from high-frequency trading to cryptocurrencies, do multiply the possibility to trade and to access financial instruments, but they also pose a threat, for the policy makers, to the control of the financial leverage; technologies that have been developed for entertainment, such as drones, have expanded to a number of no-one-envisioned-before applications and jobs, but they also enabled the possibility of physical attacks through the very same media.

Technology has drastically reduced the distance between ideas and implementation, projects, and outcomes. This is just a logical consequence of what technology is: a magnifier of our capabilities. Nowadays, a 240-character piece of news, conveyed to hundreds of millions, could sink the NYSE or skyrocket the price of a share. An induced malicious glitch in a water-desalinization or oil-extraction pressure controller could induce the outage of critical infrastructure and spur, according to the allegedly attribution, geo-political tensions in vast regions of the world. Similarly, the use of a social network by billions of young people can slowly induce, by subtle AI algorithms, new life models and different values to new generations—potentially creating domestic turmoil of an unprecedented magnitude.

As a result, the technology transformed the society so in-depth and so quickly that almost all the essential functions and services of a Nation have been digitalized; this is why even the decision on the very same adoption of an apparently neutral technology, such as the 5G, or which data can be exploited by a social network company, could lie with the Department of State as a national security matter rather than with a technical, bureaucratic desk. This means every nation needs to set appropriate cyber defenses in terms of sociological, legal, organizational, and technical issues to cope with the complexity and threats induced by the cited technology waves that could harm the very pillars of our democracies, putting at stake even the values of our new generations. While initially lagging behind these threats, States and Supranational Organizations have started to respond. For instance, at the EU level the Network and Information Security (NIS) directive and the "Cybersecurity act" are being implemented. In the USA, each government organization is involved on a daily basis to implement its own piece of a multidimensional Cybersecurity Strategy regularly revised by the White House to take both latest technology development and its social–economic implications into account. In Italy, the Parliament has recently passed a law: "National Security Perimeter for Cyber", whose mission is twofold: (1) to create a more resilient Country by reinforcing security measures for essential functions and services of the State through a complex techno-legal organization and (2) to foster a strategic plan to achieve an intended degree of digital sovereignty.

As a consequence of the previous arguments, it is true more than ever that "Information (and the technology used to manage it) is power". It is no surprise, therefore, that Information Warfare—roughly, the manipulation of information trusted by a target without the target's awareness—is a topic that cannot be anymore restricted to the battlefield. The one who is able to control or influence information within a given ecosystem (ranging from your ring of friends to industry, finance, and politics, to cite a few) can exercise a form of control over that ecosystem.

The above scenarios and considerations do pave the way to a number of fundamental questions, such as: What are the novel boundaries of Information Warfare? What technologies are today critical to that respect? To which extent the very fabric of our society, economics and critical infrastructures can be affected by Information Warfare?

All the above-introduced questions do require urgent attention and, especially, a framework that sets the tone of the discussion, highlights the assets at stakes, and suggests the objectives to be achieved. That is why I found this book a gripping read. It introduces a novel vision on Information Warfare, addressing relevant dimensions of Information Warfare so far overlooked, puts them in context, highlights the main strategical and tactical assets, and provides the tools for an educated discussion on the topic. The cited key features, combined with the clear exposition, the pleasant style, the comprehensive references and the links to real-world cases, do make this book a reference for technologists, decision-makers, practitioners, academicians and insiders. But what is more, this book also provides food for thought for all the ones who are aware that information technology and its nemesis, Information Warfare, are playing a vital role in the evolution and shaping of our Society. A Society that is in dire needs to elaborate a strategic reflection on the novel dimensions and threats posed by Information Warfare.

Deputy Director General   Prof. Roberto Baldoni*
Department of Information for Security
Presidency of Ministry Council of Italy
Rome, Italy
August 27, 2020

---

*Roberto Baldoni is currently on leave from the Sapienza University of Rome, where he is a full professor of computer science. As DIS Deputy DG, Baldoni chairs the Italian Cybersecurity Management Board (Nucleo Sicurezza Cibernetica—NSC), an inter-ministerial organization established at DIS via executive decree (DPCM 2/2017). NSC implements and oversees the prevention and management of nationwide cyber crises coordinating National CSIRT, Postal Police (Ministry of the Interior), the Inter-Force Cyber Command (Ministry of Defense) and the intelligence agencies. NSC is also responsible for national cybersecurity policy positions in international forums and for fostering cybersecurity cooperation between government, research and industry. Roberto Baldoni led the working group designing the Decree Law 105/2019 "National security perimeter for cyber", and in 2020, he is acting, on behalf of the Inter-ministerial Committee for Security of the Italian Republic (CISR), as roll-out coordinator for the Legislative Decree 105/2019.

Contents

List of Figures

List of Tables

Chapter 1
New Dimensions of Information Warfare

Since the dawn of humanity, the progress machine tirelessly introduced tools and resources that facilitated our everyday tasks. Over the years, new technologies have continually changed society with novel discoveries and inventions that proved capable of greatly improving human life. Historically, many of the processes that radically changed human lifestyle occurred gradually. However, in the past few decades, modern technology has enabled a fast and radical change of our society, modifying our habits, production means, and in some cases the very essence of work, through the widespread adoption of a plethora of new devices comprising smartphones, voice assistants, chatbots, and smartwatches that made our lives faster, easier, and funnier. Technology is also introducing new habits and addictions, changing every aspect of our society such as personal interactions, education, communication, financial services, physical goods production, logistics, and entertainment. This is happening in parallel with a wild race to the digitization of information.

Nowadays, an increasingly large share of our daily activities are performed with the help of digital devices, offering us a huge number of different Web-based services through which we manage every aspect of our lives. These services help us to learn, have fun, fulfill our work-related tasks, pay bills and manage our bank accounts, communicate with distant friends and meet with new ones, handle personal agenda, and buy items and services. On the one hand, such technologies guarantee access to a boundless range of services and information, to anyone and at any time. On the other hand, they allow service providers to access an equally boundless quantity of personal information, which are often harvested (and employed) without user awareness, let alone its consent. For instance, think of the rise of Online Social Networks: it has led to a new information ecosystem that prefers speed and immediacy to accuracy, trustworthiness, and reliability. As Meglena Kuneva brilliantly foresaw in a famous keynote speech at the European Commission in 2009—"Personal data is the new oil of the Internet and the new currency of the digital world"—we live in an era where wealth is directly linked

R. Di Pietro et al., *New Dimensions of Information Warfare*, Advances in
Information Security 84, https://doi.org/10.1007/978-3-030-60618-3_1

to the available information [1]. Within this context, Online Social Networks represent the new gold mines. Gold mines in which every technologically savvy actor can freely dig its nuggets. Digital breadcrumbs left by our daily activities thus represent a tempting opportunity for different actors—such as governments, advertising companies, state-backed organizations, hackers—opening up scenarios that would have been simply unimaginable, just a few years ago.

Online information is not only valuable per se, but it can also be used to influence other aspects of our modern societies. In fact, the ever-increasing convergence between the cyber and physical worlds is making more and more difficult to disentangle the critical systems that make up our societies. As a consequence, a single carefully crafted and perfectly timed piece of (dis)information can now potentially make or break elections, governments, economies, and infrastructures, thus granting a tremendous leverage in the hands of those who know how to weaponize and manipulate these critical systems. As a ubiquitous and striking example of this kind, think of FinTech, a growing field where finance and technology are now completely intertwined. Within this context, the interplay between Automatic Trading systems and the online chatter that feeds them for driving market decisions exposes such systems to a plethora of manipulative activities. Information reliance is also critical to business entities and industries, a problem exacerbated by the increasing adoption of outsourced ICT infrastructure (think of the cloud), with resulting increased security risks. The increased automation of information-driven modern industrial plants also exposes them to unprecedented risks. When the businesses or infrastructures at risk are those that are of critical importance for a nation—such as those responsible for telecommunications, logistics, or directly supporting military capabilities—the risks practically extend to whole countries.

The frantic technological advancement previously outlined radically changed information warfare scenarios, posing new threats, ranging from personal to national security that every actor should take into consideration [2]. Classic books on information warfare usually deal with the subject by categorizing the treated arguments based on the "warfare capabilities and directions" of the most powerful nations (e.g., the United States, Russia, China, and others) or based on the pillars of information warfare: Psychological Operations (PSYOPS), military deception, electronic warfare, physical destruction, and Operational security (OPSEC). Unlike these traditional approaches, in this book, we will discuss new threats opened up by the latest technological advancements that have never been addressed before—at least, in the dimensions we categorize them. In particular, we partition the discussion on the new dimensions of information warfare into three macro areas: Society, Economy, and Infrastructures. For each area domain, the relevant threats are contextualized with real case scenarios and explained in detail; we also provide, for each domain, insights in terms of possible future attacks and countermeasures; and, finally, for every scenario, we also highlight the related open issues.

In conclusion, we show that the genie is out of the lamp and that the ones that will tame it would likely have a strategic advantage—our aim with this book having been to provide some food for thought to enable reaching the latter objective.

1.1 Organization

1.1.1 Book Structure

The topics covered in this book are discussed following a vertical, top-down approach where we first introduce the background and the general layout of a topic, before delving into the detailed description of its characteristics. With the exception of this chapter—discussing the landscape of the new dimensions in information warfare (NDIW)—this book is organized into three parts. These parts provide the coarsest viewpoint on information warfare. In particular, they represent the pillars of a nation and the possible macro-targets for the cyberwarfare, namely, Society (Part I), Economy (Part II), and Infrastructures (Part III). Parts are organized in chapters that list and discuss different information warfare scenarios. At the finest grain, each scenario describes current and future security threats, surveys existing scientific literature on the topic, documents notable attacks, provides a list of known countermeasures, and concludes by analyzing open issues as well as proposing directions for future research, experimentation, and intervention.

1.1.2 Infoboxes

Throughout the book, two different types of *infoboxes* are used in order to highlight specific pieces of additional information that readers might be interested in. Definitions of important concepts and keywords are contained in *definition* infoboxes, as shown below.

Definitions

Information Warfare The manipulation of information trusted by a target without the target's awareness, so that the target will make decisions against their interest but in the interest of the one conducting information warfare. It involves the collection of tactical information, assurance that one's own information is valid, spreading of propaganda or disinformation to mislead the enemy and the public, undermining the quality of the opposing force's information and denial of information to opposing forces.

In addition, whenever useful resources are available, they are listed and briefly described in *resources* infoboxes. Useful resources include public, curated datasets and knowledge bases; Web portals that contain extensive detailed information on a topic; pieces of software such as packages and libraries that can be used for carrying out specific analyses; as well as full-fledged applications.

> 🖿 **Resources**
> Springer's page on *Security and Cryptology* includes links to several titles that discuss topics strictly related to information warfare.[1]

---

[1]https://www.springer.com/gp/computer-science/security-cryptology.

Part I
Society

Since the last 30 years, humanity has been witnessing an incessant global metamorphosis of society. The development and the widespread diffusion of new, faster, more powerful communication technologies—such as social media—have brought profound changes to multiple aspects of social, economic, political, and cultural life, completely redefining the concepts of time, space, and identity. We are living in an era where much of the information and knowledge of humankind can be digitally reproduced in the form of text, image, music, or video. This progress, both in the technological and in the communication sphere, is radically changing the way of living, working, as well as producing and distributing goods and services.

Besides influencing interactions among people, this information society is forcing traditional organizational structures to become more participatory and decentralized. The opportunity to timely access information eventually translated into the simplification of many organizations' processes, thus leading to an increase in both their efficiency and the overall productivity. Contemporary society is characterized by a high dynamism that places information in a central position, making it a strategic resource that can heavily affect the systems' efficiency, thus becoming a determining factor of social and economic development, growth, and cultural wealth.[1]

---

[1] http://www.treccani.it/enciclopedia/societa-dell-informazione_%28Enciclopedia-della-Scienza-e-della-Tecnica%29/ (Last checked August 2020).

✐ **Definitions**

Information Society Society in which the creation, distribution, and manipulation of information has become the most significant economic and cultural activity.[2]

Information can be seen as a new necessary capital, a valuable exchange commodity that can be accumulated—to enjoy more knowledge to be exploited, denied—to monopolize the information channels, or even imposed—to manipulate public opinion, thus becoming a new, powerful form of power.

---

[2]https://whatis.techtarget.com/definition/Information-Society (Last checked August 2020).

Chapter 2
Information Disorder

The rise of new technologies, including Online Social Network (OSN)s, media sharing services, online discussion boards, and online instant messaging applications, make information production and propagation increasingly fast. The number of Internet users, as well as the amount of available information, is continuously growing at an unprecedented pace. In 2014, 3079 billion Internet users were populating the Web. This number grew in the following years, reaching 4157 billion Internet users in December 2017, an outstanding increase of 35% in 3 years, up to 4648 billion Internet users in June 2020. The number of users populating the Web over the years is depicted in Fig. 2.1. Accordingly, user-generated content created and shared by Web users grew proportionally. To give some figures for this massive phenomenon, the indexed Web nowadays contains more than 4.45 billion pages, representing only the tip of the iceberg. The *deep Web*, also called the hidden or invisible Web, represents the part of the World Wide Web whose contents are not indexed by common Web search engines and is estimated to be 500× the size of the indexed Web, also known as *surface Web*.

People surfing the Web have an almost infinite amount of information at their fingertips. Some of this information is truthful; others are not. As a direct consequence, the ideas of individuals are no longer built autonomously (i.e., based on facts they know or elaborate on), but they are increasingly based on hundreds of thousands of opinions read on the Web, of which only a negligible part appears to be authoritative. With these assumptions, shifting the attention of the masses and changing the opinions of people is a breeze—in the former case to make events of national importance go unnoticed and in the latter one to set the agenda.

© The Author(s), under exclusive license to
Springer Nature Switzerland AG 2021
R. Di Pietro et al., *New Dimensions of Information Warfare*, Advances in
Information Security 84, https://doi.org/10.1007/978-3-030-60618-3_2

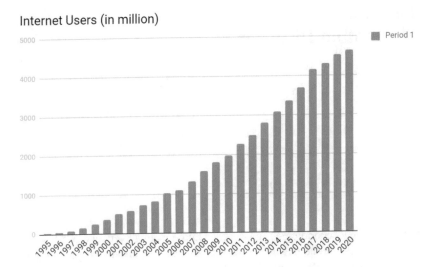

Internet Users (in million)

Fig. 2.1 Users populating the Web over the years

✂ Definitions

Misinformation Misinformation is defined as incorrect or misleading information. Regardless of any intention, misinformation is inaccurate, or incorrect information that causes people to be misinformed.

Disinformation A subset of misinformation, it is defined as false information *deliberately* and *intentionally* spread to influence public opinion or mislead the truth.

Misinformation (or worse, disinformation) grows in step with information, making it difficult to distinguish authoritative information from misleading ones. To make matters worse, people do not use to double-check the content they incur in while surfing the Web, due to either lack of time or will, and sometimes they share it without having even read or understood it, participating in an unintended spread of unauthoritative information that uncontrollably spread through the Web. Furthermore, technology is automatically separating users from the information they disagree with, virtually isolating each user in its ideological and cultural bubble.

✏ Definitions

Filter Bubble Tendency of social networks and recommendation algorithms to lock users into personalized feedback loops, each with its news sources, cultural touchstones, and political inclinations [3].

Confirmation Bias A pervasive cognitive bias resulting in the human tendency to search for, favor, and recall information that supports (or confirms) one's prior personal values or beliefs.

Homophily Tendency to form strong social connections (or to be attracted) to people with similar characteristics (e.g., ethnicity, gender, age, political leaning).

Echo Chamber Situation in which beliefs are reinforced (or amplified) by communication and repetition inside a closed system, while alternative ideas are not considered.

Polarization Sharp division into contrasting groups or sets of beliefs.

While surfing the Web, users are overwhelmed by waves of personalized content that has been artfully crafted based on their interests, their location, and their browsing history. This phenomenon tends to lower the critical spirit of individuals, placing them in front of a vision of a personalized world, absolutely not in conformity with reality. It is scientifically proven that the exposition to already known facts (or to facts people are already convinced of) exposes them to less cognitive effort if compared with the one generated when something new should be figured out. This tendency is known to the public as *confirmation bias*. Moreover, the homophily tendency explains how users are more likely to socially connect to people with similar thoughts and characteristics. With such a Web organization, people that share the same thoughts/tastes are grouped and are never exposed to ideas and contents of people who think differently from them. Similar people are closer and closer, while the "different" ones are virtually moved further and further away. This means that on every topic, instead of having confrontations with people who have different opinions, several communities with a few intersection points are formed, as if they were different clusters, i.e., the polarization concept.

In this chapter, we will first introduce the building blocks of this new social media ecosystem, analyzing what changes they are bringing to the current ecosystem. Then, two original scenarios are taken into account to describe how information warfare could pose a threat to the fabric of society of a country. Scenarios include running disinformation campaigns to cause unrest and discredit either people or governments and piloting the elections in democratic states. Finally, we report current open issues and we propose some innovative countermeasures.

2.1 The New Social Ecosystem

The latest Web technologies, including OSNs, social media, and discussion forums, are eventually leading to a process of democratization of information. News, information, and statements that years ago could only be produced by a few authoritative sources can be nowadays produced by literally everyone, without any control or restriction. Indeed, while in the past sending a message to the mass was a pretty troublesome business, nowadays there is no need to go through authoritative sources: posting a tweet would be enough to climb over them. The producers of information themselves, publicly deprived of the role of information gatekeepers, are forced to compete against every individual to obtain public attention. If on the one hand, this *disintermediation* is allowing everyone to participate in public debates and have their voice heard, on the other hand, it is bringing to a steep decrease in both the quality and the truthfulness of the information itself.

Although these episodes have always occurred throughout history, the dynamics are drastically changing. Indeed, while in the past this phenomenon could be easily dammed to prevent it from spreading, nowadays the technological catalyst is allowing it to spread on a large scale, without dams that hold. As a consequence, different entities are emerging, intending to exploit this amplified sounding board with malicious purposes. Among the most important actors, we can surely find social bots, cyborgs, trolls, spammers, and sockpuppets.

✔ Definitions

Social Bot Social bots are fully or partially automated accounts (i.e., pieces of software) that often act like humans on social media. Because of their automation, they are able to create content, share content, and interact with the other registered users [4].

Troll A troll is a human-operated account who creates and shares offensive, provocative, or inconsistent posts and comments online.

Cyborg A cyborg is defined as an account that is either a human-assisted bot or a bot-assisted human, inheriting characteristics from both.

Spammer A spammer is a person (or an organization) that sends (or spams, in the jargon) irrelevant and unwanted messages indiscriminately to a plethora of users over the Internet.

Sockpuppet A sockpuppet is a fake person employed to interact with other people, particularly in online discussions or blog comments sections.

When a social bot is used for political reasons (e.g., to artificially inflate the number of the followers of politicians or the popularity of a political post, to spread propaganda, to subtly but effectively influence people's political opinions, to target political opponents with a flood of enraged tweets), they are called political bots [5]. One significant difference between political bots and humans regards the pace of publication on social media. Indeed, even if compared with the most boisterous activists, bots do not need to sleep and have, as the sole purpose of life, the one assigned by the programmer. This makes a political bot an impressive tool when it comes to shaping public opinion , given its omnipresence in every targeted political post. The employment of political bots can be found in almost every recent political election worldwide [4], in many cases to advertise and give parties a more sonorous voice and, in others, to spread fake news about the opponent and attempt to radically change the opinion of voters.

Cyborgs fall exactly in the middle between humans and bots and are becoming increasingly present in OSNs such as Twitter and Facebook [6, 7]. Examples of cyborgs are accounts that, by exploiting RSS feeds or widgets, automatically post content on behalf of the user. When the content published is inflammatory, provocative, or offensive, these actors take the name of trolls. The reasons behind the behavior of trolls are manifold: to get attention, to start discussions, to distract from legitimate discourses, and to create unnecessary arguments, all of the reasons eventually leading to either the troll's amusement or to specific gains.[1] The online trolling phenomenon, already critical on its own, is lately getting enormous attention because of the alarming consequences it provokes. Indeed, there are several cases of teenagers who committed suicide after being victim, without any reason, of hate speeches online.

> ✐ **Definitions**
>
> **Hate Speech** A hate speech is defined as a violent and abusive speech intended to offend, insult, or intimidate an individual because of some traits, such as religion, race, origin, disability, or sexual orientation.

Other actors, in turn, have the role of spreading messages indiscriminately to the Web (i.e., spamming), with the aim of advertising products or spread malware [8]. The messages sent by spammers, often enclosed within emails, have different purposes, including the advertisement of a person/product/organization (i.e., unsolicited commercial email). The writer George Orwell in his masterpiece "1984" defined the term "spam" as "pink meat pieces," giving this word the meaning "something disgusting but inevitable."

Furthermore, the Web is becoming increasingly populated by fake profiles whose purpose is to create disagreements and, in general, to provoke chaos. Sockpuppets and meat puppets are proud representatives of this category of attackers. The term sockpuppet comes as a reference to the manipulation of a hand puppet made from a

---

[1] https://techterms.com/definition/troll (Last checked August 2020).

sock, and it was originally coined to refer to the false identities assumed by Internet users who pretend to be someone else. Nowadays, sockpuppets are employed for a variety of shady reasons, including (1) honoring, defending, supporting, attacking, insulting either people or organizations on the Web; (2) manipulating the public opinion,[2] and (3) circumventing bans/suspensions from websites.[3] A meat puppet, in turn, by pretending to have experience with the subjects discussed on the Web, can direct conversations and manipulate the public opinion.[4] Meat puppets have been defined as "guns for hire able to be marshaled at a moment's notice," and the transition from sockpuppets to meat puppets has been described as the elevation from subscribers with few fake personas to the business of invoking hundreds of automated fake followers at will [9].

Besides creating chaos and affecting online discussions, these entities are also employed to start targeted campaigns. Astroturfing campaigns allow increasing the credibility of statements and organizations without revealing the (id)entity of the supporters.[5] Political astroturfing refers to either politically motivated individuals or micro-blogging platforms that make use of centrally controlled accounts (i.e., bots, trolls, or sockpuppets) to create the impression of widespread grassroots support for a candidate or opinion and to create widespread negativity for opposing opinions. When taken to the extreme, this mechanism allows to exaggerate the success and deny the failures of individuals or governments, or even worse, to portrait opponents or critics as "traitors" or national security risks[6] [10].

> ✐ **Definitions**
>
> **Astroturfing** Astroturfing refers to the action of creating impressions of widespread support for a policy, individual, or product, where a little or (most of the time) none of such support really exists.

These actors, as soon as they find breeding ground (i.e., users that do not use to double-check content and tend to trust every information they find on the Web) can become extremely powerful tools to change the public opinion and to opportunely manipulate the thoughts of individuals. Unfortunately, the information they trust could belong to the sizeable fake news set.

---

[2]https://guardianlv.com/2013/11/china-uses-an-army-of-sockpuppets-to-control-public-opinion-and-the-us-will-too/ (Last checked August 2020).

[3]https://en.wikipedia.org/wiki/Sockpuppet(Internet) (Last checked August 2020).

[4]https://www.yourdictionary.com/meat-puppet (Last checked August 2020).

[5]https://en.wikipedia.org/wiki/Astroturfing (Last checked August 2020).

[6]https://www.thefridaytimes.com/political-astroturf/ (Last checked August 2020).

> ✐ **Definitions**
>
> **Fake News** Fake news is an ambiguous and informal umbrella term including hoaxes or disinformation purposely distributed via either traditional news media or online social media. It is used in scientific literature increasingly sporadically, in favor of more rigorous terms such as mis-/disinformation, rumors, etc.
>
> **Hoax** A hoax is defined as a falsehood artfully fabricated to conceal the truth.
>
> **Rumor** A rumor is an unverified opinion, or a talk, that has been widely disseminated without a discernible source.
>
> **Propaganda** Expression of opinion or action by individuals or groups deliberately designed to influence the opinions or actions of other individuals or groups with reference to predetermined ends [11].

Although hoaxes, rumors, and disinformation have always been around, the sounding board has never been so loud. Indeed, online social media and Web services are contributing to creating an ideal habitat for the ruthless sharing of information, allowing an immediate spread in every corner of the Web. There are different reasons behind the draft and the distribution of fake news, hoaxes, and rumors. Besides trying to convince citizens of the news itself, they may be used to manipulate the public opinion and, for example, to induce people to question democracies, states, or those entities in which we place our trust that are at the basis of the functioning of a state, thus increasing the fragmentation and the polarization.

For the sake of simplicity, in the rest of the book, the umbrella term "low-quality information" will refer to mis-/disinformation, hoaxes, and rumors, while every adversary will be called "malicious account," indistinctly.

2.2 Scenario 1: Freedom of Information

This scenario takes into account a state that does not make use of censorship techniques to silence the citizens. People are allowed to publicly express their opinion, in traditional ways as well as with modern means, such as OSNs, blogs, and online discussion forums.

The social platforms do not rely on traffic filtering techniques that are usually applied to deny access to specific websites. Users are allowed to freely adopt any communication service, such as real-time messaging applications and mail services. Moreover, the government has no control over the content of the transmitted and received information, thus allowing users to express their opinion without being incurred in fines or punishments.

In this scenario, that can be applied without loss of generality to all, and not only the western democratic countries, but citizens are free to express both their thoughts and their opinion about any topic, whatever they are. The information spreading through social media can be of any kind: true or false, trusted or not trusted, accurate or inaccurate.

2.2.1 Threat: Disinformation Campaign

One of the first documented examples of alleged low-quality information takes us to Ancient Rome in July 64 B.C. The emperor Nero set fire to an entire district of the city to make room for new buildings, accusing the Christian community of the crime. He artfully created a piece of low-quality information to not turn the public opinion against himself and to continue his persecution campaign against the Christian community. Going forward over the years, several other famous examples can be found. In 1933, the palace of the Reichstag—the seat of the German parliament—was set on fire. The leaders of the Nazi party took advantage of this opportunity to blame the opponents of the Communist party, gaining consensus that led to their final rise to power. These two cases make it clear that the invention of news and the alteration of them make it possible to maneuver public opinion and, consequently, to obtain illicit advantages out of it.

Nowadays the same principle still applies, with social media creating a sounding board that has never been so wide and loud. According to a famous study from researchers at Ohio State University, fake news probably played a significant role in depressing Hillary Clinton's support on United States' Election Day. This study, which provides a look at how fake news may have affected voter choices, suggests that about 4% of President Barack Obama's 2012 supporters were dissuaded from voting for Clinton in 2016 because of fake news stories[7] [12]. This problem was already clear some years ago when the World Economic Forum listed "the rapid spread of misinformation online" as one of its top ten problems facing the world.[8] Some years later, in 2016 and 2017, the Oxford dictionary elected "post-truth" as the word of the year, and Collins Dictionary did the same for "fake news," respectively [13].

The lack of truthfulness of information makes the recognition of truthful and false content hard for citizens, creating doubts and confusion among the population. Artfully built news is usually mixed with any size fragments of truth over time, escaping the control of the creator, who usually manages to govern the spread only

---

[7] https://www.washingtonpost.com/news/the-fix/wp/2018/04/03/a-new-study-suggests-fake-news-might-have-won-donald-trump-the-2016-election/?noredirect=on&utm_term=.d6e63f61fa06 (Last checked August 2020).

[8] https://reports.weforum.org/outlook-14/top-ten-trends-category-page/10-the-rapid-spread-of-misinformation-online/?doing_wp_cron=1583915074.7138180732727050781250 (Last checked August 2020).

for a short time. Then, this news assumes realistic contours, becoming in effect truthful news (as accepted by all as such), ignoring denials or not granting replication rights. Foreign governments, as well as terrorist groups and activists, may exploit these uncertainties on social media to undertake several kinds of disinformation campaigns, to undermine the credibility of the state, or to control public opinions, with the aim of generating chaos and destabilizing the population. In the course of history, there have been numerous cases in which the use of disinformation campaigns has caused discontent among the population, disagreements, and revolts, giving the history a presumed truth, impossible to ascertain.

2.2.2 Attacks

Throughout history, low-quality information played a determining role in the decision-making process of states and governments. This section analyzes four misinformation campaigns that have had effects on the population first, to then have heavy repercussions on the countries. The campaigns are related to (1) vaccines, (2) immigration, (3) conspiracy theories (e.g., flat earth), and (4) climate change, respectively.

It is worth to notice that several countermeasures from the psychological, social, and cultural viewpoints can be employed to mitigate the aforementioned campaigns (e.g., media literacy [14]), but we consider them out of scope for this book. Instead, technological countermeasures are evaluated in Sect. 2.4.

Vaccine Hesitancy

Even though it is a vaccine-preventable disease, measles kills over 100,000 people every year. Worldwide cases tripled in the first three months of 2019. The causes of these outbreaks are diverse: from health infrastructure to civil strife or vaccine hesitancy. In some countries, vaccine-skepticism and populism are increasing together[9]

Lola García-Ajofrín

Low-quality information has had a huge impact on the health system and, as a consequence, has heavily affected the health-related choices citizens make. According to the World Health Organization, this phenomenon threatens the progress made throughout history in tackling vaccine-preventable disease, enough to be identified as one of the top ten global health threats of 2019.[10]

---

[9]https://outride.rs/en/vaccines-fake-news/ (Last checked August 2020).

[10]https://www.who.int/news-room/feature-stories/ten-threats-to-global-health-in-2019 (Last checked August 2020).

> ✂ **Definitions**
>
> **Vaccine Hesitancy** Also known as anti-vax, it has been defined by the World Health Organization as "the reluctance or refusal to vaccinate despite the availability of vaccines".

To further highlight the benefits of being vaccinated, the US Department of Health and Human Services listed the five main reasons to vaccinate a child: (1) immunizations can save the life, protecting against diseases that vaccines have been eliminating partially or completely, such as polio; (2) safety and effectiveness of vaccines, the benefits of the disease-prevention of vaccines are greater than any possible side effect (redness, pain, or tenderness at the site of injection); (3) immunization protects others, preventing the spread of diseases; (4) immunization can save time and money; and (5) immunization protects future generations.[11] Even just looking at the numbers, vaccination is still one of the most cost-effective ways to avoid diseases, by preventing more than two to three million deaths per year. Furthermore, according to the World Health Organization, a further 1.5 million could be avoided if the global coverage of vaccinations improved.[12]

However, despite the obvious benefits and negligible consequences, whole communities are arising to protest against the immunization and to try to prevent people from doing it. There are several reasons behind the anti-vaccinationists' choice, ranging from conspiracy theories to concerns about safety. In the following, the main myths are reported.[13]

Autism Doubts about a possible relationship between autism and vaccines started as a result of the publication of a scientific paper by Andrew Wakefield, dated back 1998, defined in [15] as "the most damaging medical hoax of the last 100 years." Indeed, the scientific community, after extensive investigations, proved this theory to be false, not having found any relationship or causal mechanism between vaccines and the incidence of autism. However, the anti-vaccination activists continue promoting myths and conspiracy theories about the risk of autism, with misinformation acting as the glue between the two.

Vaccine Overload Vaccine overload, i.e., the theory that inoculating a large number of vaccines could negatively impact (e.g., damage or weaken) the immune system of children, is another myth embraced by anti-vaccination activists. According to several scientific studies, this belief is not based on solid foundations. Indeed, the improvements in the design of the vaccines of the last years have strongly

---

[11] https://www.vaccines.gov/getting/for_parents/five_reasons (Last checked August 2020).

[12] https://www.who.int/news-room/facts-in-pictures/detail/immunization (Last checked August 2020).

[13] https://en.wikipedia.org/wiki/Vaccine_hesitancy (Last checked August 2020).

reduced their immunologic load. Despite this factual evidence, vaccine overload remains one of the crucial points on which anti-vaccinationists base their campaign.

Ingredient Concerns   In 2005, Rolling Stone and Salon magazines co-published an article by Robert F. Kennedy Jr., an environmental lawyer nephew of former President John F. Kennedy, alleging a government conspiracy. According to the article, the government was trying to cover up evidence that thiomersal, or specifically, the mercury contained in thiomersal, may cause brain problems, including autism. Thiomersal is an antifungal component used in some vaccines to prevent their contamination. Endless scientific evidence excludes the fact, showing that there are no common clinical symptoms and that the phenomena are definitely uncorrelated. Another ingredient that has been considered dangerous by vaccine-hesitant people is the aluminum, used as immunologic adjuvants in many vaccines. Even in this case, several scientific studies revealed that there is no evidence of serious health risks or changes to immune systems.

Sudden Infant Death Syndrome   Sudden infant death syndrome (SIDS) is the sudden and unexplained death of a child during the first year of age. Unfortunately, such a syndrome leaves no traces, thus making autopsies fruitless. This led the anti-vax activists to think that vaccination might be a determining cause. In 1999, the ABC news program 20/20 broadcasted a story claiming that a vaccine (specifically, the hepatitis B one) was one of the causes of SIDS. The story was enriched with a picture of a 1-month-old girl who experienced SIDS only 16 h after receiving the second dose of hepatitis B vaccine. However, not only did several studies find no evidence of correlation, but also they found evidence that vaccination may protect children against SIDS.

Muslims   After several deaths among vaccinated workers, some militant groups and Islamists started seeing vaccination as a plot to either kill or sterilize Muslims. In 2003, Imams in Nigeria (i.e., Muslim leaders who lead prayers in Mosques) warned their followers and advised them not to proceed with the vaccination against polio for their children, perceived to be a plot to decrease Muslim fertility. This initiative caused a steep increase in polio cases both in Nigeria and in the neighboring countries that, in turn, stopped immunizing their children even against other diseases. As a consequence, in 2005, Nigeria reported over 20,000 cases of measles, counting 600 deaths, and in 2006 accounted for over half of all new polio cases worldwide.

Other   Other myths include the following: (1) vaccination during illness, many parents are worried about vaccinating their children if they are sick; (2) natural infection, people think that natural infection will provide their children with better immune protection against future illnesses compared to vaccination; (3) vaccine schedule, people do not agree with the schedule recommended by the Advisory Committee on Immunization Practices (ACIP) that is built to protect children when they are most vulnerable. Unfortunately, a delay in vaccinating the children will uselessly expose them to illnesses.

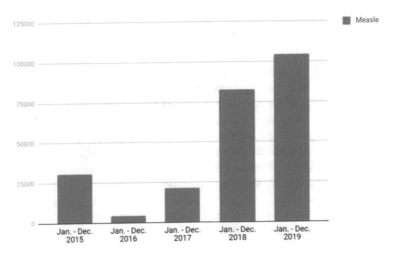

Fig. 2.2 A 5-year summary of the epidemiological data on measles disease in the European region

These myths, fueled by misinformation found on the Web and on social media, led several parents to delay (or worse, to not require) the vaccination for their children. Clearly, this behavior had several consequences. To make an example, the World Health Organization no longer considers measles to be eradicated in the United Kingdom, as well as in the Czech Republic, Greece, and Albania. Measles is a highly contagious and potentially deadly disease caused by the measles virus. Measles killed approximately 2.6 million people per year until 1963, when the first measles vaccine was introduced. From that moment on, the number of measles cases steadily declined, leading to 21 million lives saved until the end of the century. However, the widespread anxieties about vaccine safety led to a dangerous return of the disease. Only taking into account Europe, there were 4240 cases of measles in 2016, 21,315 in 2017, and 82,596 in 2018. Things got worse in 2019 where 104,248 measles cases have been identified. Figure 2.2 summarizes the trend of measles cases identified in the last 5 years in the European region, provided by the Regional Office for Europe of the World Health Organization.[14]

Immigration

I'd like to live in a world where immigration is just called moving.

Stefan Molyneux

---

[14]https://www.euro.who.int/en/health-topics/disease-prevention/vaccines-and-immunization/publications/surveillance-and-data/who-epidata (Last checked August 2020).

Although immigration has always been of crucial importance throughout history, the race for unbridled sharing of information in recent years is giving it a new and dangerous face. The presence of wars and the geopolitical scenarios led to an increasingly growing economic disparity between industrialized and developing countries. This disparity is only one of the reasons that brought people to leave their hometown and search for a better quality of life somewhere else. Among the other reasons, we may find the escape from persecution and violence, extreme poverty, and natural disasters.

In the following, some of the most widespread low-quality information about immigration are reported:

- **Migrants moving for economic reasons do not need protection.** As mentioned above, the reasons that led individuals to leave their hometown are manifold. Some think that migrants moving for economic reasons do not need any kind of protection. However, despite the reasons that led people to move, immigrants face countless difficulties during the travel: from sexual abuse (where the victims are mostly women and child) to child labor and from detention to war enrollment, not to mention the atmospheric conditions. Being aware of those risks does not change migrants' minds, having few (sometimes no) hopes in the departure country.

- **Europe is the favorite destination of migrants.** People in Europe, partly motivated by the weaponized propaganda, think that all of the migrants want to cross the Mediterranean to seek asylum in European countries. This belief does not absolutely go along with the statistics. Indeed, in 2018, more than 90% of African migrants never left their region, preferring developing countries within their borders. Even if they are facing difficulties, migrants, if allowed to choose, prefer places where they can find a similar culture.

- **Do they have a smartphone? They surely do not need help.** It is common for a newscast to broadcast images and videos of migrants piled on a boat, but intent on typing on a smartphone. The first thought of an individual would surely be "does he have a smartphone? Clearly, he does not need any protection." Even in this case, the reality is different. It is indeed crucial for a migrant to have a smartphone that is both a way to communicate with his/her family, living thousands of kilometers away, and a source of information. Information is a synonym of protection when it comes to immigration, as it allows to guide the migrants through less risky routes and to be aware of the laws of other countries to understand their rights. It is worth noting that most of the time, to afford a smartphone, the migrant has probably traded some food, clothes, or accommodation.

- **All the migrants are criminals.** Throughout history, migrants have been portrayed as criminals from media and news. Let's suppose there is a crime in the city. A possible algorithm to make immigrants look bad is the following: if the person who commit the crime is a migrant, the nationality will be specified on the news; otherwise, it will be omitted. In the medium (and long) term, viewers and listeners will be well impressed with the fact that crimes in the city have been always carried out by migrants that, in turn, will begin to be held up as dangerous and "intruding." This process may be used for different purposes: redirect hatred, manipulate the public opinion, and establish fear in people who will then be easier to control.

- **There are too many immigrants; they will end up taking the power.** For the same reasons as before, media and news may spread inaccurate information about the number of immigrants within a country. Several political parties all over the world have taken advantage of this citizens' fear to organize ad hoc election campaigns, thus inciting hatred, misinformation, and the fear toward the "different." Facebook, Twitter, and other social media platforms have incredibly increased the resonance of the rumors, thus paving the way for the spread of low-quality information such as "Illegal immigrants live in five-starred hotels entirely paid by Italian taxpayers" [16]. Such information is predictably false but nonetheless may lead voters to have a better view of a political party that is less inclined to accept migrants within the country.

Flat Earth Society

The disintermediation made possible by social media allowed everyone to participate in online debates. If on the one hand, this gives everyone the chance to speak their minds, thus enjoying the freedom of expression, on the other hand, the information authoritativeness is undergoing a considerable decrease. In the past, without online technologies, conspiracy theorists (or people who had different opinions with respect to those already affirmed) were forced to organize physical meetings or rallies to meet. These limitations did not allow them to have a direct impact on the population. As technology progressed, those rallies became groups on social networks, and meetings turned into discussion groups that millions of people can read and actively take part in. This facilitated the creation and advertisement of several "sects" which, without the echo provided by technologies, remained only local realities. An example is given by modern Flat Earth Societies.

> ✎ **Definitions**
>
> **Modern Flat Earth Societies** Organizations that dispute the Earth's sphericity by promoting the belief that the Earth is flat.

People have known that the Earth is round at least since the sixth century. However, the first doubts in people have been instilled by Samuel Rowbotham, an English writer, that published a pamphlet called "Zetetic Astronomy" based on the Bedford Level experiment. This experiment, carried out in the summer of 1838, consisted of measuring the position of the flag of a boat slowly descending a river for 9.7 km. The scientist reported that the flag constantly remained in his view for the whole journey. This made the scientist claim that the Earth is flat since, if it were not so, the top of the mast should have been below his line of sight. After Samuel Rowbotham's death, Lady Elizabeth Blount founded a Universal Zetetic Society intending to propagate the Natural Cosmogony knowledge in confirmation of the Holy Scriptures (according to [17], "Bible, alongside our senses, supported the idea that the earth was flat and immovable and this essential truth should not be set aside for a system based solely on human conjecture"), based on practical scientific-based investigations. After the Zetetic Society, several related associations came to light (e.g., Flat Earth Research Society) with a common goal: convince people (scientifically or not) of the flatness of the Earth.

The Flat Earth Society lived a severe bankrupt in the 1990s and was losing, one after the other, all of its supporters, but then the Internet appeared, transforming the group into an online global entity. Indeed, while it took 50 years for the Flat Earth Society to reach 3500 members in the pre-Internet era, nowadays their website gets 300,000 unique visits every day.[15] At the time of writing, the Flat Earth Society had gathered 89K followers on Twitter and 209K likes and 224K followers on Facebook. Among the most famous supporters of the flat Earth theory are the basketball players Shaquille O'Neal[16] and Kyrie Irving, the football players Geno Smith and Sammy Watkins, Homer (i.e., the author of the Iliad and the Odyssey), Hesiod, and Herodotus of Halicarnassus. In the Internet era, social technologies such as Facebook, Twitter, and YouTube have given activists, journalists, and people in general a new way to connect and exchange theories, stories, and ideas, no matter how illogical they are. YouTube, in particular, has been accused of allowing the spread of misinformation through its platform. Indeed the American video-sharing platform in 2019 announced changes to its recommendation algorithm, to mitigate the spread of conspiracy theories.[17]

Among the extravagant theories, Flat Earth Society claims that NASA, together with other government agencies, conspires to make humanity believe the Earth is spherical. They claim that NASA uses to edit (i.e., photoshop) the images got from its satellites. Evidence of this, according to the aforementioned society, is found in the change of the color of the ocean observed in different pictures and the position of the continents. Furthermore, they think NASA is similar to Disneyland and that cosmonauts are actors, thus taking for granted that the moon landing never happened.

---

[15]https://medium.com/s/world-wide-wtf/how-the-internet-made-us-believe-in-a-flat-earth-2e42c3206223 (Last checked August 2020).

[16]https://www.forbes.com/sites/trevornace/2017/03/28/shaq-thinks-earth-is-flat-because-it-doesnt-go-up-and-down-when-he-drives/#4ab8f4187233 (Last checked August 2020).

[17]https://edition.cnn.com/2019/01/25/tech/youtube-conspiracy-video-recommendations/index.html (Last checked August 2020).

Climate Change

Although the terms "global warming" and "climate change" are sometimes used interchangeably, they refer to slightly different concepts. One victim of the similarity of these terms was the current President of the United States Donald Trump who, according to a study conducted in 2018 [18] where his tweets have been analyzed, confuses the terms weather, global warming, and climate change. To clarify, we give the definitions of both global warming and climate change, provided by the National Aeronautics and Space Administration (NASA) agency.[18] In both cases, the changes are due to the increased levels of atmospheric carbon dioxide produced through the intensive use of fossil fuels.

> ✎ **Definitions**
>
> **Global Warming** Global warming is a long-term shift in global (or regional) climate patterns. The term is also used to define the rise in global temperatures from the mid-twentieth century to the present.
>
> **Climate Change** Climate change is an umbrella term that encompasses global warming, but, specifically, it refers to the range of changes that are happening to Earth. These changes include sea level rise, melting glaciers, and shifts in flower/plant blooming times.

At first glance, it may seem that, given its objectivity, the problem, together with the underlying causes, is universally recognized. However, if on the one hand the scientific community reached a unanimous consensus on the reality of the human-caused climate change, on the other hand, the general public is becoming increasingly polarized on the issue. Indeed, the scientific consensus is continuously questioned by ideologically motivated groups, such as the Merchants of Doubt. This group, supported and incited by others, have organized influential disinformation campaigns in which they publicly dispute the scientific consensus on several issues, including the human-caused climate changes [19], thus increasing the polarization and limiting the societal engagement with the issue.

The US President Donald Trump, besides confusing the meanings of the terms as mentioned above, is not new to episodes of skepticism toward the concepts of climate change and global warming. Indeed, he defined climate change as "mythical," "nonexistent," and "an expensive hoax" and shared tweets like "The concept of global warming was created by and for the Chinese in order to make U.S. manufacturing non-competitive"; "It's freezing in New York – where the hell is global warming"; "I don't believe it"; and "The badly flawed Paris Climate

---

[18]https://climate.nasa.gov/faq/12/whats-the-difference-between-climate-change-and-global-warming/ (Last checked August 2020).

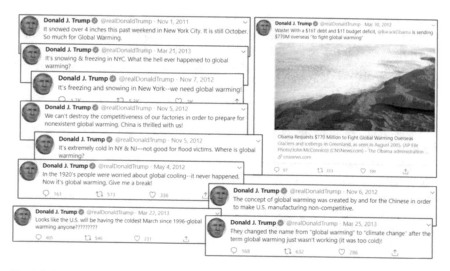

Fig. 2.3 Some of the tweets written by Donald Trump about the climate change and the global warming

Agreement protects the polluters, hurts Americans, and cost a fortune. NOT ON MY WATCH."[19] Some of the aforementioned tweets and many others are depicted in Fig. 2.3. Given the number of supporters, these statements may be dangerous and convey the wrong message, leading most Americans to underestimate and scoff at an established problem.

In the opposite extreme, the young Swedish environmental activist Greta Thunberg entered the debate. The 17-year-old girl has been internationally recognized for her determination to make humanity aware of the existential crisis the climate is facing. The straightforward and unambiguous speeches of Greta aimed at world (political) leaders are reverberating all over the world, in which she criticizes their failure to take action to address the climate change emergency. However, even against the figure of the activist, criticisms and judgments arose. Among the most popular is the question "Who is behind Greta Thunberg?". Indeed, conspiracy theorists think that Greta is only a convincing facade of a very complex marketing organization, whose goals are far from beneficial.

2.3   Scenario 2: Democratic Election in a Country

In this scenario, we will take into account the political election of a democratic country. During this election, the state promotes transparency and fairness, pro-

---

[19]https://www.bbc.com/news/world-us-canada-51213003 (Last checked August 2020).

viding the candidates with a fair media space and controlling their advertising according to principles of equality and correctness. According to the definition of Jeane Kirkpatrick, the scholar and former US ambassador to the United Nations, "Democratic elections are not merely symbolic. They are competitive, periodic, inclusive, definitive elections in which the chief decision-makers in a government are selected by citizens who enjoy broad freedom to criticize the government, to publish their criticism and to present alternatives."[20]

Democratic elections are competitive, since the mere right to participate in the ballot is not enough. Indeed, political, and other, groups involved in the elections must guarantee fairness, avoiding censorship and partisan media and respecting the rules. Both opposition parties and candidates must enjoy the freedom of speech, as well as bring alternative policies and candidates to the voters. Democratic elections are also definitive, since they determine the leadership of the government. The party leader will have the burden of leading the country, possibly respecting the political program presented during the election campaign.

2.3.1   Threat: Interference in Political Election

Political elections within a country are not only reflected in the interests of citizens. Companies and institutions (local or foreign) may have an interest in illegally interfering with the electoral campaign, with the aim of piloting its results and obtaining profits in the short, medium, or long term. Companies and institutions, especially governments, may rely on social media to profile users and manipulate their attitudes and behaviors through the use of hate speech, fake news, and manipulative campaigns. This user profiling allows the companies and institutions to build targeted (possibly fake) advertising, to manipulate the vote of individuals. Brad Smith, the President of Microsoft, realized the extent of such a threat and in a recent article that appeared in the Microsoft blog entitled "We are taking new steps against broadening threats to democracy" stated "It's clear that democracies around the world are under attack. Foreign entities are launching cyber strikes to disrupt elections and sow discord. Unfortunately, the Internet has become an avenue for some governments to steal and leak information, spread disinformation, and probe and potentially attempt to tamper with voting system."[21] In this article, dated back to August 2018, the President of Microsoft refers to the US general election in 2016, the French presidential election in 2017, and those that would have been the midterm elections in November of the same year.

---

[20]https://usa.usembassy.de/etexts/gov/democracy-elections.htm (Last checked August 2020).

[21]https://blogs.microsoft.com/on-the-issues/2018/08/20/we-are-taking-new-steps-against-broadening-threats-to-democracy/ (Last checked August 2020).

In this section, we provide a thorough analysis of the state-of-the-art studies and online articles that portray how new technologies interfered, and are continuing to interfere with many of the political elections worldwide.

2.3.2   Attacks

Over time, technological developments and innovation have provided the population with means that were unthinkable only a few decades before. Hand in hand, to not fall behind, politics needs to adapt to this new ever-increasing accelerated pace of communication. The politician on duty, if focused exclusively on offline election campaigns as in the past years, might be crushed by contenders that are more familiar with social media and that know how to rely on them to manipulate the mass. This familiarity, when placed in the wrong hands, brings to the introduction of political bots. These automatic actors may be employed to give the politician a louder voice, by automatically sharing the electoral program to a wider audience. However, political bots may also be employed to raise misinformation campaigns about the contender, by relying on credible low-quality information aimed at demolishing the credibility of the opponent. Nowadays social media turned into political war camps, where propaganda and disinformation became the most effective, modern, worldwide political strategies.[22]

In this subsection, we explain how, and to what extent, low-quality information can affect people's opinions. Finally, we describe the most impactful alleged political scandals in the literature, by reporting them within categories according to the nation in which the presumed scandal happened.

Public Naivety

In 2016, the most tweeted topics on Twitter have been revealed to the public and, not surprisingly, four out of the ten positions were occupied by political topics, with Brexit, Trump, Election 2016, and BlackLivesMatter all making the list.[23] According to a Pew Research Center article, entitled "News Use Across Social Media Platforms 2016," it emerges that 62% of US adults get news on social media. Compared to 2012, where Americans acquiring information on social media were (only) 49%, this boost gains importance and marks the beginning of a significant historical period. As depicted in Fig. 2.4, the same study highlights that 64% of Americans usually get news from one social media only, without even double-

---

[22]http://techpresident.com/news/25374/bad-news-bots-how-civil-society-can-combat-automated-online-propaganda (Last checked August 2020).

[23]https://www.independent.co.uk/news/twitter-most-tweeted-moments-2016-donald-trump-brexit-black-lives-matter-rio-a7466236.html (Last checked August 2020).

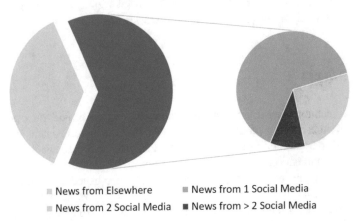

American News Consumption

■ News from Elsewhere ■ News from 1 Social Media
■ News from 2 Social Media ■ News from > 2 Social Media

Fig. 2.4 News consumption of Americans according to the study conducted by journalism.org

checking the content to assess the reliability of the news. Regarding the other 36% of the US citizens analyzed, 26% get news from two sites, while only 10% get news from three or more sites.[24] Furthermore, an interesting study published in 2016 showed that 60.66% of Twitter's users reshare articles without having read them, only relying on the "appealing" headline [20]. This information and the fact that viral fake election news stories outperformed real news on Facebook (in the last 3 months of the US presidential campaign, the fake election news stories generated more engagement than the top stories from New York Times, Huffington Post, Washington Post, etc.),[25] and the fact that fake news headlines fool US adults about 75% of the time,[26] make it possible that low-quality information can opportunely reshape people's opinion nowadays.

Many studies in the literature confirm these beliefs. To consider a practical example, in [21], the authors face the problem of identifying social influence effects in observational studies. In particular, they report results from a randomized controlled trial of political mobilization messages sent to 61 million Facebook users during the 2010 US congressional elections. The results are striking: political self-expression, information seeking, and real-world voting behavior of millions of people have changed accordingly. The messages, besides having directly influenced the recipients, also had an impact on the recipients' friends and friends of friends. However, on the other hand, several studies in the literature do not agree with

---

[24]https://www.journalism.org/2016/05/26/news-use-across-social-media-platforms-2016/ (Last checked August 2020).

[25]https://www.buzzfeednews.com/article/craigsilverman/viral-fake-election-news-outperformed-real-news-on-facebook (Last checked August 2020).

[26]https://www.buzzfeednews.com/article/craigsilverman/fake-news-survey (Last checked August 2020).

Table 2.1 Alleged political scandals documented in the literature

Country	Alleged facts	References
Argentina	Fake Twitter accounts to support politicians, astroturfing, fake news	[23, 24]
Australia	Fake tweets, social botnets, fake online users, cyborgs, sockpuppets, meat puppets to support political leaders	[9, 25]
Austria	Disinformation	[26]
France	Hacking attack that led to a massive leakage of politics-related emails, bots, disinformation	[27–31]
Germany	Political bots to influence the election campaign	[32–36]
Italy	Political bots to promote politicians, fake news, hate speech, political propaganda, misinformation	[37–42]
Mexico	Spammers, disinformation, political propaganda, political bots	[23, 43–48]
Spain	Political bots, hate speech	[49]
Russia	Political bots, trolls to manipulate the public opinion, disinformation	[50–55]
Turkey	Political bots	[56]
Ukraine	Political bots	[57]
United Kingdom	Political bots	[58–60]
United States	Fake news, disinformation, astroturfing, spammers, political propaganda, fake online users, sockpuppets, meat puppets	[61–71]
Venezuela	Political bots	[72]

these theories and suggest that Americans may not be easily susceptible to online influence campaigns [22].

Alleged Political Scandals

In the following, we report some of the alleged political scandals in the literature. To allow a more effective reading, we organize the studies in paragraphs, each referring to a different nation whose political elections have reported misinformation, fake news, or political bots employment. The results are summarized in Table 2.1

France In 2017, during the French presidential election, a hacking attack led to the leakage of more than 20,000 emails related to Emmanuel Macron's campaign. This leak immediately became viral due to the quickness in the spreading of related news throughout the Web. Indeed, US activists, WikiLeaks, and bots consistently helped to amplify the leak by spreading the information on Twitter, Facebook, and 4chan [27–29] while shifting the attention to the Russian government (under Vladimir Putin) as responsible. In the same year, Emilio Ferrara published an interesting article [30], where he provided an extensive statistical analysis of the MacronLeaks disinformation campaign that occurred in the run-up to the

French presidential election. He collected a Twitter dataset composed of 17 million posts related to the election that occurred in the period April 27–May 7, 2017. Then, thanks to a combination of cognitive-behavioral modeling and machine learning techniques, he was able to effectively distinguish humans from social bots. As a result, out of 99,378 users participating in MacronLeaks, the proposed model classified 18,324 as social bots and 81,054 as human users, respectively. Furthermore, according to the author, "prior interests of disinformation adopters pinpoint to the reasons of scarce success of this campaign," considering that most of the audience was composed of English-speaking Americans rather than French users. The author highlighted that some automated Twitter accounts had already been used to discredit Hillary Clinton during the US presidential election.

The second round of campaigning of the French presidential election has been analyzed by Desigaud et al. [31]. The authors, relying on a set of specific hashtags, collected a 3-day Twitter dataset. The analysis of these tweets led to the following interesting discoveries: (1) the Twitter content related to Macron was dominating Le Pen traffic, although the latter was slowly growing; (2) the amount of traffic generated by automated accounts doubled between the first and the second round of voting; and (3) the ratio of "professionally produced news content" to "other political content" passed from 2 to 1 (in the first round of voting) to 1 to 1 (in the second round of voting).

Italy In a series of online articles [37, 38], the story of an accusation against a famous Italian comedian and politician, Beppe Grillo, leader of the Five Star Movement is reported. According to the algorithm designed and implemented by Marco Camisani Calzolari, 54% of Beppe Grillo's 600,000 Twitter and Facebook followers might be bots. This news provoked an immediate reaction from the followers of the aforementioned politician, who started campaigns to prove themselves humans (e.g., "I am real," "I am not a bot" campaigns). The news also angered the politician who threatened to sue the Professor. Subsequent scientific studies proved that the algorithm by Camisani Calzolari was simplistic and highly inaccurate, thus likely to yield unreliable results [73].

Other articles, on the other hand, claim that bots have been adopted to help populists win elections in Italy [39]. According to a recent article named "#Election-Watch: Italy's Self-Made Bots" [40], Lega's followers are automating themselves. Indeed, some bots have been created by the account-holders themselves, a phenomenon that is called "selfbot."

Moving on to another election, Facebook intervened personally to shut down multiple Italian pages that were accused to spread fake news, hate speech, political propaganda, and misinformation in the run-up to the 2019 European elections [41]. According to Avaaz, 23 pages with 2.46 million followers were shut down, where half of the accounts supported either the League or the Five Star Movement parties.

In [42], the authors discussed the problem of detecting social spambots. By performing several experiments, they showed that neither humans nor state-of-the-art spambot detection applications can recognize them (i.e., they are erroneously labeled as genuine human-operated accounts). This study led to the construction of several datasets that the authors have kindly made available to the scientific community. One dataset that is called "social spambots #1" contains the activities of a group of almost 1000 automated accounts that was discovered on Twitter during the 2014 Rome Mayoral election. Those automated accounts were almost impossible to distinguish from genuine accounts (e.g., they had a picture, a short bio, thousands of followers/friends and used to publish few tweet posts every day, including quotes from popular people, songs, and YouTube videos). However, every time the candidate posted a new tweet in his/her personal profile, all the bots were triggered and retweeted it a few minutes later, to reach a wider audience.

> **⮞ Resources**
>
> The dataset used in [42] as well as in [74–77] for the analysis of traditional and modern, sophisticated social bots is publicly available online.[27] The dataset contains Twitter data about legitimate and automated accounts, annotated by contributors of a crowdsourcing platform.

Russia When it comes to Russia in these contexts, the Internet Research Agency fully deserves to be mentioned. The Internet Research Agency, sometimes referred to on the Web as "Troll Farm,"[28] is a Russian company known for its commitment to online propaganda operations on behalf of Russian companies and the political interests of the Kremlin. The literature boasts several interesting scientific articles that have studied the Internet Research Agency's moves and analyzed the impact it had on national and international political elections. In [78], the authors investigated the scope of the Internet Research Agency activities in 2017. The study aims to show how easy it is for malicious actors to infiltrate social media to launch propaganda campaigns. However, it also shows that it is possible to track and understand this kind of activity by fusing content and activity resources from multiple Internet services. Other studies focused on the content of the posts written by the alleged trolls. In [51], for example, the authors analyzed the content of 1.8 million images posted to Twitter by Russian trolls, as well as their posting activity. Among the many interesting findings, they (1) showed that the image posting activity is strongly coupled with real-world events, with targets that were automatically changing; (2) provided evidence of Russian trolls' general targets, like Ukraine and the United States; and (3) showed how co-occurrences of these images are found in many popular OSNs. In [79], instead, the authors analyzed 27,000 tweets from 1000 users suspected to be correlated with Russia's Internet Research Agency. The aim was to understand the differences with respect to a random set of Twitter users

---

[27]http://mib.projects.iit.cnr.it/dataset.html (Last checked August 2020).

[28]https://www.wired.com/story/facebook-may-have-more-russian-troll-farms-to-worry-about/ (Last checked August 2020).

in terms of the disseminated content, the evolution of the accounts, and the general behavior. According to the study, although Russian trolls used to stay active for long periods and reach a conspicuous number of Twitter users, the action of making viral the spreading of news has a minor effect on social platforms. In [53], the authors analyzed the relationship between Russian Internet Research Agency's organized trolling efforts and political homophilia. The analysis of the Russian troll accounts participating in the #BlackLivesMatter debate shows that these conversations were divided into political groups, where the Russian trolls systematically took advantage of these divisions to accentuate disagreement.

A New York Times article dated back to September 2017 claimed that fake Russian Facebook accounts bought $100,000 in political ads [54]. 3500 of these ads, purchased by the Russian Government and released in May 2018 by the US Congress House Intelligence Committee, have been analyzed by Dutt et al. [55]. According to the study, the ads were principally biased toward the Democratic party as opposed to the Republican party. Furthermore, the authors suggested that, given the duration and the promotion of the Republican ads effort, Russia was trying to cause racial, religious, and political ideologies division rather than swaying the election.

In [52], the authors studied how state-sponsored trolls manipulate public opinion on the Web. They analyzed ten million posts created and shared by 5500 Twitter and Reddit accounts, identified as Russian and Iranian state-sponsored trolls. Among the interesting discoveries, they pointed out that (1) during the US 2016 presidential elections, Russian trolls were pro-Trump, while Iranian trolls were anti-Trump; (2) the campaigns undertaken by both the parts are strongly influenced by real-world events; and (3) the behavior of the accounts does not remain consistent over time, leading to increasing complexity for automatic detection.

The bot activity within Russian political discussion (from February 2014 to December 2015) has been studied by Stukal et al. [50], where the authors presented a methodology that relies on an ensemble of classifiers to allow accurate detection of bots on Twitter. Among the many interesting discoveries, they highlighted how the proportion of tweets produced by bots exceeds 50% of the traffic and that one prominent activity of those bots was spreading news stories and promoting media.

However, as already mentioned above, some studies claim that troll intervention has had no impact on Americans' political attitudes and online behaviors. To make an example, in [22], the authors studied the attitudes and online behaviors of 1239 Republican and Democratic Twitter accounts from late 2017 and, exploiting Bayesian regression tree models, claimed to not have found evidence that their interaction with IRA accounts has had an impact. According to the study, "the findings suggest that Russian trolls might have failed to sow discord because they mostly interacted with those who were already highly polarized." The authors concluded by discussing some limitations of their study, including their inability to determine whether the troll accounts influenced the 2016 presidential election.

United Kingdom In [58], the authors analyzed the use of political bots during the UK Brexit referendum about the European Union membership. The two most active accounts during the StrongerIn-Brexit debate were @*ivoteLeave* and @*ivoteStay*, respectively. According to the authors, the two accounts were following a similar algorithm: they automatically retweet messages from their side of the debate, without ever creating new content. Among the many interesting bots they found, the authors discovered @*Col_Connaughton*, a pro-Palestine bot suitably repurposed to support Brexit, and @*Rotenyahu*, another pro-Palestinian bot used to retweet messages from @*Col_Connaughton*, to reach a wider audience. The behavior of bots during the Brexit debate after the 2016 referendum has been studied also by Bello and Heckel [80]. According to the analysis, more than 1962 bot accounts participated in the Brexit debate. Among them, the author identified three bots that promoted the independence of Scotland, @*StillYesScot*, @*IsThisAB0t*, and @*FAO_Scotbot*. The goal of these bots was to influence, both constructively and destructively, the opinion of their followers.

The behavior of the social bots during the Brexit referendum has been analyzed also by Bastos and Mercea [59] and Llewellyn et al. [60]. In the first work, the authors discovered the existence of a network of social bots on Twitter composed of 13,493 accounts that suddenly disappeared after actively participating. The detailed analysis of these bots led to many interesting discoveries: (1) Twitter bots were able to rapidly generate small-/medium-sized tweet cascades; (2) the retweeted content included user-generated hyperpartisan news; and (3) a botnet may follow a detailed organization (tiers or clusters) that allows a more effective replication of both active users and other bot contents. Many of these accounts are alleged to be involved in the state-sponsored manipulation of the American elections, as per a list released by Twitter. Such a list contains 2752 accounts Twitter believed to be controlled by Russian operatives. Given that a similar list for the UK referendum has never been released, the authors in [60] analyzed the behavior of the accounts related to the American election that produced UK-EU related content. They found 3485 tweets posted by 419 accounts, gathered between August 29, 2015, and October 3, 2017. According to the study, during that period the behavior of the bots changed from generalized disruptive tweeting to retweeting each other, to allow other troll accounts to reach a wide audience. Furthermore, the authors showed that some of the bots were geographically located in Germany.

United States Although Mark Zuckerberg, the Facebook's founder, considered that it is foolish to believe that fake news shared on Facebook have caused changes in the choice of the leader to be elected during the US elections [81], the fact that the most discussed fake news tended to favor Donald Trump over Hillary Clinton brought the commentators to start wondering whether, without the influence of low-quality information, Donald Trump would have been able to win the elections [4, 61]. Several studies in the literature had the same doubt and question the claim of the Facebook leader. For example, the authors in [62] studied the fake news impact on the 2016 US presidential campaign. They highlighted that (1) approximately one American out of four visited a fake news website during the presidential campaign (i.e., from October 7 to November 14); (2) the majority of users that visited fake news websites are Trump supporters; (3) almost six out of ten visits to fake news websites came from the 10% of people with the most conservative online information diets; and (4) Facebook was a key vector of exposure to fake news.

An article from Intelligencer entitled "Donald Trump Won Because of Facebook," dated back to November 2016, explains how one of the giants of social networks helped the current President of the United States to reach his position [82]. Among the reasons the article mentions, there is a massive impact the spreading of fake news had on the voters. In fact, during the election campaign, there were many fake news reports against the current President's contender, Hillary Clinton, e.g., "Pope Francis Shocks World, Endorses Donald Trump for President"[29]; "Hillary Clinton Bought $137 Million Worth of Illegal Arms"[30]; "WikiLeaks: Clintons Purchase $200 Million Maldives Estate"[31]; "Hillary Clinton's Alleged 'Lolita' Child Pedophile Sex Slave Island Ring"[32]; and many others.

In [63], the authors discovered that a large fraction of the users' population, suspected to be social bots, accounted for a considerable portion (i.e., approximately one-fifth) of the content generated during the entire political conversation. The authors stated that the presence of social bots harmed the democratic political discussions, by altering public opinion and endangering the integrity of the presidential election itself. After analyzing 14 million tweets during (and following) the presidential campaign and election, in [64] it is highlighted that (1) there is evidence that social bots were playing a key role in spreading the fake news; (2) automated accounts were particularly active and tend to target influential users; (3) many humans are vulnerable to the manipulation and tend to retweet the fake news shared by bots.

A Wired article entitled "Bots Unite to Automate the Presidential Election," dated back to May 2016, after providing an overview of the impact that bots have on the presidential elections [65], tells the story of Pepe Luis Lopez, Francisco Palma, and Alberto Contreras, three of the seven million Twitter followers of Trump. Although being actively involved in supporting Donald Trump after his victory in the Nevada caucuses, these accounts are far from representing real human beings. Indeed, they are automated accounts, employed to bring the Latino voters closer to Trump before the election. This is just one of the countless articles that claim the presence of bots among Donald Trump's supporters. Indeed, an article from Newsweek highlighted that nearly half of Donald Trump's Twitter followers are either fake accounts or bots [66] and, although many of them may be inactive, they played an active role in exaggerating the candidate's popularity during the US presidential election (i.e., astroturfing).

---

[29]https://www.snopes.com/fact-check/pope-francis-donald-trump-endorsement/ (Last checked August 2020).

[30]https://www.snopes.com/fact-check/hillary-clinton-bought-137-million-worth-of-illegal-arms/ (Last checked August 2020).

[31]https://www.snopes.com/fact-check/wikileaks-clintons-purchase-200-million-maldives-estate/ (Last checked August 2020).

[32]https://www.inquisitr.com/3682274/hillary-clintons-alleged-lolita-child-pedophile-sex-slave-island-ring-scandal-5th-of-november-part-1-claims-by-anonymous/ (Last checked August 2020).

The low-quality information content during the US presidential election has been analyzed in [67], where the authors aimed at monitoring the traffic of websites that are known to create and share fake news in the months preceding the aforementioned election. Among their interesting discoveries, they pointed out that (1) social media was the main responsible for the circulation of fake news stories, and (2) aggregate vote patterns were strongly correlated with the user visiting websites serving fake news.

In the chaos caused by fake news, there is even someone claiming to be the reason behind Donald Trump's victory, as reported by a "The Washington Post" article [83].

An interesting study [68] analyzed the real-time search option implemented by the real-time websites, such as Twitter. According to the article, when considering political topics, the search provides results that would not be found on the first page while surfing the Web. Results include fabricated content, personal opinions, unverified events, lies, and misrepresentations. To support this statement, the study provided evidence about the Massachusetts senate race between Scott Brown and Martha Coakley, showing that it is possible to predict the users' political orientation by solely relying on behavioral patterns of activity.

Other studies, as well as the US Congress, investigated Russia's possible interference in the US elections. Indeed, Russia has been accused of relying on both trolls and bots to spread misinformation and politically biased information. In [69], the authors collected a dataset containing 43 million posts shared between September 16 and September 21, 2016. Among the interesting discoveries, they revealed that (1) about 4.9 and 6.2% of liberal and conservative users were bots and most of the trolls had a conservative, pro-Trump agenda; (2) there were about four times as many Russian trolls conservative than liberal ones, and the former produced almost 20 times more content; (3) conservative users retweeting these troll messages were 30 times more than liberal users; and (4) conservative users outproduced liberal users in terms of content at a rate of 35:1. A similar study has been performed by the same authors in [70]. The study in [71] investigated the influence of misinformation during the election by analyzing one of the largest repositories of Internet Research Agency's tweets. According to the article, when the campaign reached its peak (i.e., between October and November 2016), most of the tweets drew the candidate Hillary Clinton in negative and moralizing terms, whereas Trump was depicted as a fighter and, potentially, a winner.

2.4 Countermeasures

In this section, we describe the countermeasures that have been proposed in the literature to mitigate low-quality information. Furthermore, we describe many state-of-the-art solutions that allow the identification of malicious actors, who are actively participating in the dissemination of low-quality information worldwide.

2.4.1 Low-Quality Information

Low-quality information has literally always been around, but the sounding boards are becoming wider and wider with the introduction of the latest technologies. The news that, in the past, used to circulate from mouth to mouth and could be stopped by either silencing an individual in the chain or isolating the source have now turned into seemingly unstoppable distributed processes that bounce off the Web reaching millions of people in seconds. The urgent need to defend against disinformation and low-quality information has also been identified by Microsoft that, in an online report,[33] reported "electoral attacks" as the top tech issue for 2018. To proceed in a meaningful and effective direction, they introduced the Defending Democracy Program,[34] aiming at (1) protecting campaigns from hacking, (2) increasing political advertising transparency online, (3) exploring technological solutions, and (4) defending against disinformation campaigns. According to the author, the global goal of the program is to protect the institutions and processes of democratic countries in the years to come.

The problem has also been extensively studied in the literature. Indeed, in a report called "Combating Fake News: An Agenda for Research and Action" [84], the authors proposed some possible pathways to reduce the spreading of fake news, including (1) providing the users with feedback related to the truthfulness of the news, (2) providing alternative ideologically compatible sources that confirm (or deny) the authoritativeness of the news; (3) detecting information promoted by both cyborgs and bots and tuning algorithm to manage those manipulations, and (4) identifying the sources of misinformation to reduce the promotion of information from those sources at the platform-level.

Researchers in both industry and academia are working hard to find innovative and effective ways to stop the spreading of low-quality information.

Among the most interesting approaches, it is worth to mention:

- **Fake news detection and removal**. Develop solutions to accurately identify low-quality information with the aim of clearing them out from the platform.
- **Credibility/believability news evaluation**. Implement a mechanism to evaluate the credibility/believability of both the information and the source of the information. Supposedly, information with a low score would be identified as low-quality information and might be automatically filtered out by the platform.
- **Spreading the truth to counter low-quality information**. Implement a mechanism to spread authoritative information with the aim of fighting the already-spread low-quality information.

---

[33] https://blogs.microsoft.com/on-the-issues/2018/01/02/today-technology-top-ten-tech-issues-2018/ (Last checked August 2020).

[34] https://blogs.microsoft.com/on-the-issues/2018/04/13/announcing-the-defending-democracy-program/ (Last checked August 2020).

Fake News Detection and Removal

In this section, we describe the possible steps that allow the identification of low-quality information. Since most of the existing studies that have addressed this problem are based on machine learning for the identification of fake news, in this subsection we discuss the most commonly adopted machine learning pipelines for this task. Usually, machine learning approaches require a feature extraction phase, where specific characteristics of low-quality information are identified, followed by the construction of a model, where those features are exploited to build an effective classifier.

Feature Extraction While in traditional news media the low-quality information detection could be performed by relying on the text only, in social media, there is a bunch of auxiliary information that could be exploited. This information, which will be called *features* in this section, may be divided into two categories, depicted in Fig. 2.5: News Content Features and Social Context Features.

> **✐ Definitions**
>
> **News Content Features** News content features are generally the features that consider both the information and the meta information of the news, including the source, the title, and the text of the news itself.

News content features may be, in turn, divided into two categories: *linguistic-based features* and *visual-based features*, respectively. The idea behind the extraction of *linguistic-based features* is inspired by the fact that, usually, low-quality information is linguistically different when compared to authoritative information. To make an example, if we take into account spam messages, clickbait messages, or trolls' hate speeches, we expect the text to be more appealing or more inflammatory when compared to everyday news [11]. *Linguistic-based features* may be extracted at different levels, from single characters, single words (lexical features), single sentences (syntactic features), and possibly others, according to the goal the researcher is willing to reach. *Visual-based features*, instead, are those which may be extracted from both videos and images. The rationale for this class of features stems from the growing importance of multimodal data in the spread of low-quality information and propaganda [11]. Even in this case, the intuition is that low-quality information images and videos present distinctive patterns, as they tend to impress the users to effectively attract their attention. Examples of *visual-based features* include (1) visual clarity score, (2) visual coherence score, (3) visual similarity distribution histogram; (4) visual diversity score, and (5) visual clustering score [85]. These features describe the characteristics of image distribution and allow to reveal hidden distribution patterns of images in news events.

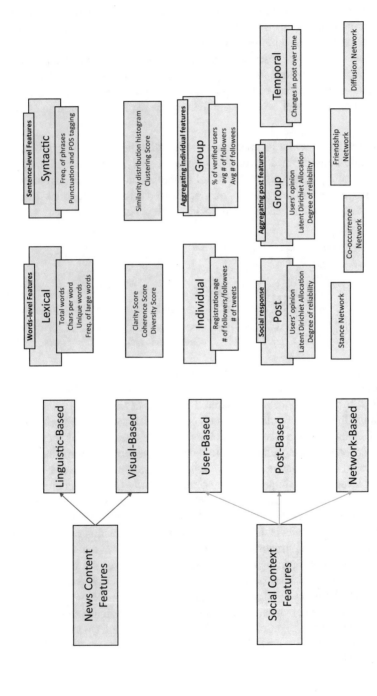

Fig. 2.5 Categorization of News Content Features and Social Context Features

We often consider low-quality information as multimedia traces (e.g., texts, audios, videos, images) from which we can extract news content features to evaluate their truthiness. Other determining roles are kept both by the author of the low-quality information and by the community that interacts with the information itself.

> ✐ **Definitions**
>
> **Social Context Features** Social context features are the features that consider the user-driven social engagements of news consumption on social media platforms (e.g., the proliferation of the news over time, the veracity of the news, etc.).

Social context features are divided into three main categories: *user-based features*, *post-based features*, and *network-based features*, respectively.

Automated malicious actors, such as bots and cyborgs, are among the biggest low-quality information creators and spreaders. Being automatic accounts, their user-based characteristics appear to be different when compared to normal users' ones. *User-based features* try to catch those differences and are divided into two categories: *individual-level features* and *group-level features*, respectively. *Individual-level features* take into account single user's features, including the number of followers/followees; the age of the user; the number of messages commented, created, or shared; and possibly others [86]. *Group-level features*, instead, capture the characteristics of groups and consider the aggregation of *individual-level features* [4].

Post-based features aim at identifying information related to the veracity of the news contained in the social media posts. The intuition is that people express either sensational or skeptical reactions when commenting on low-quality information. These features could be divided into three categories: *post-level features*, *group-level features*, and *temporal-level features*. *Post-level features* identify the stance, the topic, and the credibility of each post, *group-level features* consider the aggregate information, while the *temporal-level features* aim to catch the temporal variations of the post over time [87].

Considering that social media expose users to the echo chamber phenomenon (i.e., beliefs are reinforced or amplified by communication and repetition inside closed systems), important features may be extracted from the network, to evaluate the structural relationships. Those features are called *network-based features*. Starting from the information available on social media, several types of networks can be built, each with its unique characteristics. To make some examples, the friendship network highlights the closeness of individuals, the diffusion network helps to evaluate the trajectory of the spread of news, while the co-occurrence network shows off the user engagements with the news articles.

Model Construction After having extracted the relevant features, a low-quality information detection model can be trained. The approaches that are currently populating the literature could be divided into two categories: News Content Models and Social Context Models, respectively, according to the features they rely on.

> ✐ **Definitions**
>
> **News Content Models**   News content models refer to the models that exploit news content features to perform the classification.

News content models can be divided into two main categories: *knowledge-based models* and *style-based models*.

> 📂 **Resources**
>
> **Computational-Oriented Fact-Checking**
>
> - *ClaimBuster* [88]. Web-based automated live fact-checking tool that relies on NLP and supervised learning to identify low-quality information.
> - Karadzhov et al. [89]. LSTM-based general-purpose framework for fully automatic fact-checking using external resources.

Considering that, by construction, most of the low-quality information tends to spread false claims, *knowledge-based models* aim at classifying them by relying on the evaluation of the truthfulness of the information. The truthfulness may be evaluated by using fact-checking approaches that could be *expert-oriented* (i.e., relying on human domain experts), *crowdsourcing-oriented* (i.e., relying on the "wisdom of the crowd"), and *computational-oriented* (i.e., relying on automatic systems) [90]. In the following, some of the most important fact-checking applications are reported.

> 📂 **Resources**
>
> **Expert-Oriented Fact-Checking**
>
> - *PolitiFact*.[35] A fact-checking website that rates the accuracy of claims by elected officials and others on its Truth-O-Meter.
> - *FactCheck*.[36] Nonprofit "consumer advocate" for voters that aims to reduce the level of deception and confusion in US politics.

(continued)

---

[35]https://www.politifact.com/ (Last checked August 2020).

[36]https://www.factcheck.org/ (Last checked August 2020).

- *Snopes.*[37] A fact-checking website described as a "well-regarded reference for sorting out myths and rumors" on the Internet.
- *Full Fact.*[38] The United Kingdom's independent fact-checking organization.
- *Hoax Slayer.*[39] Hoax Slayer debunks email and social media hoaxes, thwarts Internet scammers, and combats spam.
- *TruthOrFiction*[40] *(Last checked August 2020).* A non-partisan website about eRumors, fake news, disinformation, warnings, offers, requests for help, myths, hoaxes, virus warnings, and humorous or inspirational stories that are circulated by email.

Style-based models, instead, aim at capturing the writing style that has been adopted to draft the low-quality information. The intuition is that, in order to persuade and manipulate people, the writing style of the low-quality information is different if compared with the "true" ones. There are two main categories of style-based models: *deception-oriented models* and *objectivity-oriented models*, respectively. *Deception-oriented* models capture the deceptive statements or claims from news content, while *objectivity-oriented models* capture the style signals that bring to a decreased objectivity of news content.

⮞ Resources

Crowdsourcing-Oriented Fact-Checking

- *Fiskkit.*[41] Online commenting platform that improves the discussion of online articles by allowing users to tag, or call out, incorrect facts, bad reasoning, or uncivil behavior.
- Pennycook and Rand [91]. Fighting misinformation on social media using crowdsourced judgments of news source quality.
- Pinto et al. [92]. A crowdsourcing-based process to perform the filtering, analysis, and classification of the news.

---

[37] https://www.snopes.com/ (Last checked August 2020).

[38] https://fullfact.org/ (Last checked August 2020).

[39] https://www.hoax-slayer.net/ (Last checked August 2020).

[40] https://www.truthorfiction.com/.

[41] https://fiskkit.com/ (Last checked August 2020).

> ✎ **Definitions**
>
> **Social Content Models** Social content models refer to those models who exploit social content features to perform the identification.

In social content models, auxiliary information, such as the user social engagements and the veracity of posts, are taken into account. Social content models can be divided into two categories: *stance-based models* and *propagation-based models*.

Stance-based models aim at capturing the users' viewpoints from the posts to infer their veracity, relying on stance detection. Stance detection is defined as the task of automatically determining if users are in favor, neutral, or against some target (i.e., a person, a policy, a product, an organization). For example, the task makes it possible to analyze the messages/speeches of Barack Obama to understand whether he is in favor of stricter gun laws in the United States [93].

The idea behind *propagation-based models*, instead, is to evaluate the interrelations of the social media posts to predict their credibility. The intuition is that the credibility of a news event is highly related to the credibility of relevant social media posts. The propagation process is analyzed by building credibility networks that can be both homogeneous (i.e., consisting of a single type of entities, such as post or events) and heterogeneous (i.e., consisting of different types of entities, such as posts or sub-events) [90].

Credibility/Believability News Approaches

Another effective countermeasure to mitigate the low-quality information propagation is the adoption of credibility/believability approaches. Each post shared on social media is assigned a score, according to the content and the author who posted/shared it. The intuition is that posts containing low-quality information, as well as posts shared by questionable sources, are likely to be poorly scored. This low score will adversely affect the user's decision to share the post, thus limiting its propagation in the network.

The conception of a scoring mechanism for posts is challenging. If on the one hand, truthful information posted by truthful people should have a high score, on the other hand, the concept of freedom of expression should be guaranteed. This discussion opens the door to several philosophical questions:

- Does rating a post affect the author (disparagingly)?
- To what extent does filtering out low-scored posts affect freedom of expression of individuals?

- How would it be appropriate to score posts and users? Based on the expertise of people on the topic? Based on the number of "trusted" neighbors they have? Based on other metrics?
- How does an individual influence affect the scoring mechanism?

Twitter Several studies in the literature focus on the Twitter platform which, in recent years, has conveyed several disinformation campaigns. For example, in [94], the authors introduced TURank, an algorithm to evaluate the users' authority scores on Twitter by relying on link analysis. In [95], instead, the authors introduce a machine learning-based approach to automatically identify rumors on Twitter by leveraging the concept of believability (i.e., "the extent to which the propagated information is likely to be perceived as truthful, based on the trust measures of users in Twitter's retweet network").

Expert Finding A possible way of assigning scores to posts and authors is based on the expertise the author has about the content of the post. An interesting research branch focuses on the identification of expertise on social networks. Authors in [96], for example, proposed a propagation-based model that takes into account both person's local information and network information to measure the expertise of an individual, while in [97] the authors try to solve the problem "Given an expertise need and a set of social network members, who are the most knowledgeable people for addressing the need?".

Spreading Truth

Another effective alternative consists of the spreading of truthful information to mitigate the low-quality information propagation. The intuition is to fight fire with fire; the propagation of low-quality information will be followed (or anticipated) by the propagation of truthful information, to provide the user with authoritative information immediately after (or before) receiving low-quality information. This approach, sometimes called *Rumor Debunking*, is far from being novel. Indeed, it has already been adopted by governments and other authorities throughout history, years before the introduction of social media. Their goal was to broadcast messages to the entire population to obscure any possible rumor.

However, when considering OSNs, several challenges arise, due to the huge number of users and their highly clustered network structure. In recent years, many researchers have become interested in the problem and have made significant contributions, looking at the problem from different perspectives. In [98], to make an example, the authors developed two models. In the first model, called "delayed start model," a local authority discovers a rumor after a variable number of days and decides to start an anti-rumor campaign. In the second model, called "beacon model," instead, the authors disseminate several vigilantes inside the network able to both detect rumors and respond to them effectively.

Considering the problem from a theoretical point of view, authors in [99] aim at finding the smallest set of highly influential nodes whose decontamination would help to contain the viral spread of misinformation. This study, rather than identifying low-quality information messages, exploits the propagation mechanism to restore the "truth" within the platform. According to the authors, the key difference between the low-quality information propagation and the propagation of their truthful information lies in the propagation speed. Indeed, misinformation often starts from less influential nodes, thus being inevitably constrained by the structure of the graph itself.

When implementing the aforementioned alternatives, there are several trade-offs to take into account. For example, it may be the case to avoid overwhelming users with information they may not find interesting. To do so, every user should only receive truthful information about her topics of interest. This process, however, will eventually lead to the filter bubble problem, where the user only receives material related to her knowledge and would incur difficulties when she wants to be informed about new topics.

Furthermore, even this approach hides relevant philosophical questions. Among the many, who knows the truth? The fact of knowing the truth could not be taken for granted. Indeed, most of the time, the line between the truth and the non-truth is so subtle that it is not easily perceptible. Training someone to distinguish between truth and non-truth may require them to access private (or worse, classified) documents or discuss with groups of experts. Both the resources may not be available in the time of need.

Datasets

The difficulty of finding accurate data to be used as ground truth remains one of the most critical open problems to face when it comes to creating proper classifiers. According to several studies on the Web, a dataset should be:

- *Accurate*. The dataset should not contain erroneous elements;
- *Valid*. The data collected should reflect the requirements;
- *Reliable*. The instances collected in the dataset should not contradict the ones collected in similar datasets;
- *Timely*. The data has to be collected at the right moment in time and has to be updated when the reality changes;
- *Complete*. The data collected should provide the overall picture;
- *Available*. The data should be available for further future acquisition; and
- *Detailed*. The data collected should contain as much information as possible.

The following resource boxes contain lists of datasets available in the literature, on GitHub, and the Web in general.

> **⬔ Resources**
>
> **Github**
>
> - **BuzzFeed News 2016.**[42] Dataset comprising 1627 manually fact-checked (claim-by-claim) articles written on Facebook by 9 news agencies from September 19 to 23 and September 26 to 27, 2016 (released in 2016).
> - **FakeNewsChallenge.**[43] Dataset released by fakenewschallenge.org comprising 49,972 posts associated with 4 stances: unrelated, discuss, agree, and disagree (released in 2017).
> - **BuzzFeed News 2017.**[44] Dataset released by BuzzFeed News containing the 50 biggest fake news hits on Facebook in 2016 and 2017 (released in 2017).

> **⬔ Resources**
>
> **Literature**
>
> - **CREDBANK** [100]. Large-scale crowdsourced dataset containing more than 60M tweets grouped into 1049 real-world events, each annotated by 30 human annotators, covering 96 days from October 2016 (released in 2016).
> - **LIAR** [101]. Open-source dataset for fake news detection, 12.8K manually labeled short statements (released in 2017).
> - **FacebookHoax** [102]. Dataset containing non-hoax and hoax posts, for a total of 15,500 posts from 32 pages (14 conspiracy pages and 18 scientific pages), collected by relying on Facebook Graph API (released in 2017).
> - **BuzzFace** [103]. Dataset made up by extending the BuzzFeed dataset with Facebook news articles. Among the many possible uses, the authors claim that this dataset could be used for detecting social bots (released in 2018).
> - **Goldbeck et al.** [104]. Dataset containing 283 fake news stories and 203 satirical stories from a diverse set of sources, posted between January 2016 and October 2017 regarding American politics (released in 2018).
> - **FakeNewsNet** [105]. Fake news data repository containing two comprehensive datasets with diverse features in news content, social context, and spatiotemporal information (released in 2019).

(continued)

---

[42] https://github.com/BuzzFeedNews/2016-10-facebook-fact-check (Last checked August 2020).

[43] https://github.com/FakeNewsChallenge/fnc-1 (Last checked August 2020).

[44] https://github.com/BuzzFeedNews/2017-12-fake-news-top-50 (Last checked August 2020).

- **Other datasets**. [106–108] (released in 2019).

Web German fake news dataset,[45] ISOT research lab datasets,[46] and Kaggle dataset.[47]

2.4.2 Malicious Actors

The extremely quick propagation of low-quality information is mainly due to bots (e.g., social bots, cyborgs) and malicious accounts (i.e., trolls, spammers, sockpuppets, meat puppets). Depending on the context, their goal is to share the low-quality information with as many people as possible in the shortest time. Starting from this assumption, one of the first steps that comes into mind to implement an effective countermeasure to mitigate the propagation of low-quality information consists of the distinction between malicious actors' accounts and the normal users' ones.

Social Bots

Automated accounts have an enormous presence on social media platforms, and their number is increasing every year at an unprecedented rate. According to a study conducted in 2017 by CNBC,[48] as many as 48 million Twitter accounts are not real, existing people. Although the social media operators are doing their best to identify them and clear them out from their platform (e.g., Facebook took down 2.2 billion fake accounts in the first quarter of 2019,[49] Twitter purges 174,000 fake accounts linked to the Chinese government in the first quarter of 2020), these numbers seem to represent only the tip of the iceberg. Indeed, identifying a bot is far from being trivial,[50] and there are several strategies that malicious actors can adopt to avoid (or at least slow down) detection [4]. As expected, these bots take part in political discussions and relevant events, trying to manipulate the mass or

[45]https://zenodo.org/record/3375714 (Last checked August 2020).

[46]https://www.uvic.ca/engineering/ece/isot/datasets/ (Last checked August 2020).

[47]https://www.kaggle.com/c/fake-news/data (Last checked August 2020).

[48]https://www.cnbc.com/2017/03/10/nearly-48-million-twitter-accounts-could-be-bots-says-study.html (Last checked August 2020).

[49]https://variety.com/2019/digital/news/facebook-took-down-2-2-billion-fake-accounts-in-q1-1203224487/ (Last checked August 2020).

[50]https://firstdraftnews.org/latest/the-not-so-simple-science-of-social-media-bots/ (Last checked August 2020).

divert attention. To make an example, during the coronavirus pandemic in 2020, it is estimated that half of Twitter accounts pushing to reopen America might be bots.[51] According to the study, many of the accounts have been created in February and have started spreading and amplifying misinformation including false medical advice and conspiracy theories about the virus origin, to finally push to end stay-at-home orders and reopen the country. These accounts might have an impact on the resident population who, conditioned by the misinformation campaign on Twitter, could risk to unnecessarily expose themselves to the virus, increasing the number of infections in the best case, the number of victims in the worse.

In order to mitigate the aforementioned misinformation campaigns, there is the need to understand the extent of a bot network that is, in turn, required to be able to effectively distinguish automated agents from normal users. Several researchers worked in this direction, facing the problem from different perspectives and tailoring solutions for different platforms.

Twitter Many of the studies in the literature focus on Twitter, being one of the platforms that are most populated by bots and one of the few for which collecting data is still possible. One of the first studies trying to address this challenge is discussed in [7]. To assist human users in identifying whom they are interacting with, the authors focused on the classification of humans, bots, and cyborgs accounts. During the study, they took into account legitimate bots (i.e., bots that generate a large number of benign tweets delivering news and updating feeds); malicious bots (i.e., bots that spread spam or malicious contents); and cyborgs (i.e., entities in the middle of humans and bots), respectively. The differences among humans, bots, and cyborgs have been evaluated in terms of *tweeting behavior*, *tweet content*, and the *related properties* of the account. The authors proposed a framework that is composed of four main components: (1) an entropy-based component, (2) a spam detection component, (3) an account properties component, and (4) a decision-maker. The proposed solution allows discriminating a human with an accuracy of 98.6%, a cyborg with an accuracy of 91.7%, and a bot with an accuracy of 96%.

On the same platform, the study in [109] aims at understanding (1) how the social botnet grows over time, (2) how the tweets produced by automated accounts differ from the ones produced by normal users, and (3) how social botnets may influence relevant discussions on the platform. The authors built a dataset containing about 3000 tweets in English and Arabic from the famous Syrian social botnet. They highlighted that the behavior and the content of this particular botnet did not align with the general conception of botnets portrayed in the prior literature (e.g., the Syrian social botnet was exceptionally long-lived if compared to the life span of the other reported botnets; it is still not clear if the botnet was mimicking human behavior or if it was only interested in flooding Syrian civil war-related hashtags

---

[51]https://www.technologyreview.com/2020/05/21/1002105/covid-bot-twitter-accounts-push-to-reopen-america/ (Last checked August 2020).

with topics that are not war-related), thus becoming harder to detect and interesting to study.

In [110], the authors presented a supervised machine learning framework, trained with more than a thousand features of different categories, including (1) user-based features, (2) friend features, (3) network features, (4) temporal features, (5) content and language features, and (6) sentiment features, respectively. According to the results, between 9 and 15% of active Twitter accounts are bots, and the simplest of them tend to interact with the users that present human-like behaviors. A subsequent application of unsupervised machine learning (i.e., clustering) techniques to the bots found by relying on the supervised machine learning framework described above allowed the authors to categorize the bots in several subclasses, including self-promoter bots and spammer bots.

However, not all bots have to be considered malicious. The authors in [111] pointed it out and developed a profiling framework that allows to effectively distinguish humans from consumption bots (i.e., automated agents aiming at aggregating contents from various sources and provide services for personal consumption), broadcast bots (i.e., automatic agents aiming at disseminating information), and spam bots (i.e., automated agents aiming at posting malicious content or aggressively promote content), respectively. By relying on machine learning techniques, including Naive Bayes, Support Vector Machine, Logistic Regression, and Random Forest, they reached a precision of 0.8432 with the Random Forest classifier and a recall of 0.8254 and an F1-score of 0.8228 with the Logistic Regression classifier.

Facebook Other studies in the literature focus on the Facebook platform. In [112], to make an example, the authors relied on the emotions that shine through from the posts to distinguish between bots and normal users. The work is based on the assumption that, while the posts of the real users reveal a variety of emotions such as sadness, joy, fear, and anger, dictated by life experiences, fake users' (or bots) posts, which usually aim at accomplishing specific tasks, are likely to present a limited range of emotions. The proposed approach has been trained using 12 emotion-based attributes: the first eight features (i.e., (1) fear, (2) anger, (3) sadness, (4) joy, (5) surprise, (6) disgust, (7) trust, and (8) anticipation) are Plutchik's basic emotions [113], while the remaining four have been introduced in this study and include (9) the number of categories of emotions expressed by the user in their posts, (10) the variance in the emotions expressed by the user, (11) the fraction of posts containing positive sentiment words, and (12) the fraction of posts containing negative sentiment words, respectively. Several classifiers have been trained, including Support Vector Machine, JRip, Naive Bayes, and Random Forest, and tested on Facebook users, reporting accuracies of 87.66% (Support Vector Machine), 85.71% (JRip), 83.44% (Naive Bayes), and 90.91% (Random Forest), respectively.

Unsupervised Learning Most of the approaches described above rely on supervised learning techniques to distinguish between automated agents and humans. Although these approaches show very good performance, they require a labeled dataset of bots to be trained. According to other studies in the literature, this is a limiting requirement, since finding a reliable dataset is complex and building one from scratch may take indefinite time [4, 114]. To overcome these limitations, in [115], authors proposed a seminal (unsupervised) approach to detect bots by relying on the correlation between accounts. Indeed, the approach is based on the assumption that if accounts are abnormally correlated, they are very unlikely to be human operated. They reached an accuracy of 94% and were able to identify bots that other methods did not detect. The proposed system produces a daily report about bots that the authors kindly make available online for further analysis and experimentations.[52] In [116], the authors relied on principal component analysis and K-means clustering techniques to identify Twitter bots during the 2019 Canadian elections. According to the study, the average number of daily tweets of bot accounts, as well as their percentage of retweets and daily favorites, is significantly higher when compared to human accounts. For a detailed survey of unsupervised bot detection technique, we point interested readers to the extensive literature reviews, such as [4].

Public Services Being the detection of social bots is one of the most impactful and interesting fields of study of the last years, several studies in the literature provide online services accessible by everyone to identify automated agents. Botometer [117] (formerly BotOrNot) is one famous example, a publicly available and accessible service able to measure the similarity between a Twitter account and a social bot. After 2 years of the official release, which happened in May 2014, the Botometer service served over one million requests both via the website and the APIs. Another example, already mentioned in the previous paragraph, is DeBot [118], a parameter-free, unsupervised learning method able to identify bots in the Twitter network. In February 2017, DeBot collected more than 710,000 unique bots. The valuable performance of DeBot pushed the authors to provide further services, including a bot archive API[53] and an on-demand bot detection platform.[54] The latter allows the user to detect bots related to a given topic, into a specific geographical region, or starting from a set of users. Another interesting resource is Tweetbotornot2.[55] It consists of an open-source, out-of-the-box classifier that allows the detection of bots on the Twitter platform.

Online Competitions and Web Resources The Defense Advanced Research Project Agency (DARPA), the agency of the US Department of Defense responsible for the development of emerging technologies, gave several contributions to protect the democratic processes from alarming disinformation campaigns. Indeed, they highlighted the need for identifying and eliminating the political bots before they reach a critical level of influence. In February/March 2015, DARPA held a 4-week competition where the goal was to identify influence bots within Twitter. The description of this DARPA challenge, together with the description of the method

---

[52]https://www.cs.unm.edu/~chavoshi/debot/ (Last checked August 2020).

[53]https://www.cs.unm.edu/~chavoshi/debot/api.html (Last checked August 2020).

[54]https://www.cs.unm.edu/~chavoshi/debot/on_demand.html (Last checked August 2020).

[55]https://github.com/mkearney/tweetbotornot2 (Last checked August 2020).

used by the three top-ranked teams, can be found in their white paper [119]. Another interesting challenge is the Author Profiling shared task at PAN 2019.[56] The goal was to determine whether the author of a feed on Twitter was a bot or a human. The overview of the approaches submitted by the 56 participating teams is reported in [120] in terms of preprocessing, feature selection, and classification approach.

Furthermore, the Web boosts countless interesting articles identifying ways to fight social bots on online platforms. To make an example, in [121], DFRLab reported a list containing 12 clues that can help in the distinction between automated accounts and normal users on online platforms, such as Twitter. The list is composed by (1) activity, the number of tweets divided by the number of active days may be a good indicator (72 tweets per day can be considerable suspicious, a threshold that the Oxford Internet Institute's Computational Propaganda set to 50); (2) anonymity, in general the less personal information an account gives, the more likely it will be a bot; (3) amplification, most of the bots present few or no original posts, but a never-ending list of retweets; (4) low posts/high results, bots tend to amplify single posts; (5) common content, the content of the shared and published posts is similar; (6) the secret society of silhouettes, the oldest bots did not have an avatar image, they were represented by the standard silhouette; (7) stolen or shared photo, the bots without the standard silhouette have often stolen the profile image on the Web, although nowadays modern generative adversarial networks are able to create new plausible faces, indistinguishable from real people's ones; (8) bot's in a name, many bots have a @ symbol before the name, or an alphanumeric string generated by an algorithm; (9) Twitter of Babel, many of the bots are political while others, although developed for commercial purposes, may be used to boost political tweets; (10) commercial content, advertising is seen as a classic indicator of botnets; (11) automation software, the use of URL shortener is a possible clue, a frequent use of them is an indicator of automation; and (12) retweets and likes, an indicator of a botnet can be the ratio between the number of retweets and the number of "likes" of a particular post, given that some bots are programmed to both like and retweet the same tweet.

> 🖝 **Resources**
> One of the few publicly available repositories of datasets for training bot detection methods is hosted by Indiana University.[57]

---

[56]https://pan.webis.de/clef19/pan19-web/author-profiling.html (Last checked August 2020).

[57]https://botometer.iuni.iu.edu/bot-repository/datasets.html (Last checked August 2020).

Fake Profiles

Before starting an online propaganda campaign, as well as a misinformation/disinformation campaign on social media, one of the first steps is to create a fake profile, to avoid being identified and prosecuted in any way. In each campaign, thousands of plausible fake profiles are distributed among real people, with the aim of manipulating their opinions by sharing artfully created low-quality information with them. Despite the clear repercussions that these fake profiles bring, there are still no definitive ways to prevent them from being created and used as part of information operations. To make an example, an article on Ars Technica states that social media platforms leave 95% of reported fake accounts up.[58] Other recent results reported that only 5% of sophisticated fake profiles are actually removed from Twitter [42]. Scholars are therefore working hard to make their contribution to the cause, proposing innovative solutions that could be employed by social media platforms to mitigate the issue.

Facebook Many studies in the literature are focusing on the Facebook platform to identify fake profiles. To make an example, in [122], Conti et al. explained how dangerous an adversary impersonating a real person on an OSN can be, aiming at acquiring as much personal information as possible to steal online identities. In this study, the authors investigated this problem and proposed an interesting approach to mitigate it. They first consider the time evolution of OSNs (i.e., Facebook, in this specific study), together with the characteristics of the growth rate of the network. Then, they showed that attackers aiming at impersonating a victim will eventually avoid people that are close friends of the victim in real life. This will change the evolution of the network and the interaction with the friends, thus allowing easier detection.

From Manual to Automatic Detection However, some companies prefer to rely on human employees to detect, verify, and shut down fake accounts. An example is given by Tuenti, one of the largest OSNs in Spain. According to [123], 14 of Tuenti's full-time employees have been working exclusively on that task, thus resulting in substantial monetary costs. The difficulty in capturing the behavior of both fake and real OSN profiles is the main reason behind the non-automation of the task. To cope with this limitation, the authors introduced SybilRank, a scalable tool that relies on social graph properties and allows to rank the users according to the perceived likelihood of being fake. SybilRank has been deployed in the operation center of Tuenti and proved to have very good performance. Indeed, approximately 90% of the 200,000 accounts identified by SybilRank warranted suspensions, while Tuenti's current manual approach identified only 5% of the inspected accounts to be fake.

Dark Web Fake profiles are also widespread in the Dark Web, where the anonymity guaranteed by the technology acts as additional protection for the

---

[58]https://arstechnica.com/tech-policy/2019/12/social-media-platforms-leave-95-of-reported-fake-accounts-up-study-finds/ (Last checked August 2020).

users. To make an example, by relying on The Onion Router (TOR) anonymity mechanisms, users are allowed to anonymously access anonymous services (i.e., hidden services). If on the one hand, hidden services can be meeting places where dissidents of authoritarian countries may express their opinions without incurring in censorship or prosecutions, on the other hand, they often host questionable, controversial forums (e.g., CRD Club, a Russian site on computer hacking and technology frauds; or Dream Market, a forum in which the quality of drugs and related vendors sold in the associated marketplace is discussed). The first approach to detect and geographically deanonymize communities of the hidden services on the Dark Web has been proposed by La Morgia et al. [124], where the authors, by relying on a combination of Gaussian mixture models and the expectation-maximization fitting method, have been able to identify the time zone of the users by only exploiting the timestamps of the comments they posted. The paper has been extended in [125] to validate and confirm the first results by applying Native Language Identification techniques. Native Language Identification is the task of determining the native language of an author based only on his writings in a second language. The authors applied Native Language Identification techniques to discover the geographical distribution of users in the Dark Web's hidden services by only relying on the English text of the messages they posted, thus validating the results obtained during the analysis carried out in the previous study.

Twitter Several studies in the literature focus on the Twitter platform, being one of the social media that most suffer from the presence of fake profiles. In [126], to make an example, the authors analyzed 62 million publicly available Twitter user profiles to identify automatically generated fake profiles. The authors rely on a combination of pattern-matching algorithms on screen names (with an analysis of tweet update times) and social graph analysis for detecting fake profiles on the OSN. An analysis of the characteristics of the fake profiles led to several interesting discoveries: (1) the fake profiles were created in batches, over intervals of less than 40 s, and (2) all of the fake profiles were created on some weekdays during select times of the day, thus suggesting the existence of some manual element in either the generation or the maintenance of the profiles.

Survey Many of the relevant studies in the literature about the detection of fake profiles have been collected in [127]. In this survey, the authors classified them under three major categories: network structure or graph-based defense, feature or content-based defense, and hybrid approaches, which is a combination of both. The studies, together with their assumptions, characteristics, datasets, and selection techniques, are effectively visually represented through timelines who also include their date of publication. Finally, the authors identified a list of open issues and proposed some interesting countermeasures that are worth investigating.

LinkedIn Facebook and Twitter, although among the most famous and popular OSNs, are only two of the many platforms currently affected by the fake account epidemic. Indeed, the authors in [128] proposed an approach to identify fake profiles in LinkedIn, the American business and employment-oriented service. According to the authors, the approaches that have been proposed for other social networks rely on data that are not publicly available for profiles on LinkedIn. For this reason, in this study, the minimal set of profile data required to identify fake accounts on LinkedIn is introduced, together with a suitable data mining approach for this task. The proposed approach, when applied to the 3 datasets consisting of 37 profiles each, reached an accuracy of 87% with and a true negative rate of 94%.

Astroturf

The term astroturf was coined in 1966, when a form of artificial grass was installed in Houston, Texas. This turf, although designed to look like natural grass, is fake [129]. The term has been then extensively used to refer to the action of creating impressions of widespread support for policies, individuals, or products, where a little or (most of the time) none of such support really exists. When applied to political contexts—i.e., political astroturfing—it appears as a centrally coordinated disinformation campaign in which all the participants pretend to be ordinary citizens who act independently according to their will. Predictably, political astroturfing has the potential to heavily influence electoral outcomes, as well as any other forms of political behavior [130].

The early detection of astroturfing campaigns is crucial, since it allows to timely manage a phenomenon that would soon become uncontrollable due to its ever-increasing nature. Astroturfing has been studied in the literature both from a theoretical and from a practical perspective.

Theoretical Perspective In [131], the authors were among the first to study the astroturfing phenomenon from a theoretical perspective. They provided an interesting theoretical definition of online astroturfing and discussed many of its key attributes. The motivations behind the employment of astroturfing, as well as the methods used to start an astroturfing campaign, and the mechanisms for effective astroturfing have been discussed in detail, to provide valuable insights for both practitioners and scholars.

Practical Perspective In [10], on the other hand, the authors studied astroturfing political campaigns on microblogging platforms. The study was followed by the implementation of a machine learning framework, called Klatsch, which relies on topological features, content-based features, and crowdsourced features to detect the early stages of the viral spreading of political misinformation. The proposed model reached 96% accuracy when applied in the detection of astroturfing content in the run-up to the 2010 US midterm elections. Authors in [132], instead, proposed a hidden astroturfing detection approach based on a combination of the analysis of emotions and the detection of unfair ratings. The system is composed of five modules: (1) a data crawling module, (2) a preprocessing module, (3) a bag-of-words establishment module, (4) an emotion mining and analysis module, and (5) a matching module, respectively. The results show how this approach can detect implicit astroturfing under the prerequisite of an improvement in the classification accuracy of the emotions.

There are many ways to start an online astroturfing campaign. The goal, as defined above, is to increase the credibility of statements/organizations without revealing the identity of the supporters. A politician, for example, might buy an army of anonymous bots (or fake accounts) who would start following him and retweeting the tweets he shares, to reach a wider audience. An inexperienced eye may consider those followers real and may unconsciously be affected by the ever-increasing popularity of the politician. The authors in [73] were among the first to propose an approach aiming at detecting fake Twitter followers. In this interesting paper, they (1) reviewed many of the most relevant features for the detection of atypical Twitter accounts; (2) created a dataset of verified humans and fake followers that has been released open-source;[59] and (3) trained a machine learning classifier built over the features identified. The proposed approach demonstrated the effectiveness of the selected features and correctly classified more than 95% of the accounts of the original training set.

Survey Many of the abovementioned studies, together with other interesting ones, have been gathered into a recent survey about the astroturfing techniques [133]. The authors provided a detailed taxonomy of the approaches, thoroughly summarizing the studies in the literature, and pointed out interesting research challenges and research directions for future possible contributions. Challenges and potential research directions include the need for annotated astroturfing datasets, to create an effective ground truth; the consideration of the size and the dynamicity of the OSN's data; and the study of the privacy and security in online astroturfing. Furthermore, the authors made available the set of essential characteristics they believe a generic astroturfing detection framework should present, to address the challenges identified. According to the study, a framework for detecting astroturfing should present the following characteristics: (1) generalization across multiple OSN platforms, the framework should require no (or at max, a few) modifications to be applied to different OSNs; (2) diverse feature space design, a framework relying on hybrid feature spaces would be more robust and valuable with respect to a framework that relies on a single class of features; (3) platform selection and data collection, simplicity in data collection should be a key indicator for choosing the platform; and (4) facilitation of network interaction data, the framework should facilitate the extraction of the data at the network level to identify the graph of the interactions, a data structure that is crucial for the extraction of useful features.

---

[59]http://mib.projects.iit.cnr.it/dataset.html (Last checked August 2020).

Spammers

Although apparently they seem less threatening than the other malicious actors we have considered, spammers heavily outperform contenders when it comes to the number of accounts within social media. Indeed, according to an article published on Bloomberg, experts estimated that as many as 40% of social network accounts are used for spam.[60] Social media platforms are now appearing as heavens on earth for spammers who, instead of senselessly searching for email addresses on the Web to overwhelm with their content, have the opportunity of targeting specific demographic segments, particular groups, or specific subsets of people, according to the organization of the social media they are in. Social media has implemented various mechanisms to report the accounts that exhibit these behaviors, intending to clearing them out from the platform once a given threshold of reports has been reached (or once careful investigations have been carried out on the reported account). However, spammers used to frequently change their behaviors, thus being extremely difficult to be identified [4]. The literature boasts many contributions to mitigate the problem, with solutions that consider the identification of spammers either as a classification problem or as an anomaly detection problem, respectively.

Classification Problem In machine learning and statistics, classification is the problem of identifying to which set of categories a new observation belongs, based on the features extracted during the training phase. In literature, many contributions to identify spammers treated the problem as a classification problem. In [134], the author relied on three graph-based features (i.e., the number of followers, the number of friends, and the ratio between them) and three content-based features (i.e., the number of duplicate tweets, the number of HTTP links, and the number of replies/mentions) extracted from the top 20 most recent tweets of the users. Results showed an accuracy of 91.7% by using a Naive Bayesian classifier on a dataset proposed by the author. A new dataset is also proposed by the authors in [135]. To build the dataset, they created a set of honey-profiles on three large social networks (i.e., Facebook, Twitter, and Myspace), and they logged the contacts and the received messages. From the received messages, the authors identified four categories of spam bots:

- *Displayers:* automated agents that, instead of directly sending spam messages to other users, display spam content on their profile page. This spammer is considered the least effective one in terms of people reached;
- *Braggers:* automated agents that send messages to their feed (e.g., status updates on Facebook, tweets on Twitter);
- *Posters:* automated agents that send messages to other users (i.e., on users' wall on Facebook); and
- *Whisperers:* automated agents that send private messages to other users.

---

[60]https://www.bloomberg.com/news/articles/2012-05-24/likejacking-spammers-hit-social-media (Last checked August 2020).

Having in mind these distinctions, the authors trained a classifier by relying on six features: the FF ratio (i.e., the number of friend requests sent over the number of friends), the URL ratio (i.e., the number of messages that contain URLs over the total number of messages), the messages' similarity, the friend choice (i.e., the total number of names among the friends over the number of distinct first names), the number of messages sent, and the number of friends. The classifier allowed to detect 130 spammers in the Facebook Los Angeles and New York network dataset and 15,392 spammers on Twitter.

This problem has been considered as a classification problem also by Singh et al. [136], where five types of spammers have been identified:

- *Sole spammers:* accounts created with the sole purpose of spreading malicious scripts;
- *Twitter followers market merchants:* accounts that send both information and promotional links;
- *Pornographic storytellers:* accounts that disseminate pornographic content;
- *Fake profiles:* users that impersonate the profiles of genuine users; and
- *Compromised profiles:* existing genuine profiles that have been stolen by attackers.

The dataset is composed of approximately 20 million tweets written and shared by around 100,000 users. By using a machine learning classifier that relies on Bayes Net, Logistic Regression, J48, Random Forest, and AdaBoostM1, the authors have been able to predict spammers with an accuracy of 92.1%.

Anomaly Detection All the studies described in the previous paragraph considered the detection of spammers in OSNs as a classification problem. In [137], instead, the problem is treated as an anomaly detection problem. Anomaly detection consists of identifying unexpected events or items in data sets, which differ from the norm. Besides the features identified in the previous studies (i.e., the follower count, the friend count, the favorites count, the listed count, the tweet count, the retweet count, user verified, follower ratio, link count, reply/mention count, and hashtag count), the authors took into account further 95 one-gram features extracted from the text of the tweets. Then, they modified and applied two stream clustering algorithms to adapt to the streaming nature of tweets, StreamKM++ and DenStream, respectively. Even if the algorithms were effective by themselves (i.e., StreamKM++ performed 99% recall and 6.4 false positive rate, while DenStream performed 99% recall and 2.2% false positive rate), the authors introduced a model that exploits the conjunction of the two approaches, reaching striking performance (i.e., 100% recall and 2.2% of false positive rate).

Evading Techniques Hand in hand with the introduction of machine learning algorithms to detect spammers inside social networks, several evading techniques have been developed, to allow spammers to deceive the classifiers and continue their activity undisturbed [4]. Early evading techniques have been studied in [138]. The authors analyzed the difficulties of using machine learning features to detect spammers and carried out an interesting analysis aiming at evaluating both the features used in the literature (24 features in total) and new features, proposed in the same study. Results showed that the newly designed features are more effective when it came to detecting Twitter spammers (even the ones that employ evasion techniques). Indeed, the new features allowed to increase the detection rate to 85%, a noteworthy improvement if compared with a detection rate of 51% (the worst existing detector evaluated) or 73% (the best existing detector evaluated).

Blacklisting One seminal study about spammers on Twitter is discussed in [139]. Authors found that 8% of 25 million URLs posted on Twitter are related to malware, scams, or phishing. Furthermore, according to their analysis, most of the accounts that are guilty of sending spam messages have been compromised and are puppeteered by spammers. After discovering that the URLs identified were already listed on popular blacklists, as a countermeasure, the authors proposed to rely on these blacklists to detect spammers on the social platforms. However, they pointed out several limitations: (1) 90% of visitors view a page before it is blacklisted, since the procedure to blacklist a page is too slow compared to the spreading of spam, and (2) even by reducing the delays of the blacklisting procedure, spammers might rely on URL shortening services to obfuscate the original link and circumvent the defense mechanism.

An In-Depth Analysis To analyze the behavior of spammers, together with the tools, the techniques, and the support infrastructure they boast, the authors in [140] carried out an interesting analysis of over 1.1 million accounts suspended by Twitter in a period of 7 months. The dataset is composed of 1.8 billion tweets, of which 80 million are related to spammer accounts. They discovered that (1) Twitter banned 77% accounts the same day of their first tweet and (2) less than 9% of spammers form social relationships with Twitter users, 17% of spammers performed hijacking activities, and 52% made use of unwelcome ways to reach an audience. Furthermore, the authors described that five specific spam campaigns that were controlling approximately 145,000 accounts, each of them with a different, unique spamming strategy, have been able to persist for months.

Sockpuppets

Sockpuppeting, which refers to creating fake identities to interact with other users, particularly in online discussions, may easily result in deceptions, manipulation of the public opinion, and the vandalization of online content. Sockpuppets may be semi-automated (as well as fully automated) agents whose goal is to spread lies, misinformation, and falsehood, against the target on duty. The phenomenon has been studied in the literature from several points of view.

Online Deception Knowing the reason behind online deception is a necessary step to understand the sockpuppetry phenomena. One of the studies that moved the first steps in this direction is [141]. The authors created a Web-based survey and analyzed the answers of 257 users. According to the analysis, (1) most of the users think that online deception is widespread but only one-third of them engaged in one; (2) online deception is performed by frequent (i.e., users who regularly visit the Web), young, and competent users; and (3) the identity "play" and the privacy concerns are among the most common motivation of engaging online deception.

Detecting Sockpuppets in Online Communities Several studies in the literature focused on detecting sockpuppets in OSNs/discussion communities. To make an example, in [142] the authors proposed an algorithm that makes use of a combination of authorship-identification techniques and link analysis to detect sockpuppets on the Web. They started by proposing a new social network model in which the nodes are represented by the users, and two nodes are connected if these users have similar attitudes with respect to the topics with which they interact. After building such a graph, (1) the edges are pruned according to the impact of the writing styles of the node, and (2) link-based community detection is performed. A similar graph has been built in [143]. The authors introduced a similar-orientation network where each node represents a user account and two nodes share an edge if they have similar sentiment orientations to most topics. In this case, the authors relied on multiple random walk modules to calibrate the weight of each edge and applied community detection algorithms to detect the sockpuppet gangs within the network.

Sockpuppets vs Ordinary Users In a recent work [144], the authors studied sockpuppetry across nine discussion communities to highlight the differences between sockpuppets and ordinary users. In particular, the proposed work analyzed the linguistic traits of the sockpuppets, their posting behavior, and the social network structure. The study about the linguistic traits showed that sockpuppets tend to start fewer discussions compared with normal users; they write posts that are usually shorter; they make extensive use of personal pronouns, such as "I"; and they swear more. When one person controls more than one account, these accounts are more likely to interact on the same discussions at the same time. Furthermore, the authors offered a detailed taxonomy of sockpuppets' behavior in online discussions. For example, sockpuppets could vary in their deceptiveness (i.e., whether and how the sockpuppets pretend to be different users) or their supportiveness (i.e., whether the sockpuppets support the same arguments backed by accounts controlled by the same user).

Vandalization The vandalization of online content became a serious concern over the past few years. One of the websites that took the brunt of it is Wikipedia, the world's largest crowdsourced encyclopedia. On the Wikipedia platform, every user has the opportunity to write, edit, and leave comments to articles. The registration is optional and requires only a few personal information. This led to the creation of multiple identities by malicious users for several reasons, including block evasion and block stacking. In [145] the authors carried out a case study of sockpuppet detection in Wikipedia. In particular, they made use of machine learning techniques to solve authorship attribution problems and discover who is the real puppeteer behind the documents. Wikipedia as an experimental case has been used also by Tsikerdekis and Zeadally [146]. The authors explained how the currently adopted methods to detect sockpuppets (or multiple account identity deception in general), mainly based on profile data and text lexical features, are inefficient for the social media environment, given the large volumes of data involved. Because of this limitation, they introduced a new method of detection that relies on nonverbal behavior, thus being computationally efficient for the social media environment.

Sockpuppetry on the News The impact sockpuppeting had on society has been also highlighted by an interesting article of the New York Times, called "The Hand That Controls the Sock Puppet Could Get Slapped" [147]. The article tells the story of John Mackey, the CEO of Whole Foods Market, who intervened in anonymous online discussions to promote his supermarket chain's stock.

However, it is worth noting that, although sockpuppetry could be used with malicious purposes, it may not always be the case. Indeed, according to [144], some users could create different identities to participate in different discussions and enjoy activities in different spheres of interest, without ever pretending to be other users.

Political Memes

Milner in 2013 defined memes as "multimodal artefacts remixed by countless participants, employing popular culture for public commentary" [148], while, according to Dictionary.com, a meme is "a humorous image, video, piece of text, etc. that is copied (often with slight variations) and spread rapidly by Internet users."[61] Throughout history, memes ranged from harmless and nonsensical media to dangerous and controversial ones, a transition that eventually led to endless fights, discussions, and debates, with online social media as a stage. Although, for many, they may seem harmless and superficial, memes are changing the way business operations are conducted, by shaping the popular culture while playing an extremely active role in shaping the dynamics of modern society [149].

A meme is considered a political meme when it depicts political figures. Political memes have been used in the past to reinforce an aspect of a candidate (or, conversely, to weaken or damage an opponent) enough to change the public opinion and have a severe impact on political elections. An example is given by Ted Cruz, an American politician that, during the 2016 primaries, has been declared (by a political meme) to be the Zodiac Killer (Axelrod), the pseudonym of a renowned serial killer operating in Northern California. The political meme went viral, and according to Public Policy Polling, 40% of the voters in Florida have been influenced by the meme; 10% of them had a serious thought that Ted could have been the Zodiac Killer.[62]

---

[61] https://www.dictionary.com/browse/meme?s=t (Last checked August 2020).

[62] https://en.wikipedia.org/wiki/Ted_Cruz%E2%80%93Zodiac_Killer_meme (Last checked August 2020).

This episode, along with many others, makes it clear how important it is to identify memes that can potentially affect people's public opinion. Their detection has been faced by some interesting articles in the literature that are described below.

Detection The detection of memes before their widespread diffusion and evolution became a priority, to understand the dynamics of the society and the future trends and to plan any strategic action. For this reason, several research studies started facing this problem by providing interesting contributions. In [150], the authors offer a detailed quantitative analysis of the global news cycle and a study of the information propagation dynamics between mainstream and social media. They introduced a framework for tracking short phrases and identified memes exhibiting rich daily variation, showing how such an approach could represent coherently the news cycle (i.e., "the daily rhythms in the news media that have long been the subject of qualitative interpretation but have never been captured accurately enough to permit actual quantitative analysis"). In particular, 1.6 million mainstream media sites and blogs have been analyzed for 3 months, for a total of 90 million articles analyzed. Among the many interesting discoveries, they observed a lag of 2.5 h between the peaks of attention about a phrase in the news social media compared to the same phrase in blogs. In [151], the authors introduced Truthy, a software system implemented as a website that allows to identify and analyze political memes in Twitter, helping at detecting astroturfing, smear campaigns, and other misinformation campaigns in the context of the US political elections. Some of the memes identified through this framework are characterized by small diffusion networks, representing the perfect moment for the identification, to avoid any subsequent diffusion.

It is a common belief that Internet memes spread virally but the evidence is often in short supply. This need for investigating the epidemic dynamics of memes has been fulfilled by Bauckhage [152] that, in the proposed study, analyzed the temporal dynamics and the infectious properties of 150 famous Internet memes. By analyzing several mathematical models of epidemic spread contextualized in the Internet meme domains, the author discovered that (1) traditional compartment models with constant parameters well describe the growth and the decline patterns of Internet memes but are not able to characterize short-lived bursts of Internet meme-related activities; (2) temporal dynamics of Internet memes are accurately summarized by log-normal distributions (for 70% of the 150 memes taken into account, the probability of observing a log-normal model underlying the data distribution exceeded 90%); and (3) the majority of famous Internet memes are mostly disseminated to homogeneous online communities and OSNs.

Trolls

Trolls represent Internet users that create and post offensive, divisive, provocative messages in online communities to provoke emotional responses and sow discord. Several forms of trolling can be found on social media, from the one in which trolls make statements about political debates to the ones in which trolls provoke and insult people, resulting in harmful and life-risky situations.

Among the many categories of trolls, it is possible to find the corporate, political, and special-interested sponsored trolls. Those accounts are usually employed by governments and organizations to opportunely manipulate public opinion or to start astroturfing campaigns. Another category is represented by trolls that, without any reason, rage against users, generating cyberbullying situations. Those kinds of trolls are usually found in social media, a habitat that several studies have defined much more dangerous than phone calls and messages when it comes to cyberbullying. According to the studies, victims of cyberbullying live with several feelings (e.g., depression, anger, overwhelming, powerless, humiliation) and are almost twice as likely to attempt suicide.[63]

Given these premises, the task of identifying troll accounts before they start generating chaos on social media is a priority, and the literature can boast several contributions that move the first steps in that direction.

Sentiment Analysis Since trolls represent users that usually post obscene, negative, and inflammatory comments on the Web, authors in [153] proposed a detection approach relying on the sentiment analysis of the messages. In particular, the authors decided to focus on three attributes of trolls: (1) repetitiveness, the trolls used to send a large number of messages; (2) destructiveness, the trolls used to express negative sentiments to create chaos in the online discussion; and (3) deceptiveness, the trolls' messages may be deceptive to sow discord. Starting from a limited training set (i.e., 20 users), the binary classification through a Ranking SVM classifier reached a 60% generalized Receiver Operating Characteristic (ROC). However, during the experiment, the authors were relying on a sentiment analysis model trained on a dataset written in standard English, while the messages in the forums were often written in colloquial English (from Singapore). They improved the performance by applying domain adaptation techniques to the sentiment analysis, finally reaching a ROC of 78%.

Combined Features According to some studies in the literature, an effective solution to the challenge of detecting trolls in OSNs consists of the integration of different classes of features. In [154], the authors proposed a holistic system, called TrollPacifier, that integrates the user-level features with the ones derived from the analysis of texts and the local social graph. Six groups of features have been identified in this study: (1) writing style-based features, (2) sentiment-based features, (3) behavior-based features, (4) social interaction-based features, (5) linked media-based features, and (6) publication time-based features, respectively. The introduced holistic classifier, applied on a dataset composed of 500 troll and 500 non-troll users, showed an accuracy of 95.5%.

---

[63]https://www.warrington-worldwide.co.uk/2020/04/10/the-effects-of-internet-trolling/#:~: text=Some%20of%20the%20feelings%20that,the%20person%20disinterest%20in%20life (Last checked August 2020).

Ranking Some other studies in the literature faced the problem from a different perspective. Their goal is to introduce ranking methods on the OSN that will eventually cause automatic isolation of malicious accounts. For example, the authors in [155] proposed a mechanism to compute a trustworthiness ranking of users, aiming at demoting malicious users in the ranking, thus avoiding them gaining a high reputation in the network. The idea is to allow the propagation of both positive and negative opinions about the users, which will eventually influence their global trust score. The proposed method, called PolarityTrust, has been tested by carrying out different experiments: (1) by using a real-world dataset extracted from Slashdot.org, (2) by relying on a set of randomly generated graphs, and (3) by using a combination of a real-world dataset and generation techniques. Another example is given by Cambria et al. [156] that, by exploiting natural language information of the text, defines the level of "trollness" of each post and classify the authors accordingly.

Cyberbullying To fight the cyberbullying phenomenon that, in many cases, has led to disastrous consequences in the real life, authors in [157] proposed a supervised machine learning approach for detecting troll profiles in the Twitter OSN. The assumption made in this study is that the real person behind a troll profile will follow, with the personal profile, the troll profile, to stay updated on the activity surrounding the latter. The authors relied on four features: the text of the tweet, the time of publication of the tweet, its language, and its geo-position, respectively, and applied several supervised learning classifiers, including Random Forest, J48 (i.e., a type of decision tree classifier), K-Nearest Neighbor, and Sequential Minimal Optimization (SMO). The maximum accuracy, when applied to a dataset composed of 1900 tweets written by 19 users, has been reached by the SMO and the decision trees classifier, with 68.48% and 66.48%, respectively. The proposed methodology has been applied in practice in one elementary school in the city of Bilbao (Spain). The authors have been able to attribute the authorship of the offensive messages to the culprits that, frightened by possible consequences, voluntarily confessed and apologized.

Other Machine Learning Approaches Other studies in the literature exploit machine learning techniques to distinguish trolls from normal users. To make an example, in [158], the authors developed a machine learning model to predict whether a Twitter account is a Russian troll. Starting from a dataset of 170,000 accounts and relying on both behavioral and linguistic features, they demonstrated that it is possible to distinguish a troll with an AUC of 98.9% and a precision of 78.5%. The model has been subsequently applied in the wild, specifically to out-of-sample accounts, and led to the discovery of approximately 2.6% of mentions of top journalists occupied by Russian trolls. Furthermore, according to additional analysis, the author highlighted that these trolls are not merely software-controlled automated agents and are able to manage their online identities in complex ways. In [159], instead, the authors proposed an interesting approach to analyzing both user identities and their social roles in OSNs. In particular, they developed a new text distance metric (i.e., the time-sensitive semantic edit distance) useful to classify the social roles of trolls based on the traces (e.g., tweets) they leave on the social network. To develop and evaluate their method, the authors characterized the Russian trolls that attempted to manipulate public opinion during the 2016 US presidential election, to understand their tactics based on their social roles and strategies. As a result, this study shows patterns in the similarities of tweets the Russian trolls left behind while posting online, providing useful insights into Russian troll activities both during and after the aforementioned election.

Lastly, in [160], the authors proposed an easy yet effective method to recognize opinion manipulation trolls on the Web. They assume that a user who is called "troll" by several people is likely to be one and classify them as such, reaching from 82 to 95% accuracy. A subset of the authors, 1 year later [161], proposed a classifier able to distinguish "paid trolls" from "mentioned trolls." "Paid trolls" are defined as trolls that have been revealed from leaked reputation management contracts, while "mentioned trolls" are defined as trolls that have been called such by different people. The classifier was able to distinguish a paid troll from a mentioned troll with an accuracy of 81–82%.

2.5   Open Issues and Future Directions

The advent of artificial intelligence, defined "the new electricity" by Dr. Andrew Ng, VP and Chief Scientist of Baidu and Adjunct Professor at Stanford University, is completely revolutionizing the way we work, think, and live. Institutions, companies, universities, and people in general are heavily relying on the innovation provided by artificial intelligence to automate tasks and achieve results that were unthinkable until a few years ago. Unfortunately, the undeniable benefits of this outstanding technology can also be exploited for malicious purposes: to create increasingly credible fake content or to automate fishing and disinformation campaigns on the Web, to name a few. According to several experts, the support artificial intelligence may bring to the creation of misinformation campaigns might further amplify a problem that is already difficult to manage. Indeed, spreading misinformation is way too easier than defending against it, and the support provided by artificial intelligence could even widen this gap.

One case in point is the experiment conducted by two data scientists from Zero-FOX, in which they implemented an artificial hacker able to compose and distribute more phishing tweets than humans, with a substantially better conversion rate. This experiment has shown how, with the support provided by artificial intelligence, it is possible to effectively reach a wider audience. Another fascinating—yet scary—innovative example, made possible thanks to artificial intelligence, is given by deepfakes.

> ✐ **Definitions**
>
> **Deepfakes** Deepfakes are defined as synthetic media (e.g., video, audio, text) in which, by relying on AI algorithms, a person has been replaced with someone else in a way that makes the multimedia resource look authentic.

Although this technology is being primarily used to make "fun videos" (e.g., put the face of the actor Nicolas Cage literally everywhere), there are multiple ways to exploit it for malicious (and extremely dangerous) purposes. The technology brings people to believe that something is real when it is not and, if placed in the wrong hands, could potentially endanger the credibility of individuals and allow a faster spread of misinformation [4, 11]. With this technology, everyone can make anyone saying anything at any time, and the authoritativeness of information is inevitably compromised.

"If I do not see it I do not believe it," Thomas the Apostle said incredulously in the Gospel of John, when he refused to believe in the resurrection of Jesus. With the advent of deepfakes, unfortunately, seeing is no longer enough.

2.5.1 New Directions

A detailed analysis of the state of the art allowed us to understand the current open issues, the existing countermeasures, as well as their limitations when it comes to countering these new, AI-enabled threats. In the following, we recommend some valuable directions we think are worth investigating, to stop (or at least mitigate) the wave of disinformation and donate a new, reliable, truthful face to the Web.

- *Coordinated Inauthentic Behavior.* Coordinated inauthentic behavior is a term coined by Facebook and refers to a situation in which "groups of pages or people work together to mislead others about who they are or what they are doing".[64] Valuable studies and OSNs, such as Facebook and Twitter, started focusing on the detection of coordinated inauthentic behavior, since devising techniques for spotting such behaviors is likely to provide better results when compared with the detection of individual malicious accounts. An interesting and potentially fruitful research direction thus consists of identifying suspicious coordination independently of the nature of individual accounts. However, in order to reach a valuable accuracy, several challenges have to be faced, including scalability problems of the group-based detectors and the intrinsic fuzziness of inauthentic coordination [4].

---

[64]https://about.fb.com/news/2018/12/inside-feed-coordinated-inauthentic-behavior/   (Last checked August 2020).

- *Proactiveness rather than reactiveness.* Given the quick propagation of low-quality information and the simplicity in automating the creation of fake accounts, it may be smart to push research toward proactive defenses rather than reactive ones [4, 162]. Indeed, it is very difficult to efficiently react once the propagation started.
- *Technology and policies.* At the current level of technology, machine learning makes it possible to create bots that emulate human behavior, think processes and strategies, in such a way as to be impossible to be distinguished from humans in several contexts [4]. The current machine learning techniques, once limited to responding to inputs from the users (e.g., in online reservations), are now capable of producing new synthetic content from scratch, using generative machine learning algorithms. The authenticity of these artfully created multimedia resources may be currently checked by digital forensics experts, who are able to detect the artifact by analyzing the lack of camera-induced imperfections, but the approach does not scale [163]. Many researchers think that fighting fire with fire might be the ideal solution, i.e., respond to automatic systems for propagation and diffusion with automatic systems to prevent/stop it. However, according to the analysis in [163], technological solutions alone cannot address the challenges of fake content emulating human behavior, and there is the need of "developing public policy, legal, and normative frameworks for managing the malicious applications of technology in conjunction with efforts to refine it." Some of the technological defenses proposed in the aforementioned study are described in the following resource box.

▶ Resources

Technological Defenses Proposed by Boneh et al. [163]

- **Automate the process of digital forensics [164].** A detector may be able to detect imperfections on the multimedia content to categorize it as "fake" [165, 166]. However, even if an extremely accurate detector is introduced, the GAN technology would allow creating new content to avoid the detection by construction, thus placing a tie as the maximum aspiration for the defender.
- **Improve the provenance of human forms of digital communication.** The goal is to identify deepfakes as content that was digitally synthesized. In this way, every camera should be equipped with a tamper-proof cryptographic signing key, necessary to sign the picture it takes, and every generator would not be able to sign the produced fake content. Despite the obvious advantages, the creation and the distribution of the keys, as well as their authentication, make the solution logistically hard.
- **Total accountability.** If a public figure is concerned about fake videos and wants to protect herself, she could continuously record herself with

---

(continued)

a tamper-proof camera to demonstrate its estrangement from any facts created in a fake video concerning her. As the authors mention, in this case, the cure may be worse than the disease, since it would bring to striking privacy leakages.

- *Multimodal integration of features.* The studies in the literature dealing with the detection of low-quality information or malicious actors often rely on a feature extraction phase, in which preliminary information are gathered to identify any suspicious pattern. Such information may be extracted from several sources, e.g., metadata of posts, the text of posts, profile information, the network graph, and possibly others. An interesting future direction consists of the research of efficient multimodal integrations of features to reach higher accuracy in shorter times [11].

Part II
Economy

Since the collapse of the Soviet Union and the end of the Cold War in the late 1980, the world economy has engaged in increasingly internationalized trade that progressively led to today's economic globalization. Theoretically, this process followed free trade ideals and a progressive disengagement of states, thus somehow abiding to the famous Montesquieu theory that "commerce softens manners and encourages peace" (*The Spirit of the Laws*, 1748). According to this vision, the very idea of *economic war* represents a strident oxymoron. Unfortunately, history told us that this economic globalization process rapidly diverged from Montesquieu's ideals. Admittedly, free trade has largely imposed itself as of today, but few states gave up their prerogatives of politic and economic dominance. On the contrary, economy, finance, and commerce are all increasingly seen as subtle—yet sharp—weapons for exerting influence and for amassing power. Indeed, a nation's economy—intended as the overall production, distribution, and trade of goods and services operated by different economic agents of a nation—is essential for the nation's livelihood. The more a nation's economy is flourishing, the more the nation will be able to guarantee the public services necessary for the well-being of its citizens, including public health, instruction, and infrastructures, but also military expenses, which are crucial to ensure the security against both internal and external threats. As an example, the long-lasting conflict between People's Republic of China and the United States of America reveals more than a glimpse. The two countries are waging a merciless trade war, with huge economic interests at stake. Their weapons: customs duties, industrial espionage, technological hacks, and legal tools. The very same weapons that since many years allow Americans, among others, to impose their rules outside of their national borders.

Given this picture, the aforementioned concept of economic war cannot be seen as an inconceivable oxymoron, but rather it should be regarded as a tangible reality, the one we are living in nowadays. As a paramount example of a nation's interest in economic war, France established in 1997 the École de Guerre Économique (School of Economic Warfare) as an academic institution attached to the École Supérieure

Libre des Sciences Commerciales Appliquées (Free Superior School of Applied Commercial Sciences), a renowned Parisian business school. According to the School of Economic Warfare, economic war is a process and a strategy decided by a state within the framework of the assertion of its power on the international scene. It is carried out through information on the economic, financial, technological, legal, political, and societal fields.[1] Ever since its creation, the School of Economic Warfare has been developing an academic curriculum based upon the assumptions that (i) economic conflicts have been on the rise for the past 20 years and that (ii) information warfare and management are the primary means used by contenders to gain the upper hand in such conflicts. Because of such a level of intricacy, nations and companies require a broad range of skills in order to address information warfare on the economic battlefield. The way competitive intelligence is taught is specifically tailored to analyze and deal with economic contentions that are shaped by states and private companies alike. The school currently offers postgraduate training in areas such as Strategy and Economic Intelligence, Risk Management, International Security, and Cybersecurity. According to the school itself, one of the pillars of its model has been "the transfer of methodology from the military world to the civilian world."[2]

Within the context of economic warfare and of the weaponization of the economy, external actors, such as foreign governments and terrorist groups, could attack the economy of a nation in different ways and for different goals, such as to weaken defensive capabilities before a military attack, or just to destabilize the country sowing chaos in the population. In fact, it is known that a destabilized and fragmented country is more vulnerable and that it can be more easily influenced from the outside. To this regard, the attack surface is composed of every economic asset relevant for the country, such as individuals, businesses, organizations, or the government itself. The new technologies that are continuously applied to various sectors of the economy, on the one hand, contribute to improve economic processes, optimizing and automating them, and thus decreasing costs and increasing profits. On the other hand, however, new technologies inevitably introduce new vulnerabilities. They increase the attack surface and expose the economy to unprecedented threats. Think of cryptocurrencies. Recently, they gained huge momentum and attracted a deluge of investments. However, being a new technology, the associated risks are still unclear. Any problem such as bugs in the implementation of security protocols, or possible cyberattacks could cause financial disasters. The same considerations can be carried over to High-Frequency Trading (HFT) technologies, of which experts cannot yet say whether they represent an opportunity or a threat for markets and investors alike.

Throughout the upcoming two chapters that make up this thematic section of the book, we discuss the multitude of implications that new technologies have on the

---

[1] https://portail-ie.fr/resource/glossary/95/guerre-economique (Last checked August 2020).

[2] https://www.ege.fr/index.php/l-ecole/presentation/economic-warfare-school-of-paris.html (Last checked August 2020).

economic attack surface of a nation. We particularly focus on cryptocurrencies and on FinTech at large. As for the previous section of this book, our goal is that of highlighting emerging threats, to survey existing solutions, and to outline directions for future research and experimentation.

Chapter 3
Cryptocurrencies

A cryptocurrency is a digital asset designed to serve as a medium of exchange that should be an alternative to the classic fiat currency. The idea of bringing money from the physical to the digital realm has been investigated since the 1980s, with many attempts to create digital cash systems. Over the years, several researchers have tried to implement an electronic currency disconnected from the banking system, but none of these projects have been successful until 2008. In that year, an anonymous researcher (or a group of people) known under the pseudonym of Satoshi Nakamoto published a white paper [167] that describes a peer-to-peer electronic cash system—called Bitcoin—completely independent from the traditional banking system.

Making use of existing cryptographic technologies, such as asymmetric cryptography and hash functions, Nakamoto introduces a new technology—called blockchain—which will be crucial in the development not only of cryptocurrencies but of many other applications.

✄ Definitions

Blockchain The term blockchain refers to a technology that implements an immutable and distributed database, consisting of a chain of blocks linked together. Each block, in addition to the stored data, contains the hash of its predecessor in the chain. This implies that if block n is modified, it will be necessary to modify all the other blocks of the chain accordingly, starting from block $n + 1$ until the end of the chain.

Cryptocurrency A cryptocurrency is a decentralized electronic cash system designed to work much like a standard currency, allowing users to make virtual payments, free of a trusted central authority. Cryptocurrencies leverage

(continued)

---

cryptographic functions to ensure legitimate, unique, and publicly verifiable transactions.

Bitcoin uses the blockchain to store transactions among users, which are then permanently saved in a decentralized and immutable way. New transactions are collected and verified by specific members of the network, called miners. New blocks containing only approved transactions are validated by all participants in the protocol and added to the blockchain through a consensus mechanism, called Proof of Work (PoW), that ensures the security of the network. In this way, Bitcoin implements the first decentralized and open-source payment system that does not need a trusted third party. In fact, nobody controls or owns the Bitcoin network. Anyone can join it and download the transaction ledger—which is public—to verify and validate old and new transactions.

With the introduction of the blockchain, Nakamoto not only created what is still the most famous and used cryptocurrency but also allowed the implementation of other ones. After Bitcoin indeed, numerous other cryptocurrencies were born, some of which are very similar to it while others feature different implementations of the consensus mechanism, but all characterized by the use of the blockchain. This new technology has created novel scenarios for the state economy, enabling use cases that could potentially revolutionize the world economic landscape. Although it is currently difficult to indirectly attack a state's economy by directly hitting a cryptocurrency, it may be different in the near future. The establishment of a state cryptocurrency, as well as other strategic blockchain-based state-sponsored applications, appears to be a very likely scenario [168].

In this chapter, we examine the reasons that could push the development of a state cryptocurrency, citing the nations that have already started planning it. We then describe three scenarios in which a cryptocurrency can be attacked, based on the characteristics of the currently existing cryptocurrencies and the real attacks they have experienced. Finally, we investigate the technical features that a state cryptocurrency should have to be accepted by the population and to restrict the possibilities of attacks, both internal and external.

3.1 State-Sponsored Cryptocurrency

Nowadays, more and more nations are thinking about establishing a state cryptocurrency that will support or replace the standard fiat money. This kind of scenario, on the one hand, introduces several advantages of practical nature, such as no longer having to print physical banknotes, no longer need banking institutions that keep track of balances and transactions, the faster and (supposedly) more secure transactions, and more. On the other hand, it could expose the nation's economy to a new series of cybersecurity threats. Indeed, the classical physical currency is vulnerable to several indirect attacks that mainly aim to its devaluation, such as speculative attacks. However, other kinds of attacks, such as denial of service, are very difficult if not outright impossible, due to the physical nature of the standard currency. In fact, an attacker could target the electronic systems that allow virtual transaction, causing a temporary block of this service, but there are no ways to stop transactions with cash payments. A cryptocurrency instead, as a virtual asset, is exposed to direct attacks with consequences ranging from blocking the system for a short time to its total destruction. In the first case, malicious entities could prevent legitimate users to join the network or isolate the peers that validate transactions, causing a total blockage of the network. In this eventuality, no transactions are possible in the network because users are not able to create them or the system is not able to receive them. If the attacked cryptocurrency is the only currency available in the state, citizens will no longer be able to make transactions of any kind. Consequently, the sale of goods and services among citizens would fall into anarchy, being possible only through the adoption of antiquated forms of exchange, such as barter. Table 3.1 reports the countries that—at the time of writing—have started to design, develop, or use a national cryptocurrency or have decided to support one.

3.2 Scenario 1: Trust in Maths

This scenario takes into account a cryptocurrency that relies on the intractability of certain mathematical problems to ensure the security of its protocol. To guarantee some properties like confidentiality, integrity, and availability—fundamental for the security of every communication—the cryptocurrency protocol uses different cryptographic techniques based on mathematical problems. Users trust the system because of the difficulty of the crypto-challenges derived from the aforementioned math problems, recognized as computationally hard to solve by the worldwide scientific community.

As an example, Bitcoin relies on the Elliptic Curve Digital Signature Algorithm (ECDSA) to ensure that funds can only be spent by their rightful owners. In fact, each user account is composed of a pair of addresses—i.e., the cryptographic hashes of an ECDSA private key and the derived ECDSA public key. The owner of the private key is the owner of the account and is, therefore, the only person who can spend the money contained in it. The public key is shared with the community and used to receive payments. To transfer Bitcoins from one account to another, the sender creates a new transaction addressed to the recipient's public address and signs it with the sender's private key. For this reason, the core of the security and consistency of the Bitcoin network is the security of ECDSA private keys. ECDSA relies on the math properties of the cyclic groups of elliptic curves over finite fields and on the well-known difficulty of the Elliptic Curve Discrete Logarithm Problem (ECDLP) that points the following: given an elliptic curve over a finite field and

Table 3.1 Countries that already have or are issuing national or regional cryptocurrencies

Region	State	Type	Name	Platform	Status
Caribbean	Anguilla	State sponsored			Legislation to regulate initial offerings of cryptocurrency
	Antigua and Barbuda	State supported		Etherium	No legislation, proof-of-concept
	Dominica	State sponsored			Participates in a pilot program to develop a digital Eastern Caribbean Dollar
	Grenada	State sponsored			Participates in a pilot program to develop a digital Eastern Caribbean Dollar
	Montserrat	State sponsored			Participates in a pilot program to develop a digital Eastern Caribbean Dollar
America	Venezuela	State sponsored	Petro	NEM	Implemented
Europe	Ireland	State supported	Irishcoin	MapleCoin	Implemented, currently in use
	Lithuania	State sponsored	LBChain		Final testing phase
Asia	China	State sponsored			Developing phase

two points G and H on the curve, find the scalar k such that $H = kG$. These properties ensure that deriving a private key from the corresponding public one is computationally infeasible. In the case of Bitcoin, therefore, users trust the protocol because it is based on these known properties and accept that calculating their private key in a reasonable time is an unsolvable problem for a possible attacker. However, there is no guarantee that anyone, at any time, can solve or simplify the mathematical problem from which Bitcoin's transaction security derives. In this case, an adversary could derive any user's private key from its public one, managing to spend the victim's funds without authorization. In such an event, the victim would have no way to get his funds back since the transactions are irreversible in the Bitcoin network. Furthermore, if a cryptographic protocol is not implemented correctly, it could be vulnerable even if the math behind it is still correct and the related problem difficult to solve.

In this scenario, we investigate the possibilities that an attacker can simplify the math on which a cryptocurrency bases its security and consistency. Also, we analyze possible implementation errors that could be exploited by an adversary to attack the protocol.

> **✗ Definitions**
>
> **Elliptic Curve Discrete Logarithm Problem (ECDLP)** It is a mathematical problem based on the fact that it is infeasible to find the discrete logarithm of a random elliptic curve element with respect to a publicly known base point. The ECDLP is a special case of the discrete logarithm problem. Its apparent intractability is the basis for the security of elliptic curve cryptography. Unlike the finite field discrete logarithm problem, there are no general-purpose subexponential algorithms for solving ECDLP. This implies that it is possible to choose smaller fields than those needed for cryptographic systems based on the finite field DLP, which results in keys of smaller size.
>
> **Elliptic Curve Digital Signature Algorithm (ECDSA)** The Elliptic Curve Digital Signature Algorithm is used to create the digital signature of a file, or any other digital data, to ensure its authenticity. Essentially, it is a version of the Digital Signature Algorithm (DSA) that uses the elliptic curve. It was accepted as an ANSI standard in 1999 and as an IEEE and NIST standard in 2000. Moreover, it became an ISO standard in 1998.

3.2.1   Threat: Collapse of the Cryptocurrency Foundation

Commonly used encryption methods are believed to be secure because they have been studied for many years by the most important experts in the field. Unfortunately, this doesn't mean that they are provably secure. Someone might find, at any time, a way to reduce their complexity. The two cryptographic schemes, on which the security of almost every communication protocol depends, are based on the accepted difficulty of certain arithmetic operations. In the case of RSA, it is finding the two numbers that have been multiplied together to get the modulo. In the case of Elliptic Curve Cryptography (ECC), given two points P and Q, find out the integer x that satisfies the equation $Q = xP$. Here, "difficult" means that the time spent to perform these operations exceeds the useful time of the secret to be violated. This does not apply if a shortcut is found. In this case, an attacker could be able to get around the difficulties of solving the problem, thus reaching the solution more quickly. For example, different algorithms have been developed for computing the discrete logarithm problem on elliptic curve (on which ECDSA is based) trying to optimize the resolution phase. The two most efficient ones are the "baby-step, giant-step" algorithm and Pollard's rho method. Both mechanisms, however, as well as their various subsequent optimizations, do not currently allow attacking the ECDS protocol in a reasonable time. However, there is no way to know that better shortcuts are not going to be discovered in the future.

As an example of a similar situation, we can cite the story concerning the famous Fermat's Last Theorem (sometimes called Fermat's conjecture). Formulated in 1637, it states that the equation $x^n + y^n = z^n$ has no solution in integer for $n \geq 3$. Although this conjecture is intuitively true, nobody has been able to provide mathematical proof until a British professor, Andrew Wiles, released the first successful demonstration in 1994. Just as Fermat's conjecture, which remained unsolved for three centuries before being proved mathematically, the same could happen at any time for other mathematical problems, such as ECC.

In this scenario, the major threat is represented by an adversary that reduces the mathematical complexity of the problem on which the cryptocurrency relies on, becoming able to solve it in an optimized way. This knowledge makes the adversary able to control the cryptocurrency network by exploiting its capabilities that other peers do not have. The same result could happen if an adversary discovered a 0-day vulnerability in the implementation of one cryptographic function used by the cryptocurrency's protocol and developed a methodology to exploit it.

3.2.2   Attacks and Countermeasures

The complexity of the mathematical properties that support the correctness of the ECDSA protocol has never been reduced. However, several examples of flaws in the protocol implementation that have led to serious security incidents can be found in the literature.

One of the most critical phases of the ECDSA protocol implementation is the choice of the elliptic curve and its domain parameters. These parameters, chosen by the developer at each implementation, are fundamental for the robustness of the protocol. The standard ones (widely accepted as safe) are defined by the scientific community, but every developer is free to use other customized ones. In addition, some parameters must be chosen randomly; otherwise the security of the protocol may be compromised. In 2010, a group of hackers called *fail0verflow* discovered a serious flaw in the implementation of the ECDSA algorithm used by Sony to calculate its own set of keys used to digitally sign original software for the game console PlayStation 3 [169]. The attackers were able to recover the entire private key, then using it to distribute counterfeit software. The attack works only against the algorithm used by Sony, as it used a static parameter (the variable k) instead of one randomly selected at every execution, making the private key solvable by analyzing few digitally signed files.

In some cases, the protocol could be vulnerable even if some parameters are correctly chosen randomly, as recommended by the scientific community. In fact, often the problem lies in how random numbers are generated. In [170], the authors examined the quality of the random number generated by some common Java libraries such as Android Pseudo-random Number Generator (PRNG), Apache Harmony, GNU Classpath, OpenJDK, and Bouncy Castle. They found multiple weaknesses on entropy collector components, with different degrees of severity and probability of occurrence. In particular, they showed that the overall entropy of the Android PRNG can be reduced to only 64 bits. This weakness was exploited in 2013 to steal balances from Bitcoin users' wallets generated by any Android app. The faulty component seems to be the Java class SecureRandom (used by the vulnerable wallets) that can generate collisions on the produced random numbers. The problem is that the ECDSA algorithm requires that the random number used to sign a private key is only ever used once. If the random generated number is used twice, the private key is recoverable.

In [171], the authors identified a timing attack vulnerability in OpenSSL's implementation of Montgomery's ladder for scalar multiplication of points on elliptic curves over binary fields. This vulnerability allows a full key recovery attack against a TLS server that authenticates with ECDSA signatures.

✐ Definitions

Timing Attack When the execution time of a cryptographic device or function is variable, it may leak information on the secret parameters applied. A careful analysis that includes precise time measurements could allow the reconstruction of the system key involved. The timing attack is an attack based on the leakage of information of secret parameters through variations in the running times of a cryptographic device [172].

Hash functions are another pillar of the most important cryptocurrencies available in the global financial landscape. Several attacks against hash function implementations are discussed in the literature as well as against the compression function they used. The most important are the Chabaud et al. attack against the SHA-0 algorithm [173] and the hash function attack techniques introduced by H. Dobbertin against the MD5 algorithm [174–177]. In [173], the authors presented a methodology to find collisions in SHA-0 by looking for some kind of characteristic masks that can be added to input words with non-trivial probability of unchanging the output of the compression function. They obtained a theoretical attack on the compression function used by SHA-0 with complexity 2^{61}. These techniques are not applicable against SHA-256 and SHA-512—used by Bitcoin and by other major cryptocurrencies—as investigated by several researchers in [178–180].

✐ Definitions

Hash Function A hash function is a computational method that, taking data of an indeterminate size as input (the key), returns a fixed-size string as output (the hash value). A cryptographic hash function uses one-way math functions

(continued)

to generate a hash value from a given input. The fundamental properties of these functions are (i) *pre-image resistance* and (ii) *collision resistance*. The *pre-image resistance* ensures that the function is not invertible. This means that it must be difficult to find the key starting from the hash value. The *collision resistance*, instead, ensures that is difficult to find the same hash value for two different keys. Cryptographic hash functions can be used for many different problems, ranging from integrity and authenticity to pseudo-random number generation and key derivation.

Compression Function A compression function is a one-way function that, taking two fixed-length inputs, produces a fixed-length output. Since it respects the pre-image resistance property, a compression function differs from conventional compression algorithms, which can instead be inverted. Usually, a hash function is defined by repeated applications of a compression function, until the whole message has been processed.

3.2.3 Open Issues

As described in the previous sections, the known attacks against cryptographic functions that are used by cryptocurrencies only concern weaknesses in their implementation and choice of their security parameters. For this reason, the risks associated with the use of these technologies cannot be solved or limited by individual security methodologies (such as the use of stack canary to prevent buffer overflow), but rather by a collection of best practices.

Above all, the use of open-source implementations of security protocol ensures that the code has been reviewed by several independent experts, decreasing the risk of bugs or other errors escaped by developers, which could potentially create security problems. For example, the use of a proprietary implementation of the digital signature algorithm used by Sony caused, as described above, the hacking of the system due to a parameter defined static rather than chosen randomly at each execution. In addition to using open-source software modules, the need to verify the correctness of the whole source code before releasing a software application is crucial. There are several ways to validate the correctness of the software. The most common way to check if a program works as expected is to test it. In this regard, developers submit their program to a wide range of inputs, to check if it behaves as designed. This testing methodology ensures that the software behaves correctly in most cases, which is sufficient for most applications. However, it is impossible to guarantee that the software tested in this way always works correctly, because it is impossible to test it with every conceivable input. Even when testing an algorithm with a very large set of inputs, there is always a small probability that it will fail under some unusual conditions, leading to a security vulnerability. These possible malfunctions can also be very small and difficult to find, such as memory management errors or input validation errors that can cause a buffer overflow and, even if apparently harmless, can become the weak point that could jeopardize the security of the whole application. One of the most promising approaches to solve, or at least mitigate, this problem is called formal verification. Unlike regular software, written informally and validated mainly based on its behavior, formally verified software looks more like a mathematical proof, where each statement follows logically from the preceding one. This methodology, therefore, allows validating a software with the same certainty with which mathematicians prove a theorem.[1]

The formal verification of the software dates back to the 1970s, from an idea by Edsger Dijkstra. It includes two different domains, formal specification, and formal verification. The formal specification is a methodology to describe precisely and unambiguously what a software should do. The formal verification, instead, proves beyond any doubt that a software meets its specifications and works correctly. The problem with this technology is the difficulty of application, especially regarding formal specifications. In fact, describing in plain terms what a program should do is quite easy. However, expressing the same concept using formal language that a machine can understand and execute is much more complex. As an example, in the context of cryptographic protocol implementation, it is easy to say, at a high level, that the program will never leak the private key used to digitally sign documents, but converting this idea into a mathematical definition is not trivial. This problem particularly affects cryptographic protocols, given the complex nature of the cryptographic algorithms on which they are based. In fact, it is often very difficult to design cryptographic protocols without any weakness. Even relatively simple protocols have turned out to be vulnerable. In many cases, flaws were discovered after some time of publication or even implementation. In general, it is not trivial to see whether a cryptographic protocol is secure simply by looking at it. Even in a simple protocol, the flaws can be very subtle. This has also been demonstrated in many examples in the literature on protocols that have been published, considered sound, and then discovered to be faulty. For this reason, progress has been made in recent years in developing formal methods for the design and validation of cryptographic protocols. Specifically, two types of techniques have been applied to solve this problem, also used in the analysis of conventional communication protocols. The first uses the logic of knowledge and beliefs to shape the behaviors that evolve throughout a protocol. The second one, instead, models the protocol as an interaction between a set of state machines and attempts to demonstrate a safe protocol by specifying unsafe states and attempting to prove them unreachable, mainly by using exhaustive backward state research.

One of the most used tools in this area, called the NRL protocol analyzer, was developed by the US Naval Research Laboratory. It can be used to demonstrate the security properties of cryptographic protocols and to identify security flaws.

---

[1] https://www.wired.com/2016/09/computer-scientists-close-perfect-hack-proof-code   (Last checked August 2020).

The NRL protocol analyzer managed to do both. In particular, it has been used to find previously unknown flaws in the Simmons selective transmission protocol and the Burns-Mitchell resource sharing protocol. Moreover, it has been used also to discover some hidden assumptions in the Neuman-Stubblebine reauthentication protocol and the Aziz-Diffie wireless communication protocol [181].

> **► Resources**
>
> **NRL Protocol Analyzer** A complete presentation of how the analyzer works can be found in [182], together with a description of the basic functions used for the analysis of cryptographic protocols and a working example.

However, both the NRL protocol analyzer and other similar tools have been designed to analyze cryptographic protocols most commonly used for cryptographic key authentication. This was the usual application for cryptographic protocols in the past and remains one of the most common use cases. Subsequently, cryptographic protocols were applied to new problems, including financial transactions and key negotiations. These new applications bring new security problems that put new limits on existing tools, making them less and less effective and reliable. New research efforts are needed to identify new challenges and adapt existing tools accordingly, so that they can also be used successfully in new use case scenarios. The authors investigated in [183] how far current tools could be pushed to analyze complex protocols that must meet new types of requirements and also to find out where they need to be improved. They describe six different emerging areas in the application of formal method to cryptographic protocols, highlighting challenges where more research efforts are needed: open-ended protocols, denial of service, anonymous communication, high fidelity, composability, and negotiation of complex data structures.

3.3   Scenario 2: Trust in the Computational Power

This scenario takes into account a cryptocurrency that relies on the computational power for its security. Some cryptographic protocols, computationally hard to compromise, are used to manage different security features, such as the validity and legitimacy of transactions. Any security problem related to these protocols inevitably reflects on the security of the cryptocurrency and its users, undermining the stability of the system. The most famous example of such a cryptocurrency is Bitcoin. Indeed, its protocol heavily relies on cryptographic functions to secure its network. Public-key cryptography, for example, is used to guarantee that funds can only be spent by their rightful owners. Also, a PoW schema based on a computational puzzle is used to form new blocks and reach consensus among participants.

In general, a PoW is a piece of data that satisfies some requirements, with the peculiarity of being difficult to produce but easy to verify. Bitcoin adopts the so-called HashCash algorithm to manage the block generation. This mechanism requires each miner to bring together well-formed transactions issued by users, creating a new block. The PoW then consists of finding a value, called nonce, to be inserted in the new block such that its hash is lower than a certain target value. The features of the hash function make this task particularly difficult, and, consequently, it is not possible to know who will be the creator of the next block. The difficulty of the PoW can be varied as desired simply by changing the target value. In this way, the creation rate of the new blocks can be changed.

The PoW mechanism plays a fundamental role in system stability, ensuring the correct functioning of the network and preventing various theoretical attacks through a decentralized protocol.

In such a cryptocurrency, users trust the system because of the following two considerations:

1. The cryptographic protocols used to protect the network are well known and formally proven secure. In particular, it has been proved that, at least with the technologies currently available, it is not possible to break their security or circumvent the computational work needed to solve their crypto-challenges.
2. It is difficult for a single entity to have 51% of the whole computational power available in the entire network. This assumption is highly controversial and depends strictly on the characteristics of the system in question. Generally, it is considered valid for mature systems, with a solid and stable community behind it. In young systems, instead, with a community still in the process of settling, this assumption must be considered to be not always valid.

In this scenario, we analyze the vulnerabilities of this kind of cryptocurrency, focusing on two threats in particular: (i) the emergence of new technologies and (ii) the collusion among users. In our analysis, we discussed several real-world examples of the most important cryptocurrencies available in the market. Bitcoin, as the older and most mature one, is theoretically less exposed to such problems but cannot be considered immune.

3.3.1   Threat: New Technologies

In this scenario, one of the main concerns is an attacker equipped with an unexpected computational power derived from a new technology that did not exist at the time of the design and implementation of the cryptocurrency in question. Possible threats include a new generation of hardware that could be used by an adversary to violate the cryptographic protocols used by the network, gaining an illicit advantage over other users. An example taken from the past is the ASIC hardware. The release on the market of this new technology has favored the miners who have immediately used it, compared to those who kept using general-purpose devices.

In this scenario, if the new hardware is immediately made available on the global market, it is unlikely that a single entity will be favored. Being publicly available, the new technology would be used by many distinct and presumably geographically distributed miners, balancing the benefits within the network. This immediate distribution of the new performing resource ensures that the cryptocurrency does not suffer from security issues. In the future, this scenario could repeat itself, triggered, for example, by the development of quantum computers. In this case, however, distribution on the market could be much more complex, due to the high design and development costs of this innovative technology. The company that first obtains a functioning platform may, therefore, be the only one to benefit from it, obtaining hegemony over all the systems vulnerable to its tremendous computational capacity.

Even if the research in this field is still in its infancy, quantum computing promises to efficiently solve problems which are not practically feasible on classical computers. With its huge computational power, a quantum computer could be used to attack cryptocurrency networks whose security is based on cryptographic challenges that require a certain amount of computational power to be solved. By leveraging the advantage over traditional CPUs, an attacker equipped with a quantum computer could easily solve cryptographic schemes in a relatively short time, posing serious security problems to any system based on these mechanisms.

⚡ Definitions

Quantum Computing Classical computers perform logical operations and store data relying on the definite position of individual bits, represented as binary states 0 and 1. Quantum computing, instead, makes use of quantum mechanical phenomena to manipulate and store data, acquiring the potential to process exponentially more data compared to classical computers.

Quantum Supremacy Proposed by John Preskill in 2012, quantum supremacy describes the point where quantum computers can perform a task that no classical computer can feasibly solve, regardless of whether those tasks are useful.

ASIC Hardware Application-specific integrated circuit refers to a device specifically designed for the sole purpose of mining cryptocurrencies. Each ASIC device is customized to solve a particular PoW. As a result, each device is capable of mining only a specific cryptocurrency. This specialization, in terms of both hardware and software, offers ASIC hardware a huge advantage in mining activities compared to general-purpose hardware.

State of the Art

Given that research on quantum computers, although reaching increasingly important milestones, is still in its early stages, the threat it will bring to modern cryptography is still perceived as a remote possibility. However, the scientific community has long started to wonder about the possible impact, preparing the current systems for migration to the post-quantum era.

The potential danger posed to IT security by quantum computing was first established in 1994. That year saw the publication of a quantum computer algorithm [184] by the US mathematician and computer scientist Peter W. Shor. He demonstrated that encryption techniques that were previously assumed secure could be broken in a matter of seconds by factorization or reducing a number into its constituent factors. To do so, the Shor algorithm used the computing power of quantum computers [185].

Several components of a cryptocurrency architecture could be affected by this threat, while some others are immune. Several works demonstrated that quantum computers are capable of solving complex problems unfeasible for classic computers only by using algorithms that exploit the power of quantum parallelism. For example, a quantum computer cannot be faster than a standard one in multiplications [186]. As an example, quantum computers could not be efficiently used to compute the pre-image of a hash function or to generate a collision. For this reason, the hash-based puzzles used by several cryptocurrencies to implement their PoW [187] can be safely used in the post-quantum era as long as they leverage a hash function that provides an output with an adequate length, such as SHA-2 or SHA-3 [186]. On the contrary, quantum computers could be used to efficiently solve some problems underlying the asymmetric cryptography, such as the large prime integer factorization and the discrete logarithm problem, used by several cryptocurrencies to secure wallets—that is, to ensure that funds can only be spent by their rightful owners. However, these eventualities, at the moment, remain purely theoretical. At the time of writing, there is still no real implementation of quantum devices able to run such algorithms. In October 2019, Google claimed to have reached quantum supremacy. A quantum processor with 53 qubits performed a task in just over 3 minutes that, according to Google's calculations, would have taken the world's largest supercomputer 10,000 years, or 1.5 billion times more [188]. This claim has been questioned by IBM, according to which an ideal simulation of the same task can be performed on a classical computer in 2.5 days, and with much greater fidelity.[2] However, the Google's experiment was a first proof of concept. The next step is to build quantum computers with enough qubits to solve useful problems. According to estimates by Google researchers, the methodology they are following requires a number between 100 and 1000 qubits to achieve this goal, but nobody is sure. Once this milestone is reached, an even greater evolution is needed to pose

---

[2]https://www.ibm.com/blogs/research/2019/10/on-quantum-supremacy (Last checked August 2020).

a danger to modern cryptography. In fact, it is believed that millions of qubits are needed to break the current cryptographic schemes; it may take decades to reach that point.

3.3.2 Threat: Collusion Among Miners

Another serious threat to this scenario is collusion among multiple clients. When multiple nodes organize together, sharing their processing power, entities with high computational capabilities can be created. These entities, known as "pools," are very common in today's cryptocurrency environment. In the Bitcoin network, for example, the computational power required for mining activities has become very high, making "solo mining" almost impossible. For this reason, nowadays, joining a mining pool is the only valid option to mine Bitcoin. Large mining pools could play a key role in a cryptocurrency environment, and if they exceed 50% of the total computational power available in the entire network, they could even control it, by performing the so-called 51% attack. The 51% attack is a typical threat of a permissionless blockchain-based system, due to its open nature. However, also permissioned environments are prone to this attack, as the administrators could give themselves as many participants and nodes on the blockchain as desired [189].

> ✐ **Definitions**
>
> **51% Attack** In the blockchain environment, the 51% attack, also known as majority attack, refers to a situation where an adversary, which controls more than 50% of the total computational power of the network (in case of Bitcoin, the 50% of the entire network hashing power), acts maliciously to disturb the network's operation.
>
> In the particular case of a cryptocurrency, an attacker performing 51% Attack is able to:
>
> - Spend the same coin twice, i.e., double-spend attack
> - Prevent any other transaction from being confirmed, i.e., denial of service against typical users
> - Prevent any other miner to mine new blocks, i.e., denial of service against legitimate miners
>
> An attacker performing 51% Attack is NOT able to:
>
> - Steal funds from other wallets
> - Create new coins
> - Change the default reward (coins generated per block)

Attacks

Unlike quantum computing, which is still perceived as a remote threat, collusion between miners is an ongoing problem for almost all blockchain-based systems. In fact, several real-world examples can prove the danger of this threat.

The 51% attack is often considered to be a very remote threat, with little chance of occurring. This belief is based on the extreme difficulty of performing it in the Bitcoin network. On a permissionless blockchain with the PoW as consensus mechanism, the 51% attack requires the attacker to gain 51% of the total hashing power of the network to be successful. Given the maturity reached by the Bitcoin network, in terms of the distribution of miners and the hashing power required to mine a new block, this type of attack is highly unlikely, not only for the difficulty of obtaining the necessary computing power but also for the high costs of this operation which, compared to any profits, make the attack also not very profitable. A demonstration is given by the fact that, historically, only one entity in the whole history of Bitcoin has managed to have the computing power necessary to perform the attack. In January 2014, a mining pool called Gash.io grew so much that it came close to handling 51% of the total hashing power of the network. The event caused tension among the Bitcoin community, but it was resolved very quickly. Not being an intentional growth, the mining pool solved the problem by reducing the number of participants, and therefore the total hash rate available to them, also committing to never exceed 40% in the future. Although this incident has shown the real possibility that a single entity will get more than half of the total computational power, the current conditions of the Bitcoin network make the repetition of this event unlikely. In fact, starting in 2017, the Bitcoin network has registered a tremendous increase in the hashing power available to the network, as shown in Fig. 3.1.[3]

The total hash rate of a permissionless blockchain-based cryptocurrency represents a good security metric. The more hashing power is available in the network, the greater its overall security and its resistance to attacks. The hashing power of a cryptocurrency network is, in general, unknown and difficult to compute exactly. However, it is possible to calculate an estimation given the number of blocks mined in a particular time interval and the current block difficulty. In the particular case of Bitcoin, the estimated hash rate per second (TH/s) is computed by the following formula:

$$TH/s = 2^{32} * \frac{D}{T} \tag{3.1}$$

where T is the average time between the mined blocks and D is the difficulty. Cryptocurrencies with a low total hash rate value certainly have a less negative impact on the environment, in terms of electricity consumption, and miners have

---

[3] https://blockchain.com/charts/hash-rate.

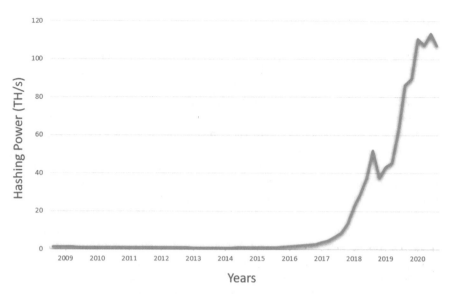

Fig. 3.1 The estimated computational power of the Bitcoin network, expressed in terahashes per second, from its origin to May 2020

a better chance of making profits. However, in this case, also the overall security level is low, exposing the network to different types of attacks.

In May 2018, an unknown malicious entity, with access to a very large amount of hashing power, performed a 51% attack on the Bitcoin Gold network. Once the attacker gained control of the network, he/she performed several double-spend attacks against different exchanges. Immediately after the attack was detected by the Bitcoin Gold community, the targeted exchanges tried to mitigate their loss by waiting for a longer amount of confirmation before approving transactions. This countermeasure does not seem to have helped, and the attacker eventually stole around $18 million. During these attacks, normal users are usually not exposed. The only parties at risk are users who accept payments (usually of large amounts) directly from the attacker. Since the cost of mounting such an attack is high, the attacker can only profit if they can quickly get something of high value from a fake payment. An actor like a cryptocurrency exchange usually accepts large deposits automatically, allowing users to trade into a different coin (including fiat currencies) quickly and then withdraw the desired amount automatically. For this reason, exchanges are more exposed during 51% attacks.

> **✦ Definitions**
>
> **Cryptocurrency Exchange** Also known as digital currency exchange (DCE), it is an online service that allows customers to trade cryptocurrencies for other assets, such as other virtual currencies or conventional fiat money.

In January 2019, the Ethereum Classic (ETC) network also fell victim to a 51% attack. From a first analysis, it emerged that the attacker has mined only empty blocks, suggesting that he/she aimed more at winning the rewards of the new created blocks rather than executing a 51% attack to double-spend coins. Subsequently, some exchanges said they blocked all ETC transactions as soon as a major reorganization of the blockchain, which included an attempt to double-spend attack, was detected by their systems. This timely reaction has certainly mitigated the damage of the attack, preventing huge losses for the exchanges.

As shown by these examples, early detection of a 51% attack is very important for limiting the damage that can result. For this reason, several research efforts have been made in this direction, also considering that this is a general problem that affects almost every blockchain-based system. As such, it is not only limited to cryptocurrencies. The systems most subject to this attack are certainly the permissionless ones, since anyone is allowed to join the network (without authentication) at any time and become a miner. However, permissioned blockchain-based systems are also vulnerable to 51% attacks, especially in the case of consortium blockchain networks. In these systems, the access is controlled, and permissions are regulated according to the role played by each user. Several institutions, such as public and private companies and governments—and possibly other actors—collaborate with each other to use the blockchain and maintain its security. However, if collusion occurs between a subset of these institutions, network security is no longer guaranteed.

One of the most promising methodologies involves the use of intelligent software agents to monitor the activity of stakeholders in the blockchain networks to detect anomalies, such as collusion. In [190], the author proposed a solution that, by leveraging supervised machine learning techniques and algorithmic game theory, reduces the chances of collusion in decentralized systems. For each new block, the proposed solution estimates the utility function based on the value of the service or goods sold in the transaction examined. Based on this function, the intelligent agent decides how fair each new transaction is, compared to the system under analysis, and therefore the probability of being generated in the context of a majority attack.

3.3.3   Open Issues

A possible solution for the threats posed by quantum computing and other advances in technologies certainly revolves around the development of PoW algorithms (or other control protocols) with information-theoretic security. This means that the security of the protocol derives exclusively from information theory. For this reason, it is impossible for an adversary to break the system, even with unlimited computational power, simply because he does not have enough information to compute.

As already discussed, youngest systems are most vulnerable to collusion and, more in general, to 51% attacks. In fact, a relatively young system is most likely characterized by an equally young community, not yet stabilized. This could create conditions, even temporary, in which obtaining 51% of the total computing power of the network is easier. This would jeopardize the stability and security of the entire network. However, even in more mature systems such as Bitcoin, the possibility of collusion between mining pools remains possible. In fact, as depicted in Fig. 3.2, very few large mining pools control a large slice of the total hashing power available in the network. Despite this, collusion between these pools seems unlikely, as the long-term profit of honest mining is higher than what they could have in a short period in which they perform a 51% attack. However, it is necessary to verify whether this balance will remain unchanged even after the next scheduled halving,

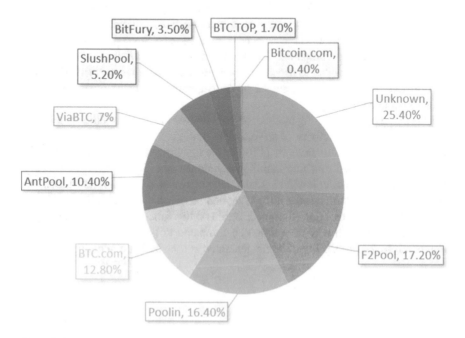

Fig. 3.2   Market share of the most popular Bitcoin mining pools (June 2020)

when the reward for new blocks is cut in half. After each halving phase, in fact, the consequences for the network and its security are unpredictable. The community of Bitcoin users often disagrees on the possible forecasts that precede a halving, with consequences ranging from the change in the price (positive or negative) to the destruction of the system. Furthermore, when the Bitcoin network reaches the available currency limit, and the miners' only profit will be the fees of the transactions included in new blocks, the equilibrium may change forever.

> ✏ **Definitions**
>
> **Bitcoin Halving** Scheduled event of the Bitcoin network, when the reward for mining Bitcoin blocks is cut in half. At the start of the network, the reward was set to 50 Bitcoins. Then, the Bitcoin protocol imposes a halving event for every 210,000 blocks added to the ledger. The criterion behind this choice was not explained in the foundational paper of the Bitcoin network. However, many believe that this mechanism serves to distribute more coins early on, attracting users, and to keep inflation in check later on.

3.4   Scenario 3: Infrastructure

As already mentioned in this chapter, the security of a cryptocurrency, as well as for any other distributed system, is closely related to the nodes that compose its network. In Sect. 3.3, we discussed the security risks related to a low total computational power available on a cryptocurrency network. When a cryptocurrency is not sufficiently mature in terms of resources to secure its ledger, the major risk is the presence of an adversary with greater resources who takes control of the system. One methodology for mitigating this risk is to increase the resources available to check network operations. In this way, taking possession of the majority becomes more difficult and expensive for an adversary. As a result, such an attack becomes unlikely and possibly less profitable. However, the increase in the number of full-nodes and their resources does not protect the network from any kind of attack. In fact, even without having enough resources to perform a 51% attack, a cryptocurrency could be attacked in other ways. For example, Denial of Service (DoS) attacks could be performed to undermine the availability of the system by targeting the whole network, individual users/entities, or specific services. These attacks can be favored by the structure of the system, exploiting both architectural weaknesses and infrastructural ones, even temporarily present in the network. As an example, in a permissionless blockchain-based system, the geographic distribution of full-nodes is really important to increase the network's stability and resistance to different types of attacks. In fact, these nodes are responsible not only for the validation of transactions and the creation of new blocks but also for maintaining and distributing the updated copy of the ledger. All these activities, in theory, can be compromised within a specific geographical area by attacking all (or most of) the full-nodes within it. As a result, the version of the ledger in use within the region under attack may differ from the one used in the rest of the network. In addition, some network services in the same area may become unreliable or completely unavailable. For these reasons, it is necessary to consider the geographical position of the full-nodes, distributing them uniformly to increase the overall security level of the network. This approach is not always easy to follow, with difficulties that vary according to the properties of the considered system. In permissioned blockchain-based systems, the institutions managing the network have full control over the privileged nodes responsible for the security of the network. Consequently, these nodes can be deployed and geographically distributed according to the level of security to be achieved. On the contrary, in permissionless blockchain systems, no details about full-nodes are known at the time of design. In fact, during the whole lifetime of the network, the number of full-nodes, their geographical distribution, and their total computational power change continuously. As a result, the network security level varies over time.

Threats that arise from physical infrastructures, such as communication networks, are often underestimated and neglected in the security analysis of a cryptocurrency. In this scenario, we consider a cryptocurrency that relies on the public communication infrastructure to manage communications between nodes provided by its protocol. We highlight the security problems and vulnerabilities that may result from its physical infrastructure. In our analysis, we consider the most important cryptocurrencies currently available, with Bitcoin, once again, as the main example.

3.4.1 Threat: Hijacking Network Infrastructure

In this scenario, the major threat is represented by an adversary that interferes with the cryptocurrency protocol by manipulating the network traffic. The malicious actor could be either an insider or an outsider. In the former case, the malicious actor actively participates in the cryptocurrency's protocol during the attack—for instance, by forging fake network packets. In the latter case, instead, the attacker does not join the protocol, performing a stealthy attack—for instance, by dropping network packets. These types of attacks are directly influenced by several factors, derived both from the technologies used by the protocol and the physical network infrastructure of the cryptocurrency. As an example, the Internet routing infrastructure could be an important attack vector, especially for permissionless blockchain-based systems. In a permissionless cryptocurrency network, anyone from anywhere in the world can join the protocol by running a full-node. Despite this, the nodes that compose the network are unlikely to be uniformly distributed across the globe. This means that, with high probability, most of the full-nodes are hosted in a few Internet Service Providers (ISP)s. Consequently, these few ISPs will route most of the network packets of the entire system. In such a scenario, several attacks could be performed to target a cryptocurrency, either directly or indirectly, by attacking the ISP's network infrastructure. In this context, we can mention few different malicious activities that could be performed by either an external adversary or a malicious ISP:

- Network packet redirection—e.g., Border Gateway Protocol (BGP) hijacking
- Network packet manipulation—e.g., eclipse attack
- Network packet filtering—e.g., blackhole attack

These malicious activities, classified as Internet routing attacks, are used to perform the following attacks:

- *Partition attack:* aims to partition the network of the cryptocurrency under attack into different disjointed portions, so that the different parts cannot communicate with each other.
- *Delay attack:* aims to delay the new block propagation so as to allow several other attacks, such as double-spending.

These attacks could be performed against any blockchain-based system that makes use of the Internet for its communications. The objectives and possible consequences are manifold and range from the double-spending attack to the Distributed Denial of Service (DDoS). The impact varies by victims: if the attack is performed against a merchant, it is susceptible to double-spending attacks; if the victim is a miner, the attack wastes its computational power; finally, if it is a regular node, it is unable to contribute to the network by propagating the last version of the blockchain.

✐ Definitions

Border Gateway Protocol (BGP) BGP is the standard (de facto) routing protocol that manages how IP packets are forwarded on the Internet. Neighboring networks or Autonomous System (AS) exchanges between each other the routes that lead to different IP prefixes. For each given IP prefix, its AS is responsible for advertising the original route, which is then propagated among ASes until all of them are aware of it.

Autonomous System (AS) An AS is a collection of connected Internet Protocol (IP) routing prefixes under the control of one or more network operators on behalf of a single administrative entity or domain that presents a common, clearly defined routing policy to the Internet.

Internet Service Provider (ISP) An ISP is an organization that provides services for accessing, using, or participating in the Internet.

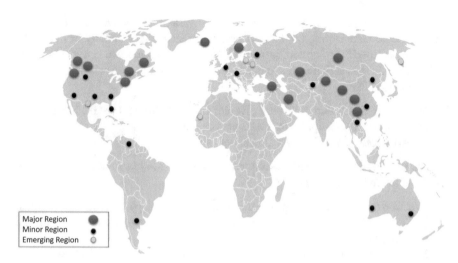

Fig. 3.3 Global overview of the Bitcoin mining regions. Data sourced from [191]

The feasibility and the success rate of both these attacks could be directly influenced by the geographical distribution of the full-nodes of the targeted cryptocurrency. In the particular case of Bitcoin, the hashing power is distributed in very few regions—as shown in Fig. 3.3—with the highest concentration in China (Sichuan region) and North America. This means that, by attacking very few ISPs, it is possible to cut a huge part of the total hashing power off the Bitcoin network, with serious consequences for the security of the system and its users.

3.4.2 Attacks and Countermeasures

In March 2014, several users of the Bitcoin network noticed suspicious activities on mining systems connected to some mining pools. For a few days, the crypto-miners' community has been in turmoil, struggling to understand what was going on. Several users reported a mysterious redirection of their systems to an unknown IP address, which responded with the same protocol—Stratum—used to coordinate the mining pools. After the redirection, everything worked as before. The miners, indeed, continued to receive work from the new server, limiting the blocking of the systems to a few seconds, caused by the server change, keeping the anomaly hidden. Only a small detail had changed: the miners no longer received any reward for their work. Following repeated reports, researchers from the Dell Secureworks Counter Threat Unit discovered several network traffic hijacking activities between February and May 2014. After subsequent investigations, 51 compromised networks, belonging to 19 different ISPs, were discovered. The hijackers exploited the hashing power of legitimate miners by redirecting their mining traffic to a malicious server disguised as the legitimate pool. The attacker used a technique called BGP hijacking, which takes advantage of the lack of authenticity in routing messages. Indeed, the BGP protocol does not verify the legitimacy of the advertisements. Consequently, any AS can advertise any IP prefix. From the miners' point of view, the attack was completely transparent. Usually, the mining hardware is continuously connected to its pool server to receive tasks. After the attack began, the miners who tried to connect to the legitimate pool server received a new BGP route, pointing to a malicious server maintained by the attackers. Once the hijacker stopped the attack, the miners who were redirected to the malicious pool continued to see activities and tasks but were not rewarded. Miners who have not been redirected remain unaffected. The attackers repeated the hijack in short rounds, allowing the activity to continue undiscovered. The attack lasted for about 4 months, involving also other cryptocurrencies different from Bitcoin. The same researchers who discovered the attack linked BGP malicious announcements to a single router owned by a Canadian ISP and estimated the attackers' profit in $83,000.[4]

The security of blockchain-based systems from a network perspective was at first underestimated compared to other attack scenarios. However, the example provided by the 2014 attack has concretely demonstrated the possibility of indirectly attacking a cryptocurrency by compromising the Internet infrastructure using routing attacks. The hijackers who carried out this attack had the sole purpose of illicitly using the computational power of honest miners to obtain rewards for creating new blocks. For this reason, technically, the Bitcoin network, its protocol, and its regular users have not been compromised. What has been compromised is the BGP routing protocol, used by the Internet infrastructure, to directly attack the Stratum protocol, used to coordinate the pools of miners. Once computational power was obtained, the attacker could have used it to perform other types of attacks against the Bitcoin network and its users, such as the 51% attack and the double-spend attack. By using this technique properly, it may be relatively easy to partition a cryptocurrency network. As shown in Fig. 3.4, the geographical distribution of the mining pools could facilitate this attack. We can observe how few main regions have more than 40% of the computational power of different cryptocurrencies. China, for example, holds 45% of the entire hashing power of the Bitcoin network, while Europe over 40% of the computational power of Ethereum, Zcash, and Monero. This observation implies that a very large chunk of the computational power of a cryptocurrency could be controlled by attacking a relatively low number of ISPs. As noted by Apostolaki et al. in [192], only 13 ASes hosted 30% of the entire Bitcoin network, while 50 ASes host about 50%. The distribution of Bitcoin nodes per IP prefixes is also surprising; only 63 prefixes contain more than 20% of the network. These observations have direct implications on both the delay attack and the partition attack. The former, indeed, becomes much more disruptive with this high concentration of nodes in a few ISPs. At the same time, the latter is much

---

[4]https://www.secureworks.com/research/bgp-hijacking-for-cryptocurrency-profit (Last checked August 2020).

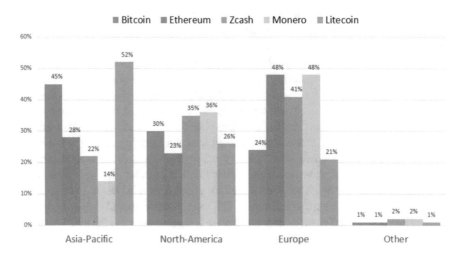

Fig. 3.4 Worldwide distribution of cryptocurrency mining in 2018

easier to execute, but the number of achievable partitions is lower. In the same paper, they also observed that only three ASes intercept more than 60% of the Bitcoin network traffic, making the delay attack much more powerful. As a known open issue, BGP's security has attracted a lot of attention. Several works have been proposed to mitigate routing attacks, mainly following two different approaches: origin validation and path validation. The former aims to filter advertisements from unauthorized ASes, while the latter digitally signs BGP packets to validate the list of ASes through which the announcement passed. To overcome this problem, a countermeasure to the partition attack in the Bitcoin network was presented in [193]. The proposed system, called SABRE, is completely transparent for both BGP and Bitcoin protocols. SABRE implements a Secure Relay Network for Bitcoin by introducing a new type of node, composed by a software module and a hardware component. The software module is a modified Bitcoin full-node (the control component), while the hardware module is a programmable switch (data plane component). The SABRE network is composed of several SABRE nodes and a number of regular Bitcoin full-nodes connected to them via UDP. When an external node advertised a new block to a node connected to the SABRE network, the new block is immediately forwarded to the SABRE data plane. If the switch does not contain the hash of the new block in its memory, the new block is forwarded to the control component. If the control plane validates the new block, the switch memory will be updated, and the new block propagated in the whole network. The proposed countermeasure is focused on Bitcoin. However, its design is general and could be applied to other blockchain systems to mitigate partition attack. Other countermeasures have been proposed to secure routing protocols preventing the attack described above [194–197]. Heilman et al. in [198] examine the eclipse attack on a single node in the context of Bitcoin's Peer to Peer (P2P) network.

Gervais et al. [199] consider other aspects of the centralization of Bitcoin and their consequences to the security of the protocol. Measuring and detecting routing attacks has seen extensive research on BGP hijack [192, 200, 201], as well as interception attacks [202].

3.4.3 Open Issues

Although the problem of attacking a cryptocurrency through the architecture of the Internet has been widely studied, we are still far from a solution. Several works have been proposed to mitigate BGP hijacking. However, none of them has been widely distributed, given the difficulty of choosing and standardizing a single solution and consequently updating all network hardware. Therefore, the Internet is still vulnerable to this attack, cryptocurrency networks included. Some countermeasures have mitigated the partition attack problem in the Bitcoin network, but they should also be extended and tested to the generic case of a permissionless blockchain-based system. Furthermore, the delay attack is still a serious threat, not only in the Bitcoin network but in all blockchain-based systems. The main challenge in solving these security problems in existing cryptocurrencies lies in the difficulty of updating an existing protocol. Usually, an important update often requires a fork of the entire project, with several practical problems. This is not always possible, especially for mature cryptocurrencies with high capitalization, such as Bitcoin. The countermeasures discussed in the previous chapter, however, should be considered in the design of a new cryptocurrency. A state cryptocurrency should consider the discussed threats, taking advantage of the available literature and lessons learned from past attacks.

3.5 Toward a State-Sponsored Cryptocurrency

When you think of a future state-sponsored cryptocurrency, it is natural to imagine it very similar to the existing ones, in particular to the most famous and used in the current crypto-exchange panorama. Bitcoin is the most popular virtual currency in the market today, with a solid technology behind it. Introduced to be the pillar of a new electronic payment technology designed to revolutionize the world of finance, Bitcoin is still suffering from some disadvantages that risk compromising its diffusion on a large scale. While several big players in the financial sector are ready to bet on its potential, the Bitcoin protocol needs several improvements to aim for the creation of a secure, reliable, and robust electronic currency. In this section, we discuss the requirements that a state-sponsored cryptocurrency should have, highlighting the features of Bitcoin (and other existing cryptocurrencies) that do not fit the identified properties.

3.5.1   Bitcoin Limitations

The Bitcoin network suffers from several architectural shortcomings that have limited its diffusion as a means of payment to be used as an alternative to traditional currencies. Consequently, the vast majority of users use Bitcoins as a speculative medium. The most important disadvantages of the Bitcoin protocol, as well as of any other Bitcoin-like cryptocurrency, that cause skepticism among users and restrain the spread of this technology are the following:

- **Fear of losing the wallet:** If a hard drive breaks or a malware corrupts/deletes the data and the wallet file is damaged/deleted, all Bitcoins contained are irreparably lost. Nothing can be done to recover them. These coins will remain in the system forever without anyone being able to spend them. Due to this limitation, a private individual could lose all his savings in seconds, just as a company could go bankrupt because of a corrupt file.
- **Irreversible transactions:** When a good or service is purchased using Bitcoin and the seller does not respect the contract (by not sending the goods or not providing the service agreed upon within the terms), the transaction cannot be canceled. This problem can be solved by using a third-party escrow service, but this implies the existence of a trusted third party, in contrast to decentralized distributed systems.
- **Volatility of the value:** The value of Bitcoins changes continuously based on demand. This constant fluctuation, in addition to lowering customer confidence, causes several problems. For example, if a purchased product is returned a week later, should the merchant return the same amount (in BTC) received at the time of purchase (even if the value has changed at the time of the refund)? What currency should BTC be tied to in this cases? These are still important open questions that the Bitcoin community does not yet have a consensus on.
- **Risk of unknown weaknesses:** The Bitcoin system may contain unknown defects, being a fairly new system based on recent technologies. If Bitcoins were widely adopted and a critical flaw was discovered, this could lead to the destruction of the Bitcoin economy.
- **Deflation:** The Bitcoin system is designed to reward early users. In fact, since the total number of Bitcoins is limited to 21 million, each Bitcoin will be worth more and more as the total number of Bitcoins available in the system reaches its maximum.
- **Poor scaling and weak architecture:** Bitcoin, like many other cryptocurrencies such as Litecoin, Monero, and Bitcoin Cash, suffers from several architectural problems that affect the scalability of the system and cause relatively high transaction fees and transaction times.

To be used on a large scale, Bitcoin must overcome the skepticism of citizens concerned by problems such as volatility of value, the usability of the system, and lack of approval from "trusted" organizations caused by the aforementioned drawbacks. Moreover, Bitcoin must also meet strict government requirements regarding money laundering and illicit trades to be accepted by a state as an official currency.

3.5.2   Develop a State-Sponsored Cryptocurrency

The best approach to the development of a state-sponsored cryptocurrency is to combine the best technological features of current cryptocurrencies with the properties of a standard fiat currency, under the supervision of a central bank. The result could be a revolutionary payment management framework which, by exploiting the advantages of a distributed system, lowers the management costs typical of a centralized structure. The objective of a state-sponsored cryptocurrency should be to support the national economic system by providing the normal functions of a banking institution, such as the payment circuit, the management of savings accounts, and the provision of loans. All these services would be provided by a secure platform, capable of reducing errors, speeding up the transfer of money, and preserving the anonymity of its customers. Unlike standard cryptocurrencies, a state-sponsored system should have the full endorsement of a government and its central bank. However, to be supported by a government, the cryptocurrency's protocol must ensure the application of specific guidelines for financial services that banks and other financial institutions must now respect all over the world, such as Anti-Money Laundering (AML) and Know Your Customer (KYC).

> ✐ **Definitions**
>
> **Anti-Money Laundering (AML)** This term refers to a collection of laws, regulations, and procedures designed to prevent criminals from concealing illegally obtained funds as legitimate revenue.
>
> **Know Your Customer (KYC)** KYC refers to an identification process used mostly by financial companies to verify the identity of their customers and assess the potential risks of illegal activities in the relationship with their client. The term often refers to banking regulations and anti-money laundering laws that govern these activities. The customer recognition processes also concern companies of other types and sizes, to ensure anti-corruption compliance for their agents, consultants, and distributors. Banks, insurance companies, and companies operating at an international level increasingly require their customers to provide the necessary detailed anti-corruption information.

The main technologies behind a state cryptocurrency could be inherited from Bitcoin and other similar protocols. Asymmetric cryptography, for example, could provide valid support for the management of payments, ensuring pseudo-anonymity to end users. Just like Bitcoin, users would use an asymmetric key pair to manage their deposit account: the public key to receive payments (such as the IBAN in the current SWIFT banking system) and the private key to authorize outgoing transactions. This then translates into the development of easy to use virtual banking applications, such as electronic wallets, already widely used to manage Bitcoin addresses and currently available for any electronic platform. One of the biggest differences between a state-sponsored cryptocurrency and the Bitcoin protocol will certainly be the owner of the ledger. In fact, almost all existing cryptocurrencies use a model called public blockchain, where anyone can join the network without authorization and the ledger does not have an owner. This model is certainly not applicable to a state-sponsored cryptocurrency, which needs to be regulated by a central bank. For this reason, the most suitable model could be a private blockchain, or a consortium blockchain, where participants need consent to join the networks. In this model, the ownership of the decentralized and distributed blockchain would be shared among all the national banks that join the network, previously authorized by the central bank. These financial institutions would be entrusted with the security of the platform. National banks would have the responsibility to provide the pair of asymmetric keys to users, and to verify and validate transactions, such as miners in the Bitcoin protocol. From a privacy point of view, since users utilize their public keys to receive money, transactions would be anonymous. National banks would be the only actors able to link a public key to an identity, having to fulfill AML and KYC requirements. However, these links would be kept confidential in accordance with the law and made public only to the judicial authority if requested. In this way, each user, once obtained his keys from the bank, is able to carry out transactions (both incoming and outgoing) safely, without any third party involved. Just like Bitcoin, users would be able to transfer money without the need for a bank to participate in the transaction. Furthermore, the transaction will be completely anonymous since the only part exposed to the public will be the participants' public addresses, which work as pseudonyms.

In summary, the actors who would participate in this hypothetical scenario are listed in the following, together with their respective duties:

- **Government and its central bank.** The central bank of the issuing state represents the entity that creates and manages the system. It has the authority to authorize national banks to participate in the network, making them part of the system and possibly miners. The central bank also has the task of regulating the amount of money available in the system, which is not created by miners as in the most famous cryptocurrencies like Bitcoin. By applying the government's monetary policies, the central bank is, therefore, able to increase the amount of money available in the system through a transfer of funds from the central bank private key to the public key of the financial institutions of the circuit. On the contrary, to decrease the money available, national banks would transfer funds to the central bank.

- **Banks and other financial institutions.** Financial institutions approved by the central bank are responsible for providing asymmetric keys to end users and possibly participating in the security of the protocol. In fact, a small group of national banks would be authorized to act as miners, collecting the transactions issued by citizens, validating the correctness of the keys involved, and checking for the presence of sufficient funds in the sender's account.
- **Citizens.** Citizens are the end users of the system. Once they have received the pair of asymmetric keys from a qualified financial institution, they can issue incoming and outgoing transactions in complete autonomy using their electronic wallet.
- **International users.** International money transfers would be much simpler. Any international user, regardless of whether he is a bank or a foreign citizen, could obtain an asymmetric key pair and start operating in the desired currency immediately.

This kind of platform would take advantage of all the benefits of a consortium blockchain, providing valuable support to the economy of the country. Transactions issued within the circuit automatically become irreversible, transparent, and auditable, making the system robust without sacrificing citizens' privacy. Also, like all decentralized systems, a state-sponsored cryptocurrency would have different properties such as fault tolerance, availability, and resilience, which help maintain its security even in the event of an attack. Considering the distrust that many users have toward cryptocurrencies, the new electronic currency could take the same name as the national fiat one. The name "virtual EURO," for example, could facilitate the acceptance of a cryptocurrency sponsored by the European monetary union, compared to a new one with an original and unfamiliar name. Most likely, a state-sponsored cryptocurrency would also be adopted to support the national fiat currency instead of replacing it [203].

Chapter 4
FinTech

Technology has, to different degrees, always been part of the financial world, starting from the 1950s with the introduction of credit cards and ATMs, passing through electronic trading floors and personal finance apps, until present days where technologies such as Artificial Intelligence (AI) , High-Frequency Trading (HFT), and cryptocurrencies are widespread. The prominent role of technology in finance has become so important as to obtain a specific term to describe the intersection between the two—that is, *FinTech*. A portmanteau of "financial technology," FinTech refers to the application of new technological advancements to products and services in the financial industry [204]. The definition is rather broad and also encompasses "innovative ideas that improve financial service processes by proposing technological solutions according to different business situations, while the ideas could also lead to new business models or even new businesses" [205]. Following the previous definitions, FinTech cannot be categorized as a brand new industry but rather as one that has evolved at an extremely rapid pace.

As of today, FinTech represents a huge industry with a momentous growth. Ernst and Young reported for 2015 that there were 1400 FinTech firms, with more than $33 billion in funding. KPMG reports a steadily growing investment trend, which topped in Q3 2019 with a record sum of $77.1 billion, as shown in Fig. 4.1. Also the scale of venture capital activities, private equity deals, as well as mergers and acquisitions is rapidly skyrocketing, as depicted in Fig. 4.2 from data collected by KPMG and reported in Table 4.1. The geopolitical distribution of FinTech firms, and of the related investments, is naturally uneven and highly skewed. The strong dependence on technology makes it so that countries featuring higher research and investment in technology, and that are more technologically advanced, also have higher adoption rates for FinTech. Indeed, one of the countries with the highest adoption rates is Hong Kong, with the United States coming second, followed by Singapore.

© The Author(s), under exclusive license to
Springer Nature Switzerland AG 2021
R. Di Pietro et al., *New Dimensions of Information Warfare*, Advances in
Information Security 84, https://doi.org/10.1007/978-3-030-60618-3_4

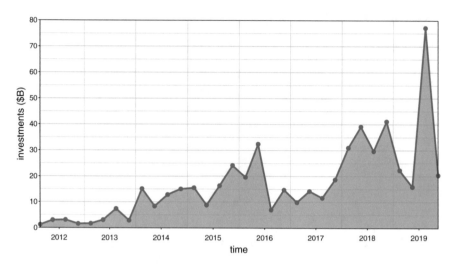

Fig. 4.1 Total worldwide investment activity in FinTech

From the applications side, financial technology is currently used in an increasingly broad array of fields. It is one of the fastest-growing tech sectors, with companies innovating in almost every area of finance. Banking and mobile banking, cryptocurrency and blockchain, investment and savings, trading, payments (e.g., Paypal, Venmo), lending (e.g., new data points and better risk modeling is expanding credit to underserved minorities), insurance (e.g., mobile car insurance, wearables for health insurance) are only some of the fields that are being deeply reshaped by FinTech. In all these scenarios, AI and Machine Learning (ML), big data, and robotic process automation are used to automate tasks and to obtain faster and more accurate predictions. In FinTech, AI algorithms are used to predict changes in the stock market and to give insights into the economy, as well as to provide insights into customer spending habits and to allow financial institutions to better understand their clients. Chatbots are another AI-driven tool that banks are starting to use to help manage customer services. Big data adds to the previous picture and can be used to predict client investments and market changes and to create new strategies and portfolios. Big Data can be employed in conjunction with AI and machine learning to analyze customer spending habits, thus improving fraud detection. Big Data also helps banks create segmented marketing strategies and can be used to optimize the operations of a company. As notable examples of this kind, Bridgewater Associates—the world's largest hedge fund—started a project to automate decision-making to save time and eliminate human emotion volatility. Similarly, Goldman Sachs now has only 2 out of 600 equity traders left in one part of its business. It found that traders can be profitably replaced by computer engineers dedicated to the development of better prediction models. In fact, it is estimated that by 2021, at least 5% of all economic transactions will be handled by dedicated autonomous software.

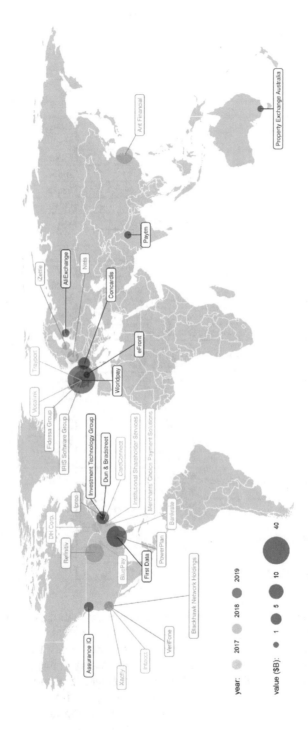

Fig. 4.2 Top 10 global FinTech deals in 2017, 2018, and 2019

Table 4.1 Top 10 global FinTech deals in 2017, 2018, and 2019. Rows are grouped by year and sorted in descending order by deal value

Firm	City	Country	Value ($B)
Year 2019			
Worldpay	London	UK	42.50
First data	Atlanta, GA	US	22.00
Dun and Bradstreet	Short Hills, NJ	US	6.90
Concardis	Eschborn	Germany	6.00
Assurance IQ	Bellevue, WA	US	3.50
AliExchange	Tallinn	Estonia	2.10
Paytm	Noida	India	1.70
eFront	Paris	France	1.30
Property Exchange Australia	Melbourne	Australia	1.20
Investment Technology Group	New York, NY	US	1.00
Year 2018			
Refinitiv	Eagan, MN	US	17.00
Ant Financial	Hangzhou	China	14.00
Nets	Ballerup	Denmark	5.50
Blackhawk Network Holdings	Pleasanton, CA	US	3.50
VeriFone	San Jose, CA	US	3.40
iZettle	Stockholm	Sweden	2.20
Fidessa Group	Woking	UK	2.10
Ipreo	New York, NY	US	1.90
IRIS Software Group	Datchet	UK	1.70
PowerPlan	Atlanta, GA	US	1.10
Year 2017			
DH Corp.	Toronto	Canada	3.60
Bankrate	Palm Beach Gardens, FL	US	1.44
Vocalink	Rickmansworth	UK	1.10
Intacct	San Jose, CA	US	0.85
BluePay	Naperville, IL	US	0.76
CardConnect	King of Prussia, PA	US	0.75
Trayport	London	UK	0.73
Institutional Shareholder Services	Rockville, MD	US	0.72
Xactly	San Jose, CA	US	0.56
Merchants' Choice Payment Solutions	Shenandoah, VA	US	0.47

Finance is currently seen as one of the industries that are most vulnerable to disruption by technology. In fact, rapid development also has a dark side, and new technologies inevitably bring new vulnerabilities and threats. For example, the interplay between algorithms (e.g., ML and AI) and security in finance is complex. On the one hand, some of the most powerful techniques to ensure cybersecurity in the coming years will be based on machine learning. On the other hand, heavy reliance on machine learning and AI—especially black-box/opaque models [206]—

can make it harder for human analysts to understand system behaviors and the associated security risks. Besides, some of the most powerful techniques leveraged by hackers are also based on ML and AI. Cybersecurity risks are particularly high in FinTech also due to the sensitive data and operations managed by companies in the financial sector. Banks, for example, collect and keep loads of sensitive information about their clients. Since the data has a direct connection to the accounts of the clients, cybercriminals deliberately target that information during attacks, intending to steal personal information of banks' customers if not directly accessing their accounts and seizing their money. The combination of fast-paced technological innovation and extremely sensitive data and operations thus creates the perfect storm for cyberattacks. In fact, a growing number of studies point out that "the unintended consequences of technology-leveraged finance include firesales, flash crashes, botched initial public offerings, cybersecurity breaches, catastrophic algorithmic trading errors, and a technological arms race that has created new winners, losers, and systemic risk in the financial ecosystem" [207]. Some even say that we are living in a "golden age for hackers," testified by gigantic data breaches occurring seemingly on a weekly basis.[1] Examples of this kind are the 2018 attack on HSBC's American operations and the 2019 Capital One data breach that affected 100 million Americans. Or even the infamous 2016 Bangladesh Bank Cyber Heist, when five huge fake money transfers were issued through the SWIFT network, totaling $101 million, of which only $38 million were recovered.[2] In that case, the bank's account at the Federal Reserve Bank of New York was hacked, and the thefts were traced to Sri Lanka and the Philippines—evidence that cybercrime in the financial sector thrives on technology and operates on a global scale. The latest survey conducted in 2019 by the Bank of Lithuania shows that cyberattacks currently pose one of the biggest threats to financial institutions.[3] IBM's 2019 Cost of a Data Breach Report concludes with similar findings and shows that the average global cost of a data breach in the financial sector is as high as €4.9 million per incident.[4]

Given this grim picture, it comes with little surprise that financial services companies are concerned about systems and data security, as well as about the concept of trust, more than organizations in almost any other sector. For instance, cryptocurrencies are completely based on trust, where trust is transferred from centralized and regulated repositories typical of fiat currencies, to trust in technology and decentralization. Without secure and trusted algorithms, FinTech will fail, and any firm developing a new FinTech business should consider how it will implement security and trust through technology [208]. In fact, FinTech entrepreneurs are

---

[1] https://www.fintechweekly.com/magazine/articles/the-cyber-security-landscape-in-financial-services (Last checked August 2020).

[2] https://en.wikipedia.org/wiki/Bangladesh_Bank_robbery (Last checked August 2020).

[3] https://www.lb.lt/en/news/survey-cyberattacks-and-re-bubbles-pose-the-biggest-threat-to-financial-institutions (Last checked August 2020).

[4] https://www.ibm.com/security/data-breach (Last checked August 2020).

constantly looking to strike the right balance between growing their business and protecting against imminent cyber threats.[5] To this end, academia recently devoted much interest toward the design and development of secure solutions for FinTech. For example, both vulnerabilities, attacks, and possible solutions were discussed for problems such as credit card and online payment fraud detection, as well as for defending against data breaches [209]. However, the majority of existing studies focused on problems of micro-security—e.g., how to enforce security for given apps or how to protect data about individuals using a given service—rather than on macro-security, which concerns with the security and trustworthiness of either whole markets or whole technologies (e.g., HFT). The former is particularly relevant to individual users, while the latter is primarily of concern for governmental entities and nations themselves, since it might have a significant impact on the whole economy.

Nowadays, regulators, innovators, and investors face an increasingly complex environment where computers and infrastructure merge, regulations allow dozens of different exchanges to coexist, and globalized business facilitates round-the-clock deals. The widening gap between innovation and regulation is acute in FinTech and particularly so with respect to cybersecurity. This is the unavoidable result of mixing solutions that are evolving at a rapid pace with regulatory frameworks that change far more slowly. Within the context of economic war, where nations look at the economy as a sharp weapon with which to pursue strategic and political goals, the aforementioned vulnerabilities of FinTech and the weak regulatory frameworks can even be put to "good" use. In fact, the very existence of the many possible ways in which FinTech firms and the underlying technologies can be hacked and tampered with implies that a nation could easily weaponize FinTech itself and use it as an attack vector pointed toward critical economic assets of competing nations. Indeed, one of the main cyber threats to financial institutions already come from state-organized actors, and the news is replete with both facts and conjectures about state-sponsored hacking [210]. In the remainder of this chapter, we investigate the different ways in which FinTech can be weaponized to attack a nation's economic assets, describing the current state of the art with regard to both attacking and defensive means.

4.1 Scenario 1: Stock Market Forecasts

The stock market of a country, also known as the equity market, is one of the most important components of a national free-market economy. It refers to a centralized place where equities or stocks of publicly held companies, bonds, and other classes of securities are issued and traded. In other words, the national stock market is a

---

[5]https://web.archive.org/web/20160110115516/http://www.whartonfintech.org/blog/protect-assets-cybersecurity-fintech/ (Last checked August 2020).

complex infrastructure that provides companies with access to capital in exchange for a slice of ownership, by offering to investors stock shares and corporate bonds. Through the course of history, several economists and philosophers argued that stock markets are the most effective way of aggregating the pieces of information that are dispersed among individuals within a society. In fact, stock markets give the opportunity to profit from information about a company, by trading that company's shares. Interested traders are thus motivated to acquire and to act on information for personal profit. In doing so, traders contribute to more and more efficient (i.e., accurate) market prices. In the competitive limit, market prices thus reflect all available information, and prices can only move in response to the news. This theory about stock markets and prices is dubbed the *efficient-market hypothesis* in financial economics. A direct implication of this theory is that it is impossible to consistently beat the market, on a risk-adjusted basis, since market prices should only react to new information. As an example, let us suppose that a piece of information about the value of a stock is widely available to investors. If the price of the stock does not already reflect that information, investors will trade on it, thereby moving the price until the information is no longer useful for trading.

Being able to predict where markets are headed is the "Holy Grail" of finance. However, if the efficient-market hypothesis alone could exhaustively model and justify the behaviors of stock markets, there would be little interest in trading because of the limited theoretical possibility to predict the market. Instead, both theoretical and empirical data suggest that markets are not completely efficient. As a consequence, prices might not accurately reflect the true value of stocks. Some economists trace back the imperfections and the irrationalities in financial markets to human factors, by citing a combination of cognitive biases such as over-confidence, overreaction, representative bias, information bias, and various other predictable human errors in reasoning and processing available information. Events such as the Global Financial Crisis (GFC) of 2007–2008 raised additional concerns on the efficiency of financial markets and led even supporters of the efficient-market hypothesis to claim that "poorly informed investors could theoretically lead the market astray" and that stock prices could become "somewhat irrational" as a result.[6]

> **📑 Resources**
> The **Billion Prices project**[7] of the Massachusetts Institute of Technology (MIT) is an academic initiative that uses prices collected from hundreds of online retailers around the world on a daily basis to conduct research in macro

(continued)

---

[6]https://web.archive.org/web/20120406035022/http://fisher.osu.edu/~diether_1/b822/fama_thaler.pdf (Last checked August 2020).

[7]http://www.thebillionpricesproject.com/ (Last checked August 2020).

and international economics. Interested scholars and practitioners have the opportunity to download several datasets related to this research study on the project website.

Perhaps even more worryingly, the same outcome can also be caused by groups of collusive traders, employing market manipulation techniques. In contrast to the properties of an efficient market, the founding idea of market manipulation is a temporary distortion of pricing. Market manipulation is a deliberate attempt to interfere with the free and fair operations of the market and to create artificial, false, or misleading appearances of the price of a product, security, commodity, or currency. Setting artificial prices for financial instruments leads to a redistribution of capital, typically in favor of the small number of participants involved in, and aware of, the manipulation. In turn, this leads to economic imbalances that hinder fair market and unaware investors, undermining confidence in financial institutions. Even though the next generation of market manipulation—e.g., those manipulations that exploit or make use of the latest technological advancements—has the same goal as their traditional counterparts, they can be much more effective due to the unprecedented velocity and interconnectedness of today's digital markets [211]. Market manipulations can take different forms, and while some target low-value and marginal securities, others involve the core of financial markets. These latter manipulations are capable of creating huge shocks in markets, thus making these security issues of concern for nations and of interest for our discussion. On May 6, 2010, the Dow Jones Industrial Average (DJIA) had the biggest 1-day drop in history, later called the *Flash Crash*. After 5 months, an investigation concluded that one of the possible causes was an automated High-Frequency Trading (HFT) system that had incorrectly assessed some information collected from the Web. In 2013, the official Associated Press Twitter account got hacked, and a false rumor was posted reporting that President Obama had been injured during a terrorist attack at the White House, as shown in Fig. 4.3. The fake news rapidly caused a stock market collapse that burned $136 billion. Then, in 2014, the unknown firm *Cynk Technology* briefly became a $6 billion worth company. Automatic Trading algorithms detected a fake social discussion and begun to invest heavily in the company's shares. By the time analysts noticed the orchestration, investments had already turned into heavy losses [212].

The previous anecdotes serve as tangible examples of how market manipulations can cause dramatic shocks capable of affecting even the strongest economy. Previous studies on this subject classified manipulations into two main categories: (1) information-based and (2) trade-based. An information-based manipulation is carried out by issuing false information or by spreading false rumors, while a trade-based manipulation is based solely on buying and selling securities without performing any other publicly observable actions or the spread of false information [211]. As for the whole FinTech domain, some of these manipulative practices

Fig. 4.3 The shocking tweet posted by the hacked AP Twitter account in 2013, which caused a $136 billion worth market crash

have always existed. However, due to the recent technological advancements, they have now become more ubiquitous, and they unfold much faster than before, thus becoming always more indistinguishable from legitimate practices. In the next three sections, we investigate these two traditional forms of market manipulation, as well as new ones that are rapidly emerging. In doing so, we discuss the next generation of manipulation-specific attacks and countermeasures inside those three sections, while in Sect. 4.1.4, we briefly outline generic countermeasures that are not designed to fight a specific type of manipulation.

4.1.1   Threat: Information-Based Manipulation

The first data sources that have been used for predicting future prices of a financial instrument were past prices themselves. In fact, stock market data naturally comes as sequences of values, such as the sequences of opening, high, low, and closing prices at different points in time, and early attempts at stock market prediction were based on the application of statistical (e.g., autoregressive models) and pattern matching techniques to these numeric market data. However, in addition to market data, there exists also a growing wealth of unstructured and heterogeneous big data outside of financial services that have a direct influence on markets. Taken in aggregate, news delivered by companies like Dow Jones, along with the blog posts by experts and analysts, and even online collective user activity gathered by the likes of Google, Facebook, and Twitter, can all be used to understand and improve upon market movements. Because of this, a growing area of FinTech revolves around the acquisition and analysis of "alternative" data. Textual data is a paramount example of alternative financial data capable of expanding the universe of available observations, thus going beyond the merely numerical market indicators [213].

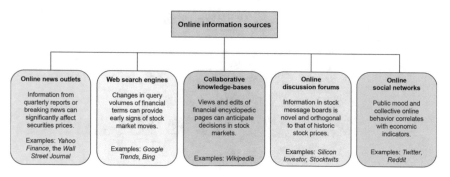

Fig. 4.4 Categorization of the online information sources most used for market prediction

A Large Attack Surface

Recent state-of-the-art market prediction systems exploit all available data, including textual data gathered online, in complex prediction systems based on Machine Learning (ML) and Artificial Intelligence (AI), to come up with more accurate predictions. Figure 4.4 shows an overview of the online information sources that are most widely used for market prediction. For instance, it has been demonstrated that collective patterns of usage of Wikipedia are informative of future stock market moves [214]. Similarly, aggregate data about queries on popular Web search engines, such as Google and Bing, can also be profitably used to predict market movements [215]. The same goes for user-generated information contained in online financial discussion boards [216]. In addition to the aforementioned online data sources, among the textual sources that are currently attracting the majority of research and development are online news (e.g., those shared by the Wall Street Journal, Dow Jones, Reuters, and Yahoo Finance) and user posts in Online Social Network (OSN) data streams (e.g., Twitter above all, but also Reddit, Facebook, and others). In detail, financial news has been proved to convey strong signals for predicting short-term market movements. The system discussed in [217] exploits news articles from Yahoo Finance to predict future prices of S&P 500 stocks. Other studies showed that information extracted from news sources is particularly informative for predicting the direction of assets volatility movement [218]. Still leveraging online financial news, several systems were developed for event-driven stock market prediction [219]. In these systems, events are first extracted from news text, and represented as dense vectors, for instance, via neural tensor networks. Then, deep convolutional neural networks are used to model both short-term and long-term influences of events on stock price movements. Furthermore, text from news articles can also be used to predict intraday price movements of financial assets [220]. Regarding the exploitation of publicly available OSNs data, the *sentiment* score of public stock-related posts has been widely used as a predictor for stock prices and other economic indicators [221, 222]. As an example, the classifier developed in [223] is based solely on the sentiment analysis of tweets and accurately predicts the next-day trend of the stock values of specific companies. Similarly, the one developed in [224] predicts opening and closing stock market prices with high accuracy. Others have instead proposed to exploit the overall volume of tweets about a company [225] and the topology of stock networks [226] as predictors of financial performance. The role of social media *influencers* has also been identified as a strong contributing factor to the formation of market trends [227]. Finally, the relationships between different companies discussed in OSNs have been found informative [228]. In detail, co-occurrences of stock mentions in online discussions have been exploited to create a graph of companies, which was subsequently clustered. It was found that companies belonging to the same clusters feature strong correlations in their stock prices. This methodology was employed for market prediction and as a portfolio selection method, which outperformed traditional strategies based on company sectors or historical stock prices. The usefulness and predictive power of online and social data are acknowledged not only by academia. In fact, there is a growing number of FinTech start-ups, as well as established companies, that are embracing this business. Companies such as Acuity Trading, Selerity, and iSentium are all harnessing data from social platforms like Twitter to give an indication of investor "sentiment", which, in turn, provides predictive signals of which way to trade. And this information-driven revolution is changing more than the investing habits of individuals or the business of emerging firms. Institutional investors are increasingly subscribing to big data information sources. The more uncommon or uncorrelated is the data source, the more valuable it is, since it is capable of bringing unsaturated information into market models. Each data source then drives a small profit in market allocations. When combined, all of the data sources deliver meaningful profitability to the data acquirers. This uncommon information model of institutional investing has become known as Smart Beta or the Two Sigma model, after the hedge fund that grew 400% in just 3 years after adopting this model.

The previous brief review of the scientific literature on stock market prediction shows that the vast majority of existing systems complement historic market data with additional data collected online, and specifically from online social platforms (e.g., first and foremost OSNs), but also blogs and discussion forums. These online data have been shown to significantly boost the predictive power of market prediction models, hence allowing to achieve larger profits, on average. Thus, if on the one hand, online and user-generated content is increasingly exploited for predicting trends in the stock market, on the other hand, we are running the risk that much of the content those systems rely on is actually fake and possibly artfully created to mislead algorithms and human investors alike. In fact, in Chap. 2 we already showed the extent to which online data can be massively fabricated to artificially support a given narrative, person, or product. Finance makes no exception, and financial spam is rampaging in our online social ecosystems since many years [8]. Because of this, without the adoption of effective defensive techniques, all market prediction systems and Automatic Trading (AT) algorithms are vulnerable to manipulation via targeted fake online content. For instance, automatic systems could be tricked into buying large numbers of stocks simply because they detected a positive sentiment or large volume of discussions in OSNs, despite the menace that those figures could have been very easily fabricated by hordes of automated accounts (i.e., social bots) or by paid human workers (i.e., trolls). In turn, these manipulative techniques could be used to unfairly favor a nation's company in a stock market against the one of a competing nation or to trick a national fund into making bad investments. In other words, the possibility to control the news and the content that circulates in OSNs currently provides a powerful leverage to influence the stock market. The previously mentioned examples of Cynk Technology and the hacked Associated Press Twitter account testify the tremendous impact that the accidental or intentional spread of false and inaccurate information, combined with AT, can have on financial markets. To our dismay, recent history is replete with such examples. In May 2020, Elon Musk tweeted about Tesla stock price being "too high," which rapidly resulted in a 10% loss by the end of the trading day.[8] To make matters worse, online information—and especially those generated within OSNs—are not only useful in the financial domain for stock market prediction. Even if in this section we specifically focus on this task, there exist many additional scenarios where these data are being actively exploited. For example, social media interactions are used to identify good customers [229]. Similarly, digital footprints are used to assess individual default risk [230], and friendship networks are exploited in peer-lending schemes [231]. As such, information manipulation can have repercussions that go well beyond stock markets. In 2017, Qatar suffered a blockade imposed by Saudi Arabia, United Arab Emirates, Bahrain, Egypt, and few other countries. The spark that ignited the Qatar diplomatic crisis was a tweet by the Qatar News Agency that later claimed to have suffered a hacking by an "unknown entity" that shared a story with "no basis whatsoever." [9]

Attacks and Countermeasures

Information manipulation attacks aimed at influencing the stock market, or other constituents of a national economy, are based on the tools and techniques that we thoroughly discussed in Chap. 2. The same consideration also largely applies to defensive means. In fact, the majority of existing countermeasures for information-based market manipulation are simply based on countermeasures to generic information manipulation, with a few notable exceptions that we discuss in detail in the following.

All research aimed at measuring and thwarting information manipulation, information disorder, strategic information operations, and the like is still relatively young, having sparked only after the shocking results of the Brexit referendum in the UK and Donald Trump's election in the United States, in 2016 [4]. Because of this, the literature on information-based market manipulation—a relatively small

---

[8]https://www.wired.com/story/elon-musk-tesla-stock-too-high-falls/ (Last checked August 2020).
[9]https://www.bbc.com/news/world-middle-east-40026822 (Last checked August 2020).

subset of all information-based manipulations—is still in its infancy, and thorough studies that investigate this issue are few and far between. Among them, some pioneering works investigated the presence of spam in online financial discussions and the role of social bots in the spread of such spam [212, 232]. The authors collected nine million tweets related to more than 3500 stocks traded in the main US financial markets (NASDAQ, NYSE, NYSEARCA, NYSEMKT). By leveraging anomaly detection algorithms, they identified anomalous discussion spikes in their dataset. Then, they turned their attention to the messages that contributed to the formation of such spikes. Surprisingly, they found that such huge discussions were mainly generated by massive retweets of a few original messages—a technique widely used to artificially increase the popularity of specific pieces of content [13] (i.e., astroturfing). The content of the massively retweeted tweets also revealed something interesting. The majority of such tweets were mentioning a few well-known and highly capitalized stocks, together with many rather obscure stocks with low market capitalization. The latter were all belonging to the OTCMKTS market, a US financial market for over-the-counter transactions with far less stringent requirements than those imposed by NASDAQ, NYSE, NYSEARCA, and NYSEMKT. Finding no apparent explanation for the massive co-occurrence of the unknown OTCMKTS with the other highly capitalized stocks, authors investigated the nature of the accounts that were responsible for a large number of retweets. They leveraged a state-of-the-art bot detection technique [75] and found that as much as 71% of all retweeters were, in fact, social bots. This finding provided the first quantitative and large-scale evidence of the existence of financial spam in OSNs. In a later work, authors went forward and analyzed the characteristics of the financial bots [233]. They found that such accounts were rather simplistic, with few profile information and social relationships. Overall, the bots did not appear as credible sources. Drawing upon these results, they concluded that the mass retweeting of low-value stocks together with some high-value ones, was targeted at Automatic Trading algorithms monitoring social conversations, rather than at human investors. Authors dubbed this practice as *cashtag piggybacking*—by leveraging the notion of piggyback used in computer networks[10]—since fraudsters were likely trying to exploit the popularity of the high values stocks to induce algorithms into buying the low-value ones [212].

☛ Resources
The dataset used in [212, 232, 233] for the analysis of information-based market manipulation is publicly available online.[11] The dataset contains social information (i.e., stock-related online conversations) collected from Twitter and price data collected from Google Finance.

---

[10]https://en.wikipedia.org/wiki/Piggybacking_(data_transmission) (Last checked August 2020).
[11]https://doi.org/10.5281/zenodo.2686862 (Last checked August 2020).

Open Issues and Future Directions

As introduced in the previous section, research on information-based market manipulation is still at its early stages. As such, many directions of research require contributions, thus depicting a pristine scientific landscape with several low-hanging fruits. One of the most important research questions, which are still unanswered, is the assessment of the impact of such manipulations. Only recently we started demonstrating the existence of information-based market manipulations, but we still have no clue about their goals and their outcomes. Measuring the manipulation impact on the markets is undoubtedly a challenging task. One possible way to achieve it consists in monitoring prices and traded volumes and by investigating the existence of possible correlations between manipulation campaigns and price movements.

Another direction of research that still requires much effort is the one related to uncovering and discussing ongoing manipulations. Until we have a sound idea of which manipulations are going on in our online social ecosystems, how they are organized, who perpetrates them, and ultimately how widespread the phenomenon is, we will not be able to put in place effective countermeasures. In this regard, several informal and anecdotal investigations have been carried out, complemented by only a few full-fledged large-scale scientific works [212, 232]. It is thus crucial to multiply efforts toward this direction in the coming years.

Lastly, we surely need to start developing mechanisms for protecting against these forms of manipulation. As we discussed throughout all this section, basically no market prediction system is currently equipped with information filters capable of protecting it from possible manipulations. As such, all the existing ecosystem of Automatic Trading (AT) algorithms is exposed and vulnerable to information-based manipulations. The quickest way to implement a possible first layer of protection revolves around the adoption of general-purpose techniques against information manipulation. For example, systems that feed on online and social data could be complemented with the latest techniques for detecting fake news and for spotting coordinated, artificial, or automated behaviors. Despite not being specifically tailored for the financial domain and financial spam, several of these techniques are readily available and demonstrated decent performance. In the medium to long term, it would however be advisable to develop specific defensive techniques for financial information-based manipulations. This would allow to obtain more accurate, reliable, and efficient countermeasures. For example, some activities are currently undergoing for exploiting labels automatically assigned to financial posts by generic fake news and bot detectors, to develop market-specific manipulation detection techniques. These next-generation tools promise the timely detection of unfolding manipulations—such as those documented in [212, 232]—at their early stages, to stop automatic systems from ingesting fabricated data.

4.1.2 Threat: Trade-Based Manipulation

A trade-based manipulation occurs when a trader attempts to artificially alter a price simply via buying and selling—that is, without releasing any false information or taking any other publicly observable action. The traditional full-information financial theory, such as the efficient-market hypothesis, asserts that such speculation actually contributes to stabilizing prices since manipulators, like all rational traders, buy when the prices are low and sell when the prices are high. In contrast, by following the theories of incomplete and asymmetric information that challenge the efficient-market hypothesis, it is possible to demonstrate that speculation can destabilize prices and increase volatility. The reason being that uninformed traders oftentimes are unable to distinguish the actions of manipulators from those of informed traders [234]. Under these conditions, it has been demonstrated that trade-based manipulation can be profitable [235]. In practice, groups of coordinated manipulators can make slightly unprofitable initial trades against the direction of available information. This initial investment, possibly complemented by corollary actions aimed at attracting additional external investments, can manage to set in motion a price trend among partially informed followers, thus turning the initial investment into a potential profit. From this point on, manipulators can profitably unwind their position against still less informed market makers and other liquidity providers.

Contrarily to information-based manipulations that thrive on the recent democratization of the information landscape, trade-based manipulations only require an open stock market. In fact, most of the techniques used for carrying out trade-based manipulations are as old as the markets themselves. Having such a long history, many nations have long developed regulations against these forms of manipulation. For instance, Section 10(b) of the Securities and Exchange Act (SEA) of 1934, Rule 10b-5, and Section 9(a)(2) of the SEA prohibit manipulation in the United States. Similar actions are taken in Section 1(2)(a) of the Market Abuse Directive (MAD) 2003/6/EC in the EU and Section 1041A of the Corporations Act (CA) 2001 in Australia. As a result of these and other laws, trade-based manipulations are fairly rare in regulated markets. Such laws, however, only apply to regulated markets, such as the main financial markets where trading takes place. However, there exist other important markets that are not subject to any of the above-cited regulations: cryptocurrency exchanges. As already introduced in Chap. 3, a cryptocurrency exchange is a business that allows customers to trade cryptocurrencies or digital currencies for other assets, such as conventional fiat money or other digital currencies. Exchanges can be brick-and-mortar businesses or strictly online businesses. The latter often operate outside Western countries so as to avoid regulations and prosecutions. Nonetheless, they do handle Western fiat currencies and maintain bank accounts in several countries to facilitate deposits in various national currencies. The largely unregulated nature of cryptocurrency exchanges represents fertile ground for all manipulations that once permeated traditional stock markets and that progressively got banned over time. In this regard, cryptocurrency exchanges are a fresh start for modern manipulators, as testified by the large number of cryptocurrency frauds. These frauds, if targeted at state cryptocurrencies such as those discussed in Chap. 3, could even endanger a national economy and be considered alike a direct attack to a nation.

Attacks

The basic mechanisms used to perpetrate trade-based manipulations did not change through the years. Here, we explain such mechanisms for a few notable manipulations.

Pump-and-Dump Pump-and-dump (P&D) is a form of security fraud that involves artificially inflating the price of an owned stock, in order to sell it at a higher price. Participants in P&D schemes collectively aim to artificially inflate a currency price through coordinated, simultaneous buying (i.e., the "pump" action). Once outside unaware investors notice the surge in price and start investing in the asset, the participants sell to them (i.e., the "dump" action), thus making a profit and causing a price collapse. Figure 4.5 sketches the typical price trend of a successful P&D operation that, interestingly, also largely follows Jean-Paul Rodrigue's phases of a financial bubble [236]. Generally, there are orchestrators behind the curtain who profit even at the expense of the witting participants themselves, let alone of the other unaware investors [237]. Historically, P&D schemes took place using email spam campaigns, through traditional media channels via fake press releases, or through telemarketing from "boiler room" brokerage houses. Often the stock promoter claimed to have "inside" information about impending news in order to lure investors into buying. In other cases, newsletters that purportedly offered unbiased recommendations then touted a company as a "hot" stock for their own

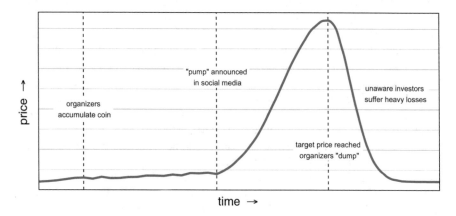

Fig. 4.5 Sketch of a successful P&D operation where organizers manage to create a surge in price, which they later exploit to make an unfair profit at the expenses of unaware investors

benefit. Other times, promoters posted messages in chat rooms or stock message boards urging readers to quickly buy the pumped stock. Nowadays, techniques for luring unaware investors and algorithms have moved from traditional media and largely involve social media, OSNs, and messaging apps. If orchestrators are successful, they will entice unwitting investors to purchase shares of the target company. The increased demand, price, and trading volume of the stock will likely convince even more people to believe the hype and to buy shares as well. When the orchestrators sell their shares and stop promoting the stock, the price plummets, and other investors are left holding a stock that is worth significantly less than what they paid for. In traditional markets, manipulators typically use this ploy with small, thinly traded companies known as "penny stocks", generally traded over-the-counter, since it is easier to manipulate a stock when there is little or no independent information available about the company or little activity anyway. The same principle also applies to pumped coins in cryptocurrency exchanges, which are typically low-value coins with little-to-no activity.

Cornering the Market Cornering the market consists of obtaining sufficient control of a particular stock, commodity, or asset so as to be able to manipulate its market price. To some, it can be defined as having the greatest market share in a particular industry, without having a monopoly. This form of market manipulation can be attempted through several mechanisms. The most direct strategy simply involves buying a large percentage of the available commodity offered for sale in some market and hoard it. However, this manipulation exposes the perpetrator to significant risks. For instance, the "cornerer" is typically vulnerable due to the size of its position, which makes it highly susceptible to market risk. Besides, by definition, cornering a market requires to purchase assets at artificial prices, thus effectively opening profit opportunities for other investors—e.g., through arbitrage. Moreover, if the price starts to move against the cornerer, any attempt to sell would cause the price to drop further, subjecting the cornerer to heavy losses. Indeed, the famous American business journalist Edwin Lefèvre once wrote that "very few of the great corners were profitable to the engineers of them" (*Reminiscences of a Stock Operator*—1923).

Wash Trade A wash trade is a form of market manipulation in which an investor simultaneously sells and buys substantially the same financial instrument, to create a misleading and artificial impression of high trading activity around that instrument. In turn, this typically raises the price of the instrument. In practice, a manipulator will first place a sell (buy) order and then immediately place a buy (sell) order at a specific price so as to buy from itself. This may be done for several reasons, such as to artificially increase trading volume, giving the impression that the instrument is more in demand than it actually is, or also to generate commission fees to brokers in order to compensate them for something that cannot be openly paid for. This form of manipulation can also be referred to as **churn**, especially when carried out to generate commission fees to brokers.

Ponzi Scheme We conclude this brief overview of market manipulation techniques with the introduction of Ponzi schemes. Although they are not strictly trade-based manipulations, Ponzi schemes benefit from the same technological advancements of the aforementioned manipulation techniques (e.g., social media for attracting investors) and often target the same financial assets, such as cryptocurrencies. A Ponzi scheme is a fraudulent investing scam that promises high rates of return with seemingly little risk to investors. The Ponzi scheme generates returns for early investors by acquiring new ones. To this end, it is similar to a pyramidal marketing scheme in that both are based on using funds from new investors to pay the earlier backers (Fig. 4.6). Both Ponzi schemes and pyramid schemes eventually bottom out when the flow of new investors isn't enough to sustain the scam. At that point, the schemes unravel. Manipulators that engage in a Ponzi scheme typically focus all of their efforts into attracting new clients to profit from their investments, hence the renewed interest in this fraud since the rise of social media that makes this task way easier. The Ponzi scheme is named after a swindler named Charles Ponzi, who orchestrated the first one in 1919 in the United States, promising returns of 50% in 45 days or 100% in 90 days. Due to his (legit) success in previous investment schemes, investors were immediately attracted by his new business. However, instead of actually investing the money, Ponzi just redistributed new incoming funds to old investors, telling them that they made a profit. The scheme lasted until August 1920 when The Boston Post began investigating Ponzi's company. As a result of the investigation, Ponzi was arrested by federal authorities and charged with several counts of mail fraud.

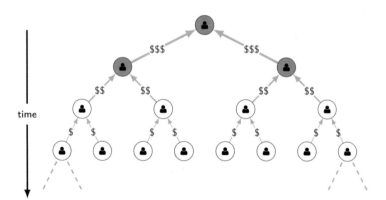

Fig. 4.6 Pyramidal structure of a typical Ponzi scheme. Organizers (red-colored) at the top of the pyramid make a profit at the expenses of subsequent investors (white-colored)

Countermeasures

All previous forms of market manipulation are well-known to regulators and have been banned from regulated markets for many years. For some of them, specific mechanisms have also been put in place in order to automatically prevent fraud. For example, several markets now make it impossible to buy or sell one's own stocks, thus making it more difficult to carry out wash trading and churning manipulations. However, as anticipated, the relatively new and decentralized cryptocurrency exchanges still lack deployed technological tools and regulatory frameworks to prevent some of these frauds. In particular, the combination of cryptocurrency exchanges with the speed and anonymity offered by new media, such as OSNs and encrypted peer-to-peer messaging apps, set the stage for the comeback of frauds, such as P&D and Ponzi schemes. A new stream of research is tackling this recent wave of trade-based market manipulations.

Given that modern trade-based market manipulations deeply leverage social media, some preliminary studies aimed to characterize online social media discussions about cryptocurrencies. In detail, the study in [238] investigated Reddit discussions about a few notable coins—namely, Bitcoin, Ethereum, and Monero. Authors obtained interesting results particularly with regards to Monero, a coin that is often used for shady transactions in the Dark Web. They find that information cascades about Monero are longer and wider than those of the other coins, implying a larger and prolonged interest. In turn, this stressed that one of the main reasons for online interest and debate around cryptocurrencies are indeed cryptocurrency frauds. Furthermore, modeling the discussion patterns around legitimate cryptocurrency transactions, a byproduct of the study in [238] also paves the way for future systems capable of detecting suspicious online discussions, thus possibly leading to the development of automatic fraud detection techniques. Another pioneering study is discussed in [237]. Here, the authors collected a large unbiased sample of online cryptocurrency conversations on Twitter, Discord, and Telegram. Contrarily to the majority of other works, the study did not focus on specific coins or specific frauds, but is aimed at mapping the online cryptocurrency ecosystem considering both legitimate discussions as well as possible manipulations. In addition, they also mapped the interplay between the different platforms by collecting and analyzing invite links to Discord and Telegram closed groups that were shared on Twitter. The analysis in [237] ultimately uncovered the existence of many users and channels/groups involved in P&D and Ponzi schemes. In detail, they estimated that around 20% of all Telegram channels related to cryptocurrencies are in fact involved in either P&D frauds or Ponzi schemes. On the contrary, Discord appears to be a rather healthy online ecosystem, for what concerns cryptocurrencies, with only one Discord channel involved in manipulative activities. Authors also found that more than 56% of the Twitter users that shared invite links to Telegram and Discord were in fact social bots. Such bots were used as a cheap, large-scale, expendable way of luring unaware investors into the secluded Discord and Telegram groups, thus efficiently fueling the P&D and Ponzi frauds [237].

> **Resources**
> The dataset used in [237] for documenting P&D fraunds and Ponzi schemes
> is publicly available online.[12]The dataset contains cryptocurrency-related
> messages collected from Twitter, Telegram, and Discord, as well as network
> information about invite links shared on Twitter for joining Telegram and
> Discord channels.

In contrast to the two previous large-breadth studies, the majority of other works focused on investigating given manipulations for a given set of coins, typically on a single social media. As an example, the work presented in [239] provided a detailed analysis of how P&D schemes occur in Telegram. The authors also developed a basic machine learning model for predicting the likelihood of a coin being the target for manipulation. Then, they used the trained model to inform a simple trading strategy. Interestingly, they empirically demonstrated that the strategy based on early investments on coins that are likely to be pumped allowed to generate a return as high as 60%, within a period of 2 and a half months. This result goes a long way in demonstrating the effectiveness of P&D frauds. Other studies observed that P&D phenomena are widespread on both Discord and Telegram [240] and evaluated the effects of such fraud on the liquidity and price of cryptocurrencies. Among the main findings of the study, large importance is played by coin ranking in predicting the success of the pump operation. In fact, while there are attempts to pump coins spanning a wide range of popularity, pumping obscure coins gave the pump scheme the potential for greater success at the expense of increased risk, such as volatility. The study in [241] is among the few ones that adopted a predictive approach, which focused on detecting the presence and on estimating the success of P&D scams. Based on Twitter and Telegram data, the authors evaluated a computational approach to automatically identify P&D scams as they unfold. Besides, they also developed a multimodal (i.e., textual and visual) approach for predicting whether a particular pump attempt will likely succeed or not, in terms of meeting the expected price target. Finally, they also analyzed the prevalence of bots in cryptocurrency-related tweets, uncovering a significant presence of bots during coin pumping operations, thus corroborating results obtained in [237]. Another predictive study is described in [242]. The authors analyzed trading data related to P&D manipulations, identifying anomalous behaviors. Based on this finding, they proposed the application of anomaly detection techniques to locate points of anomalous trading activity, thus flagging potential P&D attempts.

P&D manipulations are not the only financial fraud under scrutiny. In [243], the authors investigated online Ponzi schemes publicized on the *Bitcointalk* discussion forum. They used survival analysis to identify factors that affect the success of Ponzi scams, finding that credible and active scammers are more likely to succeed than

---

[12]https://doi.org/10.5281/zenodo.3895021 (Last checked August 2020).

newer and less active ones. In [244] is proposed an automatic approach for detecting Ponzi schemes. The authors analyzed the Bitcoin blockchain and extracted features related to known Bitcoin Ponzi schemes. Then, they used the known schemes as the ground-truth for training a machine learning classifier.

Open Issues and Future Directions

As testified by the previous literature review, the majority of existing studies about modern trade-based market manipulation are descriptive in nature. This approach is motivated by the recency of these frauds and by the need to understand how manipulations are orchestrated, in order to start designing defensive mechanisms. In this regard, current studies are building the knowledge that is required for subsequent predictive works. In addition, results of these studies have important implications for regulatory policies, which are still lagging behind, and that greatly benefit from sound evidence of the different forms of market manipulation, including manipulated assets, targeted markets, involved groups, and platforms.

Despite the generalized focus on descriptive and observational approaches, some scholars already moved forward and tried proposing automatic techniques for detecting widespread frauds such as P&D and Ponzi schemes. Although preliminary, these endeavors contribute to the development of early warning systems that are capable of promptly detecting coins and other assets that are likely to become targets of manipulation, for instance, to temporarily suspend trades involving those assets, thus negating any benefit to fraudsters. For the future, additional efforts will likely follow this research direction. More predictive studies are to be expected, putting to good use the preliminary findings of previous works.

Finally, we also highlighted that the majority of existing studies focused on specific frauds (e.g., P&D and Ponzi schemes), platforms (e.g., Twitter and Telegram), and coins (e.g., Bitcoin). Given this narrow focus, we currently lack a thorough understanding of the whole extent of these market manipulations. For the future, it would be advisable to broaden the scope of subsequent studies or to concentrate on those frauds, platforms, and coins that have not been investigated before, thus contributing to the sketch of a complete picture.

4.1.3   Threat: Algorithm-Based Manipulation

In the two previous sections, we covered the main types of market manipulation, which are either information-based or trade-based. Over the course of the years, market manipulation techniques belonging to these two families represented the main threats to fair and free markets. However, the recent advancements in algorithmic trading, as well as the growing adoption of Artificial Intelligence (AI) in almost all corners of FinTech, anticipate the advent of unprecedented forms of manipulation. Before digging deep into the new perils posed by automated and AI-driven markets, we first take a step back by discussing the current penetration of algorithms and AI in financial markets and in FinTech at large.

Algorithms Taking Over

As discussed throughout this chapter, the FinTech revolution gradually brought more data, algorithms, and computational power into the hands of financial analysts, which, in turn, led to the development of always more complex data-driven models. *Quant* (short for *quantitative*) traders and portfolio managers were the first to deploy data analysis to improve financial operations in an algorithmic framework. Using mostly daily data and armed with the latest inferences from statistics and physics, the quants sought answers to challenges associated with portfolio risk management, derivative pricing, and diversification. Their early work paved the way for modern Exchange-Traded Funds (ETFs): passively managed, yet actively traded indexes. Motivated by the early success of quantitative approaches, algorithms spread through all the corners of finance. Counterparty risk computation deals with the quantification of the risk of payment by a money-sending party. As an example of the algorithmic takeover, in early 2000s counterparty risk was managed by human traders, and all settlements took at least 3 business days to complete, as multiple levels of verification and extensive paper trails were required to ensure that transactions actually took place as reported. Fast-forward to today, fast technology and fully automated systems enable transfer and confirmation of payments in just a few seconds, fueling a growing market for cashless transactions. Algorithms are making their presence felt in wealth management as well, as *robo-advising* (or robo-investing) is taking over the job of traditional portfolio managers. Although the idea has been around for a while, since around 2015 the momentum has started to grow. The core concept of robo-advising is that a computer, equipped with cutting-edge predictive algorithms, is capable of delivering portfolio optimized solutions faster, cheaper, and at least as good as its human counterparts (i.e., the old-school portfolio managers). Robo-advising now enables investors to use technology to place their money in well-diversified asset pools, at a much lower cost. Given a selected input of parameters to determine the customer's risk aversion and other preferences (say, the customer's life stage and its personal aversion to given stocks), algorithms then output an optimal and personalized investing plan. Automation of investment advice enables fast market risk estimation and the associated custom portfolio management. For example, investors of all stripes can now choose to forgo expensive money managers in favor of investing platforms such as Motif Investing. For less than $10, investors can buy baskets of ETFs preselected based on particular themes. Moreover, companies such as AbleMarkets offer real-time AI-driven risk evaluation of markets, aiding the judgment of market-making and execution traders with real-time inferences from the market data, including the proportion of high-frequency traders and institutional investors present in the markets at any given time. Algorithms and AI are also permeating the operations of hedge funds. BlackRock is replacing human stock pickers with machine algorithms, using deep learning neural networks. Sentient Technologies is a hedge fund run entirely using AI. It is supposed to have a proprietary algorithm with adaptive learning that uses thousands of machines for computation. Numerai is a hedge fund that makes ensemble trades by aggregating trading algorithms submitted by anonymous contributors. Prizes are awarded to contributors in a cryptocurrency called Numeraire, which resides on the Ethereum blockchain. The latest data shows that funds using AI outperform others quite handily,[13] with a gap that is only bound to widen. Consequently, increasing shares of money are marching into AI-driven funds, as Numerai raised more than $1 million in short order.[14]

Loose Cannons on the Automation Deck

The previous examples, which are just a few out of an immense spectrum of financial applications, highlight the usefulness of algorithms and AI for solving a plethora of real-world tasks. This usefulness is well motivated by the exceptional—even beyond human-like—performance of recent ML/AI algorithms. Especially with the recent progress in AI, which relies on increasingly complicated artificial neural network architectures, the predictive power of algorithms advances in contrast with their interpretability [206], as summarized in Fig. 4.7. On the one hand, we have a large set of different neural network architectures, configurations, and learning algorithms that allow us to effectively automate and speed up many challenging tasks. On the other hand, however, oftentimes we have no clue as to why our latest intelligent system managed to obtain state-of-the-art performance on a specific benchmark dataset or why it yielded *that* particular prediction in the face of a given input instance. This issue is particularly acute in finance, where the trade-off between predictive power and interpretability is completely in favor of the former. Our understanding of the inner functioning of these complex techniques is such that, to many eyes, AI just *automagically*[15] solves increasingly challenging tasks.

Moreover, the performance of AI algorithms is far from being easily generalizable. In fact, almost all such techniques manage to obtain exceptional results only when they operate in their best conditions (i.e., in their sweet spots), such as when analyzing data that is very similar to those used for training them. Since the early days of ML and AI, it is known that instances analyzed at "test" time (i.e., after the model has been trained, when it is deployed) might have somewhat different statistical properties than those used for training the model. This issue

---

[13]https://www.preqin.com/insights/research/blogs/the-rise-of-the-machines-ai-funds-are-outperforming-the-hedge-fund-benchmark (Last checked August 2020).

[14]https://www.sec.gov/Archives/edgar/data/1667103/000166710316000002/xslFormDX01/primary_doc.xml (Last checked August 2020).

[15]A colloquial portmanteau used in computer science to indicate something effective, yet unintelligible.

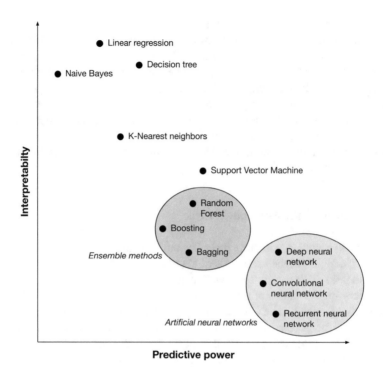

Fig. 4.7 The trade-off between performance (i.e., predictive power) and interpretability in machine learning and artificial intelligence algorithms. Latest advances (e.g., deep neural networks) provide unparalleled performance at the cost of limited interpretability

naturally occurs in many applications and results in degraded performance. For example, in a computer vision system (i.e., such as those used for automatically "reading" and "interpreting" road signs in self-driving vehicles), two different cameras could be used to take pictures at training and test time, thus leading to a trained model achieving degraded performance on test images. Generalizing the previous example, this detrimental effect on performance occurs because the vast majority of algorithms are designed to operate in stationary and neutral (if not even in benign) environments. In practice, however, there are many situations in which the working environment is neither stationary nor neutral. When the previous assumptions on the environment are violated, algorithms operate in sub-optimal conditions and even the best ones start making big mistakes, thus yielding inaccurate and unreliable predictions. In the previous computer vision example, using two different cameras violated the stationarity assumption, since the properties of the images changed when switching from training to test data.

An even more worrying scenario, however, occurs when an attacker deliberately manipulates training or test instances, in order to cause the algorithm to make mistakes. In fact, one can easily imagine several situations in which attackers could have an interest in fooling a machine learning system. Think for example

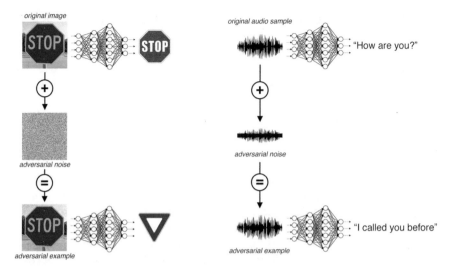

Fig. 4.8 Adversarial examples used to fool computer vision and speech recognition systems. The deceptive adversarial examples are obtained by adding a carefully crafted adversarial noise to the original data instances

of all security applications of machine learning. By definition, the goal of security systems is to keep at bay unwanted accesses (i.e., to data, systems, etc.). Attackers— or adversaries, as they are often called—are thus obviously motivated to fool security systems. One straightforward way to reach their goal is by modifying their data footprint in such a way that security systems misclassify them as legitimate and genuine users. In other words, adversaries make it so that the neutrality assumption of machine learning algorithms is violated. Moreover, they often also violate the stationarity assumption by modifying their behavior through time in order to continually evade detection, thus creating data instances with evolving characteristics. Such intentionally modified data instances are called "adversarial examples", since they are generated by an adversary. Figure 4.8 shows two simple examples of adversarial attacks that can be mounted against computer vision and speech recognition systems. In each case, the original data instance is modified by adding a carefully crafted, subtle adversarial noise, so as to induce classification errors. Interestingly, it is often possible to produce adversarial examples that appear to humans as almost identical to the original data instances, but that nonetheless produce completely wrong classifications in automated systems, as in the examples shown in the figure. As demonstrated by the previous examples, the presence of adversaries is not only related to security systems but rather to all systems that could be gamed in order to gain an advantage, such as an economic or an information advantage. Quite obviously, trading algorithms are a paramount example of this kind of machine learning systems.

The current situation with AI and ML is one where algorithms are like *loose cannons on the automation deck*. On the one hand, when working in the best conditions, they are capable of providing unparalleled performance. On the other hand, however, their power is "unstable." What's more, it can be weaponized, since it can be easily manipulated by knowledgeable adversaries. The pervasiveness of ML/AI and of algorithmic decisions—both in finance and elsewhere—combined with their vulnerabilities, thus represent an explosive mixture for our increasingly automated world.

Attacks

Because of the huge range of existing situations where adversaries are potentially motivated in fooling a machine learning system, a recent branch of research started focusing on the development of robust ML and AI algorithms, capable of withstanding attackers. Adversarial machine learning, also known as machine learning in hostile environments, is a paradigm that deals with the development of algorithms designed for withstanding the attacks of an adversary. It focuses on the study of possible attacks (e.g., how to modify an image in order to fool a computer vision system) and on the design of countermeasures to those attacks (e.g., smoothing the decision boundary of a classifier so as to make it more robust against adversarial examples). That is, adversarial machine learning studies possible attacks to build more robust and more secure systems. The idea of considering the presence of adversaries for improving the robustness of existing systems has been embraced by the ML community only recently. In fact, despite the original ideas date back to 2004–2005, adversarial machine learning is considered to be still in its infancy [245]. Nevertheless, it is currently regarded as one of the most promising directions of research on ML and AI. The reasons for the great interest around this novel paradigm are partly due to the pervasiveness of the weaknesses it aims to overcome. Indeed, it has been demonstrated that almost every ML system is potentially vulnerable to adversarial attacks, since adversarial examples often transfer from one model to another. In fact, adversarial attacks can be successful even when adversaries have only limited knowledge of the model's characteristics.

In the remainder of this section, we provide a high-level overview of the types of attacks that can be mounted against ML and AI systems. For a detailed analysis of the technical and mathematical foundations of both attacks and countermeasures, we point interested readers to any of the extensive surveys on this topic [246, 247]. Figure 4.9 sketches the landscape of the existing classes of attacks that can be categorized according to the attacker's goals, capabilities, and information. Regarding attacks to machine learning models, an adversary can attempt to manipulate either the collection or the processing of data to corrupt the target model, thus altering the intended output. A first taxonomy categorizes adversarial attacks according to the capabilities of an attacker, in growing order of attack complexity, as detailed in the following.

Exploratory Attacks Given a "black-box" access to the model, exploratory attacks aim at gaining as much knowledge as possible about the learning algorithm of the

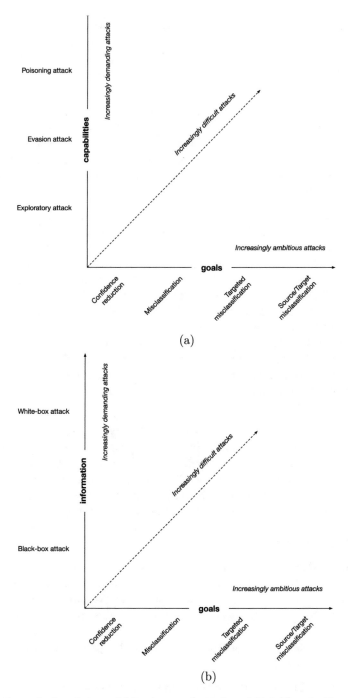

Fig. 4.9 Categorization of adversarial attacks according to the attacker's (1) goals, (2) capabilities, and (3) information. Attacks that are more ambitious and that require better capabilities or more information are considered to be more difficult. (**a**) Goals vs. capabilities. (**b**) Goals vs. information

underlying system and the data patterns exploited by the model. For example, this can be done by feeding a diverse set of inputs to the model in order to reverse engineer its functioning. In turn, acquiring knowledge about the model can help the attacker to circumvent detection. Exploratory attacks require modifying neither the training nor the test data.

Evasion Attacks The adversary tries to evade detection by the system by maliciously adjusting its data footprint at testing time. Evasion attacks evade the ML model by passing an adversarial example so that the model misclassifies it. This setting does not assume any influence over the training data. However, it assumes influence on the test data, and it represents the most common type of attack in the adversarial setting.

Poisoning Attacks This type of attack, also known as contamination of the training data, takes place during the training phase of the machine learning model. An adversary tries to poison the training data by injecting carefully designed data samples, so as to compromise the whole learning process. The attacker adds such adversarial examples to the training data so that the model's decision boundary can be manipulated. For example, the malicious training samples could cause the model to learn a wider decision area for the legitimate class, thus possibly including also some malicious input that the attacker could later exploit. This type of attack represents the most demanding one, since it requires the attacker to be able to tamper with training data—that is, with the training process of the model.

Another categorization, orthogonal to the one presented above, organizes attacks according to the information that the attacker has access to.

White-Box Attacks In white-box attacks on a machine learning model, an adversary has total knowledge of the model (e.g., the type of neural network along with the number of layers and the internal weights). The adversary utilizes this information to identify the feature space where the model may be vulnerable, such as those areas of the feature space for which the model has a high error rate. Then, this information can be used at test time by feeding the model with artfully crafted adversarial examples that lay in the high-error area, thus triggering inaccurate predictions. The possibility to access internal model weights for a white-box attack represents a very powerful adversarial attack.

Black-Box Attacks Black-box attacks, on the contrary, assume no knowledge about the model and use information about the settings or past inputs to analyze vulnerabilities. For example, in an oracle attack, the adversary exploits a model by providing a series of carefully crafted inputs and observing the corresponding model outputs.

Finally, attacks are also categorized based on the goals of the adversaries, as shown in the following.

Confidence Reduction The adversary aims to reduce the confidence of the prediction of the target model. For example, a modified instance (i.e., an adversarial example) of a given class can be correctly predicted, but with lower confidence than the unmodified one.

Misclassification The adversary aims to alter the output classification of an input to *any* class different from the correct class.

Targeted Misclassification The adversary produces adversarial examples that force the system to yield *a given* target classification. In other words, this goal aims at forcing a target output class, without putting restrictions on the input data.

Source/Target Misclassification The adversary aims to force the output of the classification for a given input to be of a given target class. This is the most ambitious goal since it is the one having the strictest requirements, involving both input data and the output class.

Countermeasures

Given the previous attacks to ML and AI systems, several defense strategies have been developed. While some of them are high-level, generic guidelines for training robust models, others are low-level and tailored for specific types of models, such as Support Vector Machines and deep neural networks [247]. In the reminder of this section, we briefly describe the most widely adopted of such defense strategies.

Adversarial Training The primary objective of the adversarial training is to increase model robustness by injecting adversarial examples into the training set. Adversarial training is a generic and broadly applicable brute force approach where the defender simply generates many adversarial examples and augments the targeted model with these examples during its training phase. The augmentation can be done either by feeding the model with both the original data and the crafted data or by learning with a modified objective function. This defense strategy can be easily implemented, since it only requires the generation of adversarial examples.

Gradient Hiding A large family of adversarial attacks exploits the known characteristics of the attacked model. Among the most important of such characteristics is the gradient of deep neural network models, which is used during the training phase of the model to tune the model's parameters. However, the same information can also be used at test time to tune adversarial inputs so as to trigger wrong classifications by the model. The gradient hiding technique represents a natural defense against gradient-based attacks and attacks using adversarial crafting methods (e.g., FGSM [248]) and simply consists of hiding the information about the model's gradient from the adversary. For instance, if the model is non-differentiable (e.g., decision trees, nearest neighbor classifiers, random forests), gradient-based attacks are rendered ineffective.

Defensive Distillation Let us assume that we already have a neural network that classifies a training dataset into the target classes. The final softmax layer of the neural network produces a probability distribution over the target classes. Let us also assume that we want to train a second neural network on the same dataset, achieving the same performance. Now, instead of using the target class labels of the training dataset, we use the output of the first network to train the second neural network. Notably, the second network has the same architecture as the first one and uses the same input dataset. The new labels used for training the second network thus contain more information about the membership of input data instances to the different target classes, compared to the simple crisp labels used by the first network. The advantage of training the second model using this approach is that of obtaining a smoother loss function, which better generalizes for an unknown dataset, with high classification accuracy even for adversarial examples.

Feature Squeezing Feature squeezing is another model hardening technique. The main idea behind this defense is that it reduces the complexity of the data representation so that the adversarial perturbations disappear because of the low sensitivity of the new data representation. Though these techniques work well in preventing adversarial attacks, they might have the collateral effect of worsening the accuracy of the model on the true examples as a consequence of the coarse-grained data representation.

Basis Function Transformations This broad family of techniques investigates various defense mechanisms like Principal Component Analysis (PCA), low-pass filtering, JPEG compression (for images), and soft thresholding that alter input data based on basis function representations. All these mechanisms are applied as a preprocessing step on both adversarial and legitimate data instances. The efficiency of each technique is evaluated in terms of its success at distinguishing between adversarial and real inputs.

NULL Labeling One of the main reasons behind the defeat of most of the well-known defense mechanisms is due to the strong transferability property in neural networks. This property implies that adversarial examples generated on one classifier are expected to cause another classifier to perform the same mistakes. This property holds true even if the classifiers have different architectures or even if they have been trained on disjoint datasets. Hence, one profitable way for protecting against black-box attacks is to block the transferability property of the adversarial examples. NULL labeling is a method organized in three steps to prevent the adversarial examples to transfer from one network to another. The main idea behind the proposed approach is to add a new "NULL" class in the dataset and to train the classifier to reject the adversarial examples by classifying them as NULL. The advantage of this method is the labeling of the perturbed inputs to the NULL class, instead of classifying them into their original labels. This method is accurate to reject an adversarial example while not compromising the accuracy of the clean data [249].

> **✐ Definitions**
>
> **Generative Adversarial Network (GAN)** Machine learning framework where two competing deep learning networks are jointly trained in a game-theoretic setting. A GAN is composed of a *generator* network that creates data instances and a *discriminator* network that classifies data instances. The goal of the generator is that of creating synthetic data instances that resemble the properties of real organic data, while the goal of the discriminator is to classify input data instances as either synthetic or organic. The discriminator is evaluated based on its binary classification performance, while the generator is evaluated in terms of its capacity to induce errors in the discriminator, hence the competition between the two networks.

Defense-GAN Another family of defensive techniques is based on the application of Generative Adversarial Networks [250]. In particular, the core idea of defense-GANs is to project each input instance onto the range of the generator of a GAN by minimizing the reconstruction error, before feeding the input instance to the classifier. Due to this preliminary step introduced by defense-GANs, all adversarial perturbations are greatly dampened and with reduced efficacy.

Open Issues and Future Directions

The previous attacks and countermeasures represent one of the most novel advancements in ML and AI. As such, their application to diverse practical scenarios is still limited. For example, many of the discussed techniques have been originally developed for fields such as computer vision [251], speech recognition [252], and Natural Language Processing (NLP) [253]—that is, those areas where deep learning and AI thrive the most. Recently, the application of adversarial machine learning has also started in fields such as automation detection on the Web (e.g., social bot detection) [254–256] and fake news detection [257]. Some recent works have also seen the application of GANs as data generators for the task of stock market prediction [258–261]. However, in all these studies, the focus was on improving the performance of market predictions systems, rather than on assessing their vulnerabilities or improving their robustness. Unfortunately, as previously anticipated in this section, in FinTech the trade-offs between predictive power and security, robustness, and interpretability are totally in favor of the former. Therefore, we can confidently claim that adversarial machine learning has never been applied to ML and AI systems employed for market prediction, nor for other finance-related tasks, for improving their robustness and reliability. On the one hand, it might appear reassuring that no vulnerability has still been found in market prediction, or in other similar, systems. However, on the other hand, the reason for this is to be attributed to the lack of investigations rather than to the robustness of such systems. In fact, all theoretical and practical results obtained so far suggest that basically all ML and AI systems are vulnerable to adversarial attacks, unless adequately defended. It is thus just a matter of time before some knowledgeable attacker will exploit the algorithmic vulnerabilities of Automatic Trading systems for its own profit, or worse, for starting an economic war.

Given this situation, the main effort to be expected for the coming years revolves around the assessment of the vulnerabilities to adversarial attacks of the existing algorithm-driven FinTech systems. Based on the results of this assessment, it would then be of the utmost importance to devote efforts toward the deployment of existing defensive techniques, such as those we previously discussed, or toward the development of new, specific ones—all with the ultimate goal of safeguarding our financial systems from targeted algorithmic manipulation.

4.1.4   Other Countermeasures

In the previous sections, we separately addressed different types of market manipulation, describing the main attacks and the corresponding specific countermeasures. Here, we conclude our discussion on financial market manipulation by briefly surveying generic and context-agnostic defenses to market manipulation.

The first, and simplest, generation of generic market manipulation detection methods leverages only raw market data. These are simply anomaly detection techniques implemented via unsupervised algorithms or via rule-based systems that analyze the time series of market data. In case of an anomalous deviation from the expected values or the permissible intervals allowed by the model, an alert is triggered. This alert signal can be used to automatically halt transactions around a given financial instrument or to solicit manual investigations by human analysts. These methods are very generic and simple, and, as a result, they are easy to calibrate and to apply for any market, time granularity, and financial instrument [211]. However, this simplicity is counterbalanced by a limited capability of detecting sophisticated manipulations. The second group of methods still leverages market data, but this time the core idea is that of building a model of a specific market or instrument and using that model to spot anomalous behaviors. In particular, the model is used to forecast the market (or part of the market). Contrarily to the majority of market prediction systems, these forecasts are not used for driving investments but as a baseline against which to compare the actual market movements. As such, these models need not be exceptionally accurate. Then, at any given point in time, the actual market behavior is compared with the prediction given by the model for the same time. If the observed behavior diverges significantly from the expected one, as predicted by the model, an anomaly is detected. Among the algorithms that can be used to create market models are many well-known supervised machine learning techniques such as decision trees, neural networks, regression models, and Support Vector Machines. Contrarily to the first family of manipulation detection techniques, some of these methods require a large number of parameters to be correctly tuned, in order for the algorithm to be effective. This means that the increased detection performance of these methods is counterbalanced by the need for continuous and accurate model calibration [211].

Market manipulation often requires the coordinated activity of several different actors that work in conjunction to alter the value of a financial instrument. Leveraging this notion, another broad group of detection techniques is based on similarity analyses. In particular, trade networks have been analyzed with the goal of spotting pools of manipulators via graph clustering algorithms [262]. Similarly, other graph clustering techniques, such as Markov cluster algorithm, have been used to detect cyclical trading [263]. Finally, the individual trading activities of different investors have been compared to one another in order to spot suspicious similarities, and the detection of colluding investors was carried out via spectral analysis [264, 265].

The previous techniques leverage raw market data and coordinated behaviors to detect market manipulation. In addition to these, other interesting techniques also exploit human psychology. In fact, it has long been demonstrated that catastrophic market crashes, such as those that are potentially dangerous for a national economy, are driven by panic as much as by economic factors. Because of this, predicting panic is of critical importance not only in many areas of human behavior but also in the context of market dynamics. For the latter case, studies demonstrated that panic may be due to specific external threats but also to self-generated nervousness among investors [266]. It has been shown that both long-lasting economic crises as well as sudden single-day crashes were preceded by extended periods of so-called *market mimicry*—an abstract concept related to the extent to which investors look at one another for cues. When the mimicry is high, the market becomes less influenced by external news and more so by internal dynamics, which are often driven by uncertainty and nervousness. In addition, many stocks follow each other's movements, thus setting the stage for extensive panic to take hold. Ultimately, it has been shown that high levels of mimicry represent a quite general indicator of the potential for self-organized market crises [266]. As such, continuous monitoring of market mimicry can allow to anticipate and, possibly prevent, large market crises.

4.2   Scenario 2: High-Frequency Trading

"Move fast and break things" was an early motto at Facebook, intended to push developers to take risks. The inspirational phrase appeared on office posters and even featured in a letter from Mark Zuckerberg to investors in 2012. Over time, it came to be embraced as a mantra broadly applicable to all technological disruption, and, as such, it was adopted by countless entrepreneurs. As we already investigated in the previous sections of this chapter, the unfolding technological revolution that propels FinTech brought massive changes to the way paying, trading, and investing are done. FinTech thrives on technology, and, in fact, looking back at the last decades of technological advancements, one can confidently say that this revolution disrupted and reinvented the FinTech landscape multiple times.

✐ **Definitions**

Automatic Trading (AT) occurs whenever a computer algorithm automatically determines when to initiate or cancel orders, with limited or no human interaction.

In addition to the previous characteristics, **High-Frequency Trading (HFT)** also demands an infrastructure that minimizes network and other types of latencies using specific facilities as co-location, proximity hosting, or high-speed direct electronic access. HFT is thus a subset and a specialization of AT [267].

One crucial dimension along which technological advancement unfolds is *speed*. Nowadays, thanks to High-Frequency Trading (HFT) and Automatic Trading (AT), transactions happen in microsecond timeframes and unprecedented volumes. Trading strategies based on HFT and AT were even dubbed "flash trading," in recognition of the sheer speeds involved, which at times, can be orders of magnitude faster than the blink of a human eye. To reach such inhuman peaks in trading speed, FinTech giants moved mountains—almost literally. In his bestselling book *Flash Boys* [268], Michael Lewis describes a 2011 $300 million project for the construction of an 827-mile (1331 km) tunnel, hosting fiber optics cables, that cuts straight through mountains and rivers from Chicago to New Jersey. This once titanic endeavor allowed to reduce the roundtrip time from 14.6 to 14.1 ms. This was later rendered obsolete by the construction of a microwave link, which follows an even straighter route. The new air route also takes advantage of the faster speed of signal travel that is possible through the air, as compared to signal travel speed through glass fibers, which slows light down. With these two advantages, this new link shaved 4.5 ms off the fiber optics cables. As copper cables got replaced by fiber optic cables and as radio waves did the same by microwaves, also the latter was eventually rendered obsolete by laser beams. In the EU, the laser beam link between London and Frankfurt is currently being rerouted via Dunkerque and away from Calais, in an effort that is bound to save a few nanoseconds [269]. If you think these tiny gains are not worth the huge investment, think twice.

✐ **Definitions**

Arbitrage is the legit practice of capitalizing upon a price difference between two markets. The profit results from the difference between the market prices at which the unit is traded.

(continued)

> **Front running** (or **tailgating**) is the illicit practice of issuing a trade based on nonpublic knowledge of other pending transactions that will influence the price of the traded security.

By leveraging (1) high-performance computers; (2) co-location services, as well as individual data feeds, to minimize network and data latencies; and (3) extraordinary high-speed algorithms for generating, routing, and executing transactions, HFT is capable of simultaneously analyzing different global markets and establishing and liquidating positions in very short timeframes, based on real-time market conditions. HFT is thus an advanced technology that opens up new trading possibilities for its adopters, by profiting from lightning-fast analyses and transactions with respect to slower traders. This results in the possibility to profit from even minor price differences across different markets. In fact, high-frequency traders typically benefit more from a large number of minor transactions than from a few particularly significant ones, as manual traders do. Obviously, this is only made possible by the opportunity to monitor markets at large and to immediately benefit from the slightest price differences. Because of this advantage over traditional traders, HFT is often used to perform arbitrage. In addition to the legit practice of arbitrage, HFT has also been used to obtain unfair advantages. One way to do so is via front running, sometimes done even at the expense of one's own clients. This occurs when an HFT firm races ahead of a large client order, scooping up all the shares on offer at various other exchanges (if the client is issuing a buy order) or hitting all the bids (if it is a sell order) and then turning around and selling them to (or buying them from) the client and pocketing the difference [268].

> **📂 Resources**
> The existing literature on HFT is based on datasets of four different types [267]:
>
> * Data for equity trading on NASDAQ.
> * Data on trading in the E-Mini.
> * Data used by CFTC and SEC to release their report on the market disruption that occurred in the case of the 2010 Flash Crash.[16]
> * Datasets made available to researchers by exchanges and regulators. These require proxies for identifying HFT activity.

Given the disruptive changes brought by HFT and its uses, sometimes shady, it comes with little surprise that there exists a vast academic literature and a heated

---

[16]https://www.sec.gov/news/studies/2010/marketevents-report.pdf (Last checked August 2020).

debate on AT and HFT and on their effects on markets. Many papers discuss their roles in capital markets as well as their trading strategies and consequences for market quality. Similarly, market regulators have expressed concerns about the growing participation of HFT and the costs associated with monitoring their activities. Among the existing literature, it is striking that the majority of the most cited papers actually link HFT to positive market effects. In fact, it has been found that HFT tends to reduce information asymmetry between buyers and sellers over time. Despite frequent accusations of arbitrage, many empirical studies demonstrated a general improvement in market liquidity, measured by the reduction of spreads or the increase in depth, and a general reduction of the intraday price volatility [210]. Some examples are in the following studies, showing evidence that HFT stabilizes markets [270], improves market quality and reduces bid-ask spreads [271], and reduces trading costs [272]. These results ultimately seem to suggest that any regulatory action introduced to curtail this activity may have serious negative implications for liquidity and market participants, as also demonstrated recently both in France and in Italy [267].

The previous results reported overall positive effects of HFT on markets, when markets operate under "normal" conditions. However, radically different results have been obtained when studying the role of HFT in markets during distressed times, such as in the case of flash crashes. The signs that HFT could play a negative role in the emergence of systemic crashes surfaced since the infamous 2010 Flash Crash. Years of investigations led to trace back a possible cause of the crash to the London-based trader Navinder Singh Sarao, who used an automated trading program to manipulate the market via spoofing—offering $200 million worth of fake bets that drove prices down, modifying them 19,000 times, and then canceling all of them before they could be completed. As the market fell, he sold futures contracts. When the market began to recover, he bought futures back and sold them again at a higher price [273]. On a large scale, this behavior can have potentially catastrophic effects if a chain reaction of instability sets in. In the years following the 2010 Flash Crash, several studies reported that HFT is not beneficial to the stock market during flash crashes and actually consumes liquidity when it is most needed. HFT exacerbates the transient price impact, unrelated to fundamentals, typically observed during a flash crash [274]. Other studies report that HFT functions essentially as an accelerator and a catalyst to already existing market dynamics, such as bubbles and crashes. More flash crashes, involving additional markets and instruments, can be expected in the future, resulting from the increasing interdependences between various financial instruments and asset classes. Within this evolving scenario, the technological race involving AT and HFT is not expected to provide a stabilization effect. On the contrary, the most recent results support the hypothesis that HFT can in fact lead to catastrophic market crashes and it could do it even more frequently in the future [275]. In light of these findings, the old Facebook motto *Move fast and break things* appears to suit HFT particularly well.

4.2.1   Threat: Technological Bias, Divide, and Monopoly

The preceding paragraphs highlighted the role that HFT can have in the formation of market crashes. They also discussed the strong dependence of HFT on the underlying technologies, which are responsible for its exceptional speed and performance. Similarly to our discussion about possible algorithmic manipulation of financial markets, the combination of technology in HFT and flash crashes opens up the possibility for state actors to perpetrate targeted manipulations. If the most performing (i.e., the fastest) HFT technologies are publicly available and all actors in the financial market rely on them, the single agent advantage is negligible. However, if one actor manages to develop or to acquire a system that is much more performing than those available to the other actors, it will gain a huge and unfair advantage. In fact, the major open problem with respect to the possible weaponization of HFT is related to technological bias and divide.

Here, we define technological bias as an asymmetry or an imbalance in the technology that is available to different economic actors. Similarly, technological divide represents the gap between the technology available to different actors. Although a certain degree of technological bias has always existed, if the resulting gap exceeds a certain threshold, its effects on financial markets may become significant. This asymmetry can even widen up to a point where the leading actor finds itself in a position of monopoly, derived from its enhanced capabilities of driving the market. To complicate matters, the fight for obtaining the upper hand in this situation of technological bias is highly dynamic. In fact, the technology behind HFT, and FinTech at large, is in constant evolution and those who adapt faster to new technology will inevitably hold a higher ground.

4.2.2   Attacks and Countermeasures

Until now, to the best of the existing knowledge, the technological bias in HFT has never been exploited to carry out massive manipulation operations or attacks to national assets and economies. In recent years, despite its growing significance, technological bias failed to attract much interest from academics. Nonetheless, it has worried other stakeholders that are more directly exposed to market dynamics, such as market traders and state decision-makers. For example, "slow traders" have been actively trying to avoid markets that are polluted by high-frequency traders, to not succumb to their greater firepower. Many finance professionals are constantly debating market structure and whether a new exchange can help slow traders to avoid high-frequency ones. Some firms even based their business on providing this sort of information, as AbleMarkets that delivers daily estimates of aggressive high-frequency traders acting across different markets. The negative effects of technological bias have been reported also for other areas of FinTech, in addition to HFT. For example, the improvements in market forecasting opened up by

AI and deep learning are often regarded as another potential factor for technological bias. In turn, this high-tech progress may create challenges for market efficiency, along with information asymmetry and irrationality of decision-making. Skilled traders can leverage this technological division for netting excess returns, at the expense of traders that adopt more traditional technologies [276]. Results reported in [276] for Forex trading are in contrast with the efficient-market hypothesis. The author concludes that with the progressive enhancement in computational methods and software, trading strategies will be vastly improved, with the inevitable result that some traders will be more successful than others. This process contradicts the classical definition of a market with perfect competition. However, it complies with the so-called adaptive-market hypothesis [277], according to which markets are not seen as efficient ecosystems, but rather as fiercely competitive ones. Since the market *ecology* changes over time, adaptation mistakes can occur as a consequence of the different degrees of adaptation of the participants. As a result, some of them will obtain more significant returns than others. Within this context, the technological shift is considered as a primary driver for change in market ecology [276].

While the previous considerations account for direct harms (e.g., immediate financial loss) caused by AT and HFT, others also raised attention on the indirect consequences (e.g., diminished confidence in financial markets). The latter might even have a bigger and worse impact than the former. In particular, HFT has changed those whom trading can harm, how they might be harmed, and the scale of the harm [278]. Therefore, a generalized loss of confidence derived from systemic crashes and failures may even reduce investor appetite for risk, thereby stalling economic growth [278]. To support this grim hypothesis, the authors considered the case of Knight Capital Group. On August 1, 2012, the firm lost $440 million in less than 30 min due to its new AT software flooding the market with orders and forcing the temporary closing of the New York Stock Exchange. The direct harm to the firm and its shareholders was catastrophic and almost led to bankruptcy. The accident, however, also had an indirect impact on the investing public's confidence in the structure of financial markets.

Countermeasures to the aforementioned issues are still being debated, and existing proposals come mainly from the regulatory and ethics communities, rather than from the computer science and engineering ones. This is also reflected in a lack of papers discussing security issues of HFT from a technical standpoint. Regarding regulations, some of the proposed solutions aim at reducing the effectiveness of HFT by changing how markets evade pending orders. In detail, some have argued that the priority rules which determine the execution sequence of submitted orders are designed to prioritize speed. Here, the regulatory conundrum is whether time-price priority unduly rewards high-frequency traders and leads to risky overinvestments in the technology arms race [279]. The greatest benefit of current priority rules is that they treat every order equally. However other priority rules have been proposed, such as one where every order at a price gets a partial execution, independent of time [280]. Others have proposed to replace the continuous trading model by periodic auctions, which can be designed to minimize the advantage of the speed and to mitigate other negative outcomes of continuous trading such as manipulative strategies [281]. The main benefit of periodic auctions would be a reduction of the speed of trading and the elimination of the arms race for speed discussed throughout this section. Many markets already have auctions at the open and close times and are now considering the introduction of midday auctions, in addition to the continuous trading segment [280].

In addition to the previous regulatory countermeasures—anyway not bound to be deployed at large anytime soon—some politicians also hinted at the possibility to introduce more radical initiatives. For example, Hillary Clinton once suggested the introduction of a small tax on all cancellation orders, in an attempt to quell the practice of spoofing.[17] Introducing comprehensive financial transaction taxes would however face great difficulties, also in light of the potential risks and undesirable consequences that this might cause [282]. On the contrary, specific taxes aimed at thwarting HFT are seen as a more sensible and desirable possibility, although difficult to implement [280].

4.2.3   Open Issues and Future Directions

The growing stack of papers on the topic of AT and HFT indicates a developing academic interest in the potential contributions and limitations of HFT activity. However, many open questions remain unanswered. First and foremost, it is still not clear if the systemic risk of financial markets is embedded in electronic trading or if it is really caused by HFT. Existing studies showed that High-Frequency Trading is a multifaceted, complex, and secretive practice and that it has surely been implicated in nefarious market events. However, correlation does not necessarily imply causation, and isolating causal mechanisms from interconnected automated trading is highly challenging for regulators and scholars alike, seeking to monitor AT and HFT across multiple jurisdictions and markets [283]. For both ethical and practical reasons, markets must remain fair and orderly. Deciding how best to ensure this—in light of the huge growth of HFT in the last decade, also expected to continue in the next—requires additional endeavors of careful thoughts and discussions.

The growing interconnected and automated nature of financial markets also raises additional technology-driven questions. For instance, given that corporate disclosure is progressively moving toward machine-readable reports [267], can firms anticipate HFT trading strategies at the time of disclosure? Then, assuming that such strategies could actually be anticipated, would it be possible to exploit this mechanism to drive HFT toward specific strategies, thus somehow manipulating the market? More in general, despite the recent development of a new generation of network facilities, high-performance computers, and powerful forecasting algorithms, it seems that

---

[17]https://mechanicalmarkets.wordpress.com/2015/10/14/could-hfts-benefit-from-a-cancellation-tax/ (Last checked August 2020).

academia is still not paying enough attention to technological bias and its potential consequences. Moreover, the technological shift is likely to become even more significant in the coming years. Because of this, the key role of technological bias toward market efficiency deserves to be examined in more depth in future research efforts.

By looking back at where it all started—the 2010 Flash Crash—it's easy to understand that the AT software that initiated the market collapse simply executed the tasks requested by Navinder Singh Sarao. Though suggestive of the kinds of harm that AT and HFT might cause, the crash itself could only partially be blamed on such technologies. Containing, stopping, or even promptly detecting such unfolding market failures exceeds the boundaries of existing scientific and regulatory tools. In addition to calling for renewed efforts, this also inevitably escalates the problem to an ethic and philosophic plane, forcing a debate over "whether it is more important to move fast, or to avoid things being broken" [273].

4.3 Scenario 3: Remote Stock Market

The New York Stock Exchange (NYSE) is the world's largest exchange by market capitalization of its listed companies. Since its founding in 1792, it was the living heart of New York City's financial district, and it gradually became the core of American and world finance. For centuries, the NYSE and all other exchanges that contributed to the rise of Wall Street as an icon of trading and finance have been a place rooted in vast physical rooms. Trading floors have been thriving on hectic human activity and have always been filled with tightly packed rows of desks with hundreds of workstations and monitors, specialized phones called "turrets," and other ad hoc trading equipment. This streamlined organization survived each and every calamity—man-made or otherwise—to happen to New York, the United States, and the world. The shift to decimalization in stocks, the 9/11 attacks, the financial crises, the rise of passive investing, and Hurricane Sandy are just some of the notable shocks that affected Wall Street in the last decades.[18] However, none of this fundamentally changed the way trading was done. More importantly, none of these events caused trading floors to be closed while markets were opened, not even for a single day, not even in the case of a World War. This was only until Monday, March 23, 2020. On that day, the NYSE closed its trading floor—at that time, indefinitely—in the wake of the spreading COVID-19 pandemic. Two workers in the premises had tested positive to the virus, and the NYSE decided to switch to electronic-only trading for the first time since the current trading floor opened in 1903 and since its very founding in 1792. Traders and market makers started working remotely, as concerns of contagion continued to disrupt every facet of our

---

[18]https://www.cnbc.com/2020/04/30/goldman-sachs-trader-says-wall-street-never-the-same-after-coronavirus.html (Last checked August 2020).

society and everyday life, financial markets included. The US Financial Industry Regulatory Authority (FINRA) confirmed that traders could work remotely and that firms might need to implement alternative supervisory systems to support this switch. FINRA also temporarily waived some record-keeping requirements and opened to some flexibility for firms facing difficulties in meeting other filing obligations. The same decisions were taken worldwide by other exchanges, banks, and by all sorts of financial operators. Amid fears that COVID-19 could further spread, dealers and employees of brokerages have been temporarily permitted to log into trading systems from remote locations. In the United Kingdom, the Financial Conduct Authority said it had no objection to brokerage staff working from home if certain standards—like the recording of conversations and prompt execution of orders—could be met.[19] The London Metals Exchange, despite already having most of its traffic handled electronically, moved its once physically driven price-setting mechanisms to its electronic trading system as well, for the first time after 143 years.[20] Banks sent traders home in the second week of March as the pandemic was wreaking havoc, causing a historic surge in stock volatility and dislocations across credit markets, and IT departments worked around the clock to equip thousands of traders for the task. Similarly, brokers of the National Stock Exchange of India (NSE)—the leading stock exchange in India, in Mumbai—have been allowed to access the market from their homes.

As all activities suddenly moved online while markets stayed opened, traders had little time to come up with a new "normal." This is when technology came to the rescue, with the latest apps and appliances that allowed traders to feel so connected to coworkers and clients alike, as to rarely miss trading floors. Dedicated messaging platforms for investment banks such as Symphony, which is similar to the widely known Slack, became the *de facto* standard for creating chat rooms for internal teams and clients. Each trader had about tens of different chats simultaneously opened, efficiently connecting them with hedge funds and asset managers. The teleconferencing application Zoom also recorded a surge in use, as it became widely adopted for setting up calls with clients and with other traders and for coordinating entire teams. Then, telecommunication companies, such as Cisco, promptly delivered dedicated phones that conveniently provided the possibility to record calls, as demanded by most regulatory agencies. With all these workplace tools at their disposal, it comes with little surprise that many traders even experienced a rise in productivity. And in fact, the five biggest US investment banks reported their best trading quarter in nearly a decade, as both bond and stock desks handily beat expectations. For the first time in history, stock markets had gone fully remote. In the end, the COVID-19 pandemic raised the question as to whether exchanges should retain trading floors at all. Some consider them to be costly and

---

[19]https://fortune.com/2020/03/22/coronavirus-nyse-trading-floor-closed-stock-market/   (Last checked August 2020).

[20]https://www.economist.com/finance-and-economics/2020/05/25/covid-19-forced-trading-floors-to-close-theyll-be-back (Last checked August 2020).

overhead heavy businesses. Moreover, also human brokers are considered by some
to be slower and more error-prone than algorithms. In addition, some researchers
also argued that fully electronic markets are more efficient than those featuring a
certain degree of human intervention [284]. Researchers analyzed NYSE's hybrid
auction structure, which normally allows floor traders to submit their last orders
of the day up to 10 s before the market's close, whereas those coming through
electronically have to make theirs 10 min before its end. This difference gives
floor traders an advantage in end-of-day auctions. Then, to evaluate the effect of
an electronic-only market, scholars compared market efficiency while the NYSE
was operating only remotely, with its normal (i.e., hybrid) mode of operation.
Interestingly, they found that auctions have become more efficient since the NYSE
moved entirely online [284].

Despite these results, once the curve of COVID-19 contagions had been "flat-
tened," all exchanges slowly and gradually started to revert back to pre-pandemic
work conditions. At the same time, however, it was clear from the beginning that
some of the changes caused by the pandemic were bound to remain. In fact, in the
few months of extensive lockdown, many businesses had to adapt, sometimes even
for the better. With respect to electronic-only trading and remote stock markets,
the pandemic only accelerated a trend that was already in place. Many exchanges
already had the majority, if not all of their trades, handled electronically. Examples
of this kind are the stock markets in Hong Kong, London, Tokyo, Toronto, and
Mumbai that have long scaled back the respective trading floors. The NYSE was
undergoing the same process as well, with roughly 80% of its trade volume already
managed electronically through a data center in suburban New Jersey. On top of
this remotely driven scenario, when the NYSE reopened, only a few floor traders
actually came back, and they were allowed to do so only after abiding by several
requirements including social distancing norms and the need to wear face masks.
With the gloomy prospect that COVID-19 was just one in a series of pandemics
to test our societies for the coming years,[21] it is quite natural that worldwide stock
markets are accelerating their transition to remote- and online-only. An outlook that
raises renewed concerns for the security of stock markets.

4.3.1   Threat: Attacks Against Availability

As we have already seen in Chap. 3 with cryptocurrencies that are replacing physical
fiat currencies, the switch from physical to virtual inevitably introduces several
security challenges. Online and remote stock markets make no exception to this rule.
The first concern about a fully online stock market is related to potential attacks on
its availability. Stock markets play an important role in modern economies, easing

---

[21] https://theconversation.com/coronavirus-is-a-wake-up-call-our-war-with-the-environment-is-
leading-to-pandemics-135023 (Last checked August 2020).

the access to capital and allowing its allocation from those who have a surplus to those who are in need, and contributing to stabilizing security prices. They represent a hub for a multitude of financial services. As such, limiting or denying access to these services would have tremendous repercussions on a national economy. In the past, when it has been suggested the possibility of a market holiday in the United States, or when other countries have suspended trading, people reacted with widespread panic. In the United States, continuous liquidity is a hallmark of equity markets and assuring investors that they will have the capability to access their money is mandatory for maintaining confidence in the system. It is thus crucial that people continue to have confidence that the markets will be open to both express their investment thesis and to access their savings.[22]

Among the most common types of cyberattacks that are designed to limit the availability of a resource to its intended users are Denial of Service (DoS) attacks. These are typically carried out by flooding the target resource with bogus requests, thus overloading it and preventing some or all legitimate requests from being fulfilled. Some of the most effective DoS attacks are carried out in a distributed fashion—that is, by using multiple machines, typically in the region of thousands, to send the bogus requests. Large-scale, Distributed Denial of Service (DDoS) attacks are more difficult to defend against, since the victim would need to shut down a significant portion of all the machines involved in the attack, instead of a single one.

Attacks and Countermeasures

Typically, DoS and DDoS attacks are perpetrated for profit, as in the case of groups of hackers blackmailing their victims; for obtaining an industrial advantage on a competitor; or for ideological reasons by groups of activists. However, we have also seen a few cases of state-backed actors involved in DDoS attacks for political and economic reasons. One of the biggest DDoS attacks in history occurred in 2007 and targeted government services, media outlets, and financial institutions in Estonia. This had a crushing effect on Estonia, since the country was an early adopter of e-government and was practically paperless at the time, to the point that even national elections were held online. This attack is considered by many to be the first case of cyberwarfare and came in response to political conflict between Estonia and Russia, which is suspected to be responsible for the attack.[23] More recently, during the 2019 Hong Kong protests that are part of the long-lasting Hong Kong-China conflicts, the messaging app Telegram suffered a large-scale DDoS attack aimed at preventing protesters from coordinating their efforts. Investigations by Telegram found that the attack was carried out by a State-sized actor and via IP addresses originating from China.[24]

---

[22]https://www.iflr.com/Article/3926218/Inside-nyses-response-to-the-Covid-19-crisis.html (Last checked August 2020).

[23]https://www.cloudflare.com/learning/ddos/famous-ddos-attacks/ (Last checked August 2020).

[24]https://www.pcmag.com/news/chinese-ddos-attack-hits-telegram-during-hong-kong-protests (Last checked August 2020).

The previous examples demonstrate how cyberattacks can be weaponized by a nation as a mean to fulfill its political and economic goals. Past attacks mainly targeted governmental Web services and communication facilities, and, until now, there have been no records of state-driven attacks targeting national stock markets. This was partly due to the physical component that stock markets have always had— e.g., their frenzied trading floors. However, with the progressive dehumanization of stock markets resulting in all-electronic trading, this scenario might rapidly change. Since markets are so sensitive to uncertainty, halting trading even for a limited amount of time could send stock prices plummeting. In fact, the online components of stock markets and other financial institutions (e.g., online banks) have a long history of small- to medium-scale DDoS attacks carried out by hackers and fraudsters. In a 2013 survey of 46 stock exchanges, the International Securities Commission Association (IOSCO) reported that more than half had already suffered a DoS cyberattack that year [285]. The majority of such attacks were considered to have had no effect on the proper functioning of the market and only resulted in minimal costs (less than $1 million) for the targeted market. As an example, in 2012, a wave of DDoS attacks led by activists hit the NYSE, NASDAQ, and BATS stock exchanges in the United States, but trading systems were not affected. Instead, in the fall of 2019, the Hong Kong Stock Exchange (HKEx) admitted to have suffered a series of DDoS attacks. The attacks overwhelmed HKEx's website and affected its ability to display prices and publish filings. More importantly, at the same time, the exchange also suffered an extended shutdown of derivative trading. This was later attributed by HKEx's chief executive to an unspecified "software bug," which however did not lift suspicions that the halt was due, or at least linked, to the cyberattack.[25] This scenario could even become more complex than this, if we consider that an attacker could preemptively sell (buy) some shares on a market, only to subsequently carry out a targeted attack aimed at lowering (increasing) the value of the manipulated shares, thus obtaining a direct unfair profit from its attack. This could be achieved by targeting a specific company and manipulating the price of its stocks or even by targeting a market and inducing a flash crash.

While there are only a few recent cases of attacks against the availability of a stock exchange, the scenario is completely different for cryptocurrency exchanges. Having always been online-only, cryptocurrency exchanges naturally attracted all sorts of cyberattacks. In [286], scholars analyzed the impact of DDoS attacks on the volume of Bitcoin traded on the Bitfinex cryptocurrency exchange. The study shows that for most attacks, Bitfinex suffered a significant impact in the aftermath of the attack, but also that it was able to recover within a single day. This proves that a long-lasting DDoS attack can severely cripple the revenues of any given exchange. Also, the study in [287] investigated the impact of DDoS attacks on the Mt. Gox Bitcoin currency exchange. The study concluded that on days where DDoS attacks or other shocks occur, the distribution of daily transaction volume

---

[25]https://www.finextra.com/newsarticle/34352/hong-kong-exchange-suffers-cyber-attack   (Last checked August 2020).

shifts in such a way that fewer large transactions take place, with detrimental effects for the exchange itself. DDoS attacks have also been investigated with respect to the competition between different mining pools. In particular, the study in [288] applied a game-theoretic approach and found that pools have a greater incentive to attack large pools than small ones. They also observed that larger mining pools have a greater incentive to attack than smaller ones. These results suggest that small-scale attacks are unlikely to be profitable, while large-scale ones are instead more profitable for the attackers—a result that raises concerns on the overall stability of stock and cryptocurrency exchanges. The theoretical result of [288] was also later confirmed in [289], which empirically measured that big mining pools are much more likely to be DDoS-ed than small pools. The extensive study in [289] also found that currency exchanges, mining pools, gambling operators, eWallets, and financial services are much more likely to be attacked than other services. They also found that currency exchanges and mining pools are much more likely to have DDoS protection, such as that provided by CloudFlare, Incapsula, or Amazon via AWS Shield.

> **☛ Resources**
> Main DDoS protection solutions:
>
> - **Project Shield**[26] by Jigsaw, a technology incubator created by Google
> - **Microsoft Azure**'s DDoS solution[27]
> - **AWS Shield**[28] by Amazon Web Services
> - IBM's DDoS protection as part of **IBM Cloud Internet Services**[29]
> - **Cloudflare**,[30] one of the most popular DDoS solutions to date
> - **Imperva Incapsula**.[31]

Regarding countermeasures to DDoS and other availability attacks, there already exists an extensive literature on the topic [290, 291]. These attacks are not new and have long been studied by academia. Accordingly, also many industry leaders are already providing their DDoS protection solutions. In Sect. 6.2.2 we present, among other solutions, an overview of several DDoS protection strategies. The challenge related to securing the availability of remote and online stock markets is thus more toward applying the countermeasures that already exist, rather than devoting research and development efforts to propose new ones.

---

[26]https://projectshield.withgoogle.com/ (Last checked August 2020).

[27]https://azure.microsoft.com/ (Last checked August 2020).

[28]https://aws.amazon.com/shield/ (Last checked August 2020).

[29]https://www.ibm.com/cloud/cloud-internet-services (Last checked August 2020).

[30]https://www.cloudflare.com/en-gb/ (Last checked August 2020).

[31]https://www.imperva.com/products/ddos-protection-services/ (Last checked August 2020).

4.3.2   Threat: Work-from-Home Perils

The COVID-19 spreading and the switch to fully remote stock markets forced organizations around the world to enact remote, work-from-home policies. While some organizations have maintained robust remote work practices for years, many others have had limited experience in this regard. Even for organizations that have long maintained a remote workforce, the breadth and depth of remote work have dramatically increased. Business units and functions that have never been done remotely are now required to operate in a fully remote mode. As a consequence, many that have never experienced remote work—think, for example, of trading floor workers—are now suddenly forced to do so. During these rapid, unplanned, and unprecedented changes, security experts are pondering what new risks may have been introduced.

For instance, many office workers have been originally only provisioned a desktop computer from their employer. How did these workers connect to the network after the switch? How many of them were forced to utilize an unmanaged personal system or an insecure connection in order to keep up their work? On the workers' side, this raises a plethora of security concerns. Some of these concerns are related technical security risks, such as the inevitable increase in computer-mediated communications that could be sniffed by an attacker, or even the vulnerability of the system and the applications (teleconferencing and messaging apps) that employees need to use for their remote work. Other additional concerns are related to the psychological effects of work from home. First of all, operators that start working remotely immediately become more valuable targets for attackers, which exposes them to increased risks. At the same time, they might feel safer at home or even be more carefree as a consequence of the informal work environment. The combination of increased risks and diminished attention represents the recipe for security breaches. The situation also became more complicated on the companies side. In fact, the security perimeter previously established by the company, weakened or even vanished. In addition, security teams are now left with limited visibility and control over remote workers' appliances and actions. If not adequately addressed, these work-from-home security risks might cause a rapid surge in attacks.

Attacks

Here, we discuss in more detail some of the risks that this new remote connectivity paradigm brings. To do so, we consider a sample of the remote access implementations that are typically being used.

Direct Access The simplest and least secure remote access method revolves around directly exposing networking protocols, such as Microsoft Remote Desktop Protocol (RDP), to the Internet. This scenario represents a baseline case, since most mature organizations prohibit direct access through proper firewall configurations and other restrictions. However, a few cases of this type nonetheless still exist. Here, the main attacks consist of the traditional means of gaining access to externally facing services. Network scanning of external ports and exploitation through brute-forcing, credential spraying, and spear phishing are among the most widely used attacks. Further increasing the risk of this direct network access is that these services likely allow unmanaged devices direct access, providing little visibility into the hosts that are connecting to the services.

Given the lack of control and the risks introduced by the previous model in exposing RDP and other remote protocols to the Internet, organizations have centralized remote access to a few technologies. Two widespread implementations are based on Virtual Private Network (VPN) or virtualized desktops and the so-called zero trust model. These solutions allow for improved access management, logging, and security controls.

VPN/Virtual Desktop In the first solution, which also represents the most widely used one, a VPN or a virtualized desktop interface such as Citrix or VMWare is placed within the organization's Demilitarized Zone (DMZ). Threats to this model include unauthenticated attacks, compromised credentials, and compromised systems. Moreover, attackers often chain-control deficiencies together, by exploiting the initial access they obtain to the VPN or virtualized desktop, to gain further access.

Endpoint Remote Access Endpoint remote access is one of the vulnerabilities of this model, for which mail filtering, endpoint hardening, and reduced administrator privileges and visibility should be enforced. In addition, security teams should validate that endpoint visibility remains consistent for users that switch from in situ to remote and for any new users or third parties.

Multifactor Authentication Bypass Many organizations have implemented Multi-factor Authentication (MFA) to reduce the success of brute-forcing or credential spraying. However, carefree users might still accept push notifications, thus enabling remote access. Against this issue, remote employees should be adequately trained to identify and report unauthorized push notifications.

Unmanaged Device Access Organizations often conduct limited validation checks to identify unmanaged devices, including attacker systems connecting to remote access solutions. Oftentimes, the checks performed by VPN solutions can be bypassed by modifying VPN software responses or registry key settings. In addition to attacker systems connecting to the network, security teams should also consider users connecting from unauthorized systems.

Tunneling Configuration To handle the increase in remote connectivity caused by the switch to remote markets, some organizations passed from a full-tunnel configuration to split tunneling. With a full tunnel, all traffic traverses the VPN, allowing Web proxies to filter traffic and security teams to identify unauthorized activity. Instead, split tunneling reduces this visibility unless appropriate endpoint agents are installed to provide sufficient visibility and control.

Remote Access DoS Entire organizations are moving toward a remote access model. As such, the potential impact of a DoS attack on these remote access portals has significantly increased. An attacker could be able to generate multiple failed password attempts on an account and lock the user out. If this attack runs at scale, it might even cause widespread account lockouts, thus impairing the organization's activities.

Zero Trust Model In contrast with VPNs and virtual desktops, the emerging zero trust model leverages an identity provider to provide access to the applications. Then, authorization rights are determined based on both the user and device, via a series of identity checks. Given that this model is based on device trust as a component of authentication and authorization, issues such as the protection of certificates establishing device trust and access limitations to unmanaged devices, are of the utmost importance. These add to some of the previously mentioned concerns that still apply, such as endpoint visibility and hardening, MFA bypasses, and DoS attacks.

Countermeasures

In light of these threats and in order to adapt to a remote and distributed workforce, organizations need to create a strong set of defenses at the edge of their networks for protecting both identities and applications, regardless of whether they are in the corporate network or in the cloud.

Regarding the problem of authentication, organizations must implement MFA on all external corporate resources to reduce the effectiveness of attacks such as credential spraying, password stuffing, and phishing—which are bound to become increasingly common. However, as previously outlined, MFA alone is not sufficient to ensure secure authentication. Because of this, it is also becoming increasingly important to validate the device establishing connectivity, for instance, by relying on device identity certificates. Then, regarding endpoint control, endpoint visibility should be enforced, and employee endpoints should be hardened in order to reduce the ability for an attacker to gain access to systems and to escalate privileges. Moreover, default configurations of virtualized interfaces should be avoided as they may allow to break out of virtual sessions, thus opening access to the underlying operating system. The switch to remote work also implied an increased dependence on third-party cloud services, as thoroughly analyzed in Chap. 6. Here, contrarily to the current trend, organizations should strive to develop suitable corporate alternatives for cloud services. In all those (alas, many) cases in which this is not possible or not yet available, organizations should at the very least ensure that security teams regularly receive logs from cloud providers so as to review them for unauthorized access and data exfiltration. Moving on, regarding network control and visibility, off-network communications from virtual desktops should be limited to whitelisted resources, in order to reduce potential exposure. Similarly, shifts from full-tunnel to split-tunnel VPN should be limited and possibly also complemented by augmenting network visibility with a cloud proxy or with a similar solution. Finally, special care should be devoted to providing adequate security awareness training for remote workers, especially for those that are new to this paradigm. In addition to computing hygiene topics such as phishing and password guidance, employees should be trained on physical security topics such as using a privacy screen, limiting work on confidential material in public spaces, and securing physical computing assets. Still, regarding physical security, the possibility for appliances to be lost or stolen should be also taken into account, for instance, by ensuring that all employee computing resources have full disk encryption.

4.3.3 Open Issues and Future Directions

Given the recency of the switch to online- and remote-only markets, the full extent of new security risks and their impact on the market and financial stability is yet to be fully understood. Nevertheless, the analysis that we developed in this section still allows to draw some preliminary conclusions. On the one hand, we have a rapidly evolving situation where multiple voices are advocating the advantage of fully online markets. Among them are those in favor of reducing costs and delays imputable to trading floors and those striving for greater market efficiency, which appears to require less human intervention in favor of more algorithmic decisions. These forces, combined with current digitalization trends and with the possibility of future pandemics or other shocks impairing physical human interactions, are bound to progressively reduce the importance of trading floors and human brokerage. On the other hand, we already collected extensive evidence of the volume and scale of cyberattacks that continuously affect online exchanges, such as cryptocurrency exchanges. For the future, it is thus foreseeable that an increased number of cyberattacks will be targeting stock markets. Solutions for defending against or for mitigating the majority of existing attacks already exist. What we are actually missing is however a greater understanding of the vulnerabilities of fully remote markets and the assessment of the practical impact that a large-scale attack, such as one carried out by a state-sized actor, could cause. Moreover, development and deployment endeavors for applying current solutions to stock markets are still lagging behind.

4.4 Scenario 4: Complex Financial Networks

In the previous sections of this chapter, we discussed many novel technological means that could be used to attack an individual financial entity (e.g., a company) or a single component of a complex financial system (e.g., a market). We surveyed previous attempts at each of those attacks, and we highlighted the impact they could have on the financial ecosystem at large. Despite showing the potential to endanger a national economy, such attacks would nonetheless be less dangerous and detrimental than a full-fledged systemic failure—that is, a severe widespread financial crisis affecting many components of a financial system. The latter would, in fact, cause widespread and long-lasting dramatic effects, possibly including prolonged recession, severe lack of liquidity, country defaults, and even small- to medium-scale humanitarian crises.

This was exactly the case with the Global Financial Crisis (GFC) that started in 2007–2008. As it happens with all systemic problems, also this crisis had deep roots. In the aftermath of the 2001 9/11 attacks, the US economy faced a mild recession. To contrast the downward trend, the Federal Reserve lowered interest rates up to a minimum of 1% in 2003, the lowest ever reached in 45 years.[32] This injection of liquidity allowed subprime (i.e., risky) borrowers to have mortgages and, with them, houses. House prices raised and homeownership reached a peak of 70% in 2004. At that point, interests started rising again, and few people were asking for houses, due to the high homeownership. By the end of 2005, home prices started to fall. As interests raised and home value decreased, for a growing share of subprime borrowers, it simply became more advantageous to give the home back instead of repaying the mortgage. Between 2006 and 2007, as borrowers started defaulting on their loans, so did an increasing number of subprime lenders. In April 2007, the well-known New Century Financial filed for bankruptcy. Since then, problems spread also outside of the United States, with the British Northern Rock eventually taken into public ownership in 2008. At that time, issues were emphasized also by the number and pervasiveness of securities that were backed by the now massively failing subprime mortgages, such as the extremely popular Collateralized Debt Obligations (CDOs) that also imploded as a result of the subprime mortgage crisis. These massive losses either resulted in investment banks going bankrupt or being bailed out by governments. In the United States, all this led to Lehman Brothers filing for bankruptcy, Indymac bank collapsing, Bear Stearns being acquired by JP Morgan Chase, Merrill Lynch being sold to the Bank of America, and Fannie Mae and Freddie Mac being put under the federal government control, to name but a few notable cases. Figure 4.10 shows the number of failed banks in the United States, comparing aggregate counts for 10 years before the GFC (1997–2007), with yearly data after the crisis. The devastating effects of the GFC are strikingly evident, and, in fact, it took almost 10 years to revert the situation to pre-crisis conditions. The spillovers of the global financial crisis beyond the US borders were equally catastrophic.

Given the devastating impact of global crises, many scholars have long studied the risk of systemic failure that affects financial ecosystems. In many of these studies, global financial systems are modeled as *large complex networks* in which banks, hedge funds, and other financial institutions are interconnected to one another through a series of financial links (e.g., those representing money that has

---

[32]https://www.investopedia.com/articles/economics/09/financial-crisis-review.asp (Last checked August 2020).

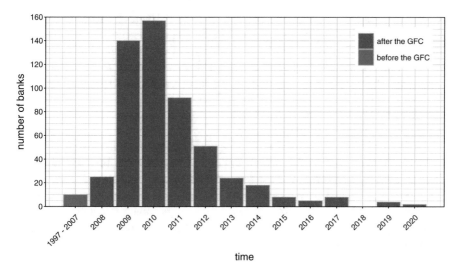

Fig. 4.10 Number of US banks failed per year, before and after the 2007–2008 Global Financial Crisis

been borrowed and lent). Then, grounding on this model of financial ecosystems, attention was directed toward the understanding of those mechanisms capable of triggering network breakdowns, such as those that led to the 2007–2008 GFC. For instance, this can happen when the financial links turn from being a means of risk diversification to channels for risk propagation [292]. Under these circumstances, the failure of a single entity (i.e., a node in the network) can start a cascade of failures that propagates through the financial network by traversing the existing links between entities. Depending on the properties of the financial network and the starting conditions, the shock can rapidly spread and engulf the majority of the network. Until now, manipulation attacks targeting individual entities—such as those discussed in the previous sections of this chapter—and complex financial networks have been studied separately and by different communities. However, it is crystal clear from the previous description that they are nonetheless related. A single targeted attack to a weak node of a financial network could in fact trigger a cascading effect on the network, with much bigger—and likely, much worse—consequences than those expected for the individual entity under attack.

4.4.1 Threat: Systemic Risk and Cascading Failures

In the wake of the 2007–2008 GFC, there has been increasing recognition of the need to address risk at the systemic level, as opposed to the traditional way of focusing on individual banks or single financial entities [293]. *Systemic risk* refers to the risk of a breakdown of an entire system rather than the failure of individual parts of the system. In a financial context, it denotes the risk of *cascading financial failures*, caused by linkages within the financial system and resulting in a severe economic downturn. The basic mechanics of distress propagation that lead to cascading failures are very simple: when a financial entity suffers a loss, distress propagates to its creditors who, in turn, suffer losses, which propagate further on in the network. Systemic risk has some universally accepted characteristics. It is a risk that has (1) a large impact, (2) is widespread, and (3) creates a ripple effect that endangers the viability of the whole financial system. Systemic risk is an attribute of the financial system and not that of a single entity. However, financial institutions individually contribute to the overall systemic risk and those that provide large contributions to the overall risk are deemed "systemically important." Thus, a key question for policymakers is how to limit the build-up of systemic risk to contain crises if and when they do occur. Instead, the key question for scholars is how to accurately measure and quantify systemic risk in the first place. This is the focus of the subsequent section.

4.4.2   Measures of Systemic Risk

Policymakers, scholars, and practitioners have yet to reach a consensus on how to precisely define systemic risk. Given that systemic risk is not yet fully understood, its measurement is obviously challenging and many competing and contradictory definitions of threats to financial stability exist. As such, a large number of diverse measures for systemic risk have been proposed so far. Indeed, a single agreed-upon measure of systemic risk may be neither possible nor desirable. As in all cases where there exists the need to measure a complex phenomenon, we are often better off leveraging multiple indicators than a single one. In fact, more indicators give higher guarantees to capture the multifaceted and adaptive nature of complex financial systems [294].

Economics and Finance Approaches

Early and traditional approaches to measuring systemic risk quite naturally arose from the economics and finance literature. In the years following the 2007–2008 crisis, a plethora of measures was proposed, which are mainly based on game theory, finance, and macroeconomic modeling. These can be classified according to the data required for computing the measure, to their supervisory scope (e.g., micro- vs. macroprudential measures), or to the relative time when the measure is available with respect to a crisis (e.g., ex ante, contemporaneous, and ex post measures) [294]. For example, according to this latter categorization, many systemic risk measures were proposed for being adopted as ex ante measures of early warning. Among them, there are measures based on predictions of costly aggregate asset price boom/bust cycles [295], macroeconomic early warning indicators for banking sector crises [296], statistical models for the timing of banking defaults [297], and many others. Other ex ante measures are based on stress tests, such as the 10-by-10-by-10 approach [298] or the marginal and systemic expected shortfall [299]. Then, among the measures for nowcasting systemic risk (i.e., contemporaneous measures), there are measures aimed at assessing the fragility of the system and those aimed at providing tools for monitoring an ongoing crisis. Finally, ex post measures are based on forensic analysis [300] or on the "risk topography" of the financial system [301], derived from a data acquisition and dissemination process that informs policymakers, researchers, and market participants about systemic risk.

Network Approaches

More recently, the assessment of systemic risks involved the scientific communities beyond economics and finance. Complex system scholars, in particular, were attracted by the interconnected and multifaceted nature of financial networks. As a result, a novel stream of research on systemic risk modeling led to the proposal of several new metrics grounded on network science and graph analysis principles. The financial networks needed by these studies can be obtained and built in different ways. In these networks, nodes typically represent banks or other financial institutions, and directed edges represent lending relations weighted by the amount of the outstanding debt. Some simple networks are based on public data released by the FED and assume a star structure with the FED positioned at the center of the network [302]. Other networks also model the many financial dependencies between institutions themselves, leading to more complex structures such as multiplex, bipartite, core periphery, and time-varying networks, depending on the properties of the considered financial links. One possible way to build these latter networks is by applying text mining techniques to SEC filings or financial news, to automatically extract inter-bank loan transactions representing the weighted edges of the financial network [303]. For example, it has been shown that the equity investment network of transnational corporations has a bow-tie structure with financial firms in the core forming a tightly connected component [304]. In addition, other studies focused on the characteristics of bipartite networks between banks and bank assets [305].

   After having built a network model of the financial system with any of the approaches just described, the goal consists of designing a metric for quantifying the systemic risk of the network. This is typically achieved by a careful combination of graph theory and economic principles. Among the most widely used metrics of systemic risk is DebtRank. In detail, the DebtRank score of a node (i.e., an institution) in a financial network is a number measuring the fraction of the total economic value in the network that is potentially affected by the distress or the default of that node [302]. The original DebtRank assumes that losses are propagated linearly between connected nodes. However, in other subsequent studies, this assumption was relaxed with the introduction of nonlinear propagation functions, which led to even more accurate estimations of systemic risk [306]. Other studies found that the measure of the scalar assortativity of a financial network correlates well with the level of systemic risk. In particular, network structures with high systemic risk are scalar assortative, meaning that risky banks are most exposed to other risky banks. Conversely, network structures with low systemic risk are scalar disassortative, with interactions of risky banks with stable banks [307]. Others adopted a model of shock propagation to investigate the bipartite network of US mutual fund portfolios and their assets, to identify a systemic risk component stemming from the similarity of portfolios [308]. By following the evolution of the 2007–2008 GFC, they showed that portfolios became more diversified during the crisis. Nonetheless, a large overlap in portfolios was measured to be far more likely than expected from random baseline models, demonstrating a strong correlation between fund investment strategies. The results of the study ultimately showed that diversification and similarity should be jointly taken into account to properly assess systemic risk. Also the work discussed in [309] focuses on overlapping portfolios and expectation feedbacks to study systemic risk. The model obtained from the study showed that risk expectations play a crucial role in the systemic stability of the financial system. In particular, wrong risk expectations may create panic-induced reduction or over-optimistic expansion of balance sheets. Other works studied Granger-causality tail risk networks to identify periods of distress in financial markets and possible channels of systemic risk propagation [310]. As part of the study, a novel market turbulence indicator is proposed, based on a measure of connectedness of the networks. By retrofitting the indicator to data about the 2009 European Sovereign Debt Crisis, authors showed its informativeness demonstrated by a peak of the indicator at the onset of the crisis, thus signaling the instability of the financial system.

4.4.3   Countermeasures

The multitude of methods for measuring systemic risk that we briefly surveyed in the previous section provides useful indicators for the stability of financial systems. As such, the analysis of the dynamics of financial models carries potentially far-reaching implications for the design and implementation of public policy [293]. Such tools thus represent a convenient control panel for regulators and policymakers interested in the healthiness of our economies. In other words, measures of systemic risk can inform decisions by regulators and policymakers, who can monitor the evolution of such indicators to avert financial crises and to have precious feedbacks on their regulatory activity. In fact, if academia is actively involved in proposing estimations of systemic risk, policymakers and regulators are deputed for acting upon such estimations to come up with effective countermeasures for avoiding financial breakdowns. The majority of policy interventions are aimed at reducing the existing systemic risk, thus reducing the possibility of cascading failures to occur. In the following, we briefly discuss a series of intervention strategies that have been proposed to reduce systemic risk in financial ecosystems.

Setting Capital and Liquidity Thresholds Ratios of capital have been in secular decline in banking institutions for at least the past 150 years, despite their strategic importance as buffers for absorbing external shocks. Reversing these trends by setting higher required thresholds for capital ratios would strengthen the absorptive capacity for each of the nodes in a financial network. As importantly, it would also lessen the risk of idiosyncratic defaults cascading around the system. Broadly, the same arguments apply to the setting of regulatory requirements on bank liquid assets.

Adjusting Requirements to Superspreaders There has been a significant rise in the size and concentration of the financial system over the past two decades. This leads to the emergence of superspreader institutions in financial networks, which are too big, too interconnected, or simply too important to fail. As a testimony of the damage that can be caused by the failure of a superspreader, it is enough to think of the consequences of the Lehman Brothers failure in October 2008. Protecting financial systems from future such events would thus require that superspreader nodes obey to much higher regulatory thresholds—in proportion to the system-wide risk they contribute—with respect to those applied to smaller players.

Regulating Derivatives Markets As discussed at the beginning of this section, the rapid growth in the size and complexity of the derivatives market (e.g., CDOs) was partially responsible for further destabilizing the already heavily stressed system on the onset of the 2007–2008 financial crisis. This inevitably questions the underlying structure of the derivatives market. One means of simplifying the complex Web of interactions between banks in derivatives markets is to centralize the trading and clearing of these instruments.

Shaping the Topology of Financial Networks While discussing measures of system risk, we highlighted the importance of diversification strategies for disentangling network nodes, thus reducing the possibility of cascading failures. However, if overall little effort has been devoted to assessing the system-wide diversity of balance sheet and risk management models, even less effort has been put into providing regulatory incentives to promote such diversity. In rebuilding and maintaining the financial system, the objective of systemic diversity is to be given much greater prominence by the regulatory community. Similarly to the previous point, modularity measures the extent to which a network can be partitioned in different communities. Modular network configurations contribute to preventing cascades from infecting the whole network in the event of an individual node failure. That is the reason for the long-lasting debates on the advantages and drawbacks of splitting banks, either to limit their size—to curtail the strength of cascades following failure—or to limit their activities—to curtail the potential for cross-contamination within firms [293]. In any case, network modularity should also be given greater importance in regulatory activities.

4.4.4   Open Issues and Future Directions

In pretty much all fields of science, it generally takes three subsequent and increasingly difficult steps for any given area of study to become a mature scientific field. The first step mandates to understand and *model* the mechanisms behind a real-world phenomenon. The second step concerns the *forecast* of the future dynamics of the phenomenon. The third and last step challenges to *control* the phenomenon so as to avoid undesired events. Most of the efforts discussed in this section for studying systemic risk are still at the first stage [292]. As such, avenues for future research and experimentation are manifold. On the one hand, we still need more accurate indicators for measuring systemic risk and more efficient policies for regulating financial systems. On the other hand, we also need to push the boundaries of current research by experimenting with forecasting models and by using existing and future models for simulating possible intervention strategies. Only through this iterative process of modeling and simulation we are likely to obtain more secure and stable financial systems.

As shown in our brief survey, the majority of recently proposed indicators for measuring systemic risk are based on network and graph theory approaches, applied to financial networks. However, recent works also demonstrated the importance of social and informational networks, and their interplay with financial networks. For example, pioneering studies showed that house price experiences in OSNs can drive contagious risk-taking in the US housing market [311], and others exploited epidemiological models to examine the interplay between social and informational contagion in driving financial cycles [312]. Despite these compelling results, the study of the interplay between social dynamics and financial risk remains almost completely unexplored. Consequently, much theoretical and empirical work is still needed to gauge the extent to which social contagion matters for aggregate financial system risks. In this regard, early results seem to suggest that "social network approaches could potentially have as much influence on cyclical macroprudential policies over the next decade as financial network approaches have had on stress-testing and structural macroprudential policies over the past decade" [312].

As the concluding section of Chap. 4, here we aimed to bridge the gap between the micro-security level discussed in Sects. 4.1, 4.2, and 4.3, and the macro-security level discussed in this section. In particular, throughout the previous sections of this chapter, we discussed several technology-enabled ways to manipulate companies and markets. Here instead, we took a more systemic point of view, and we showed how a local shock, such as one caused by one of the aforementioned attacks, could result in dramatic system-wide consequences by propagating through financial networks. Defending against such striking events thus involves both increasing the robustness of individual components of financial networks, by reducing the leverage and effectiveness of manipulation techniques, as well as shaping financial networks that are intrinsically more resistant to cascading failures. These challenges currently represent the battlegrounds that will decide the fate of worldwide economic warfare in the coming years.

Part III
Infrastructure

The evolution of Information and Communication Technologies (ICT) systems has triggered a radical change that has affected several sectors of modern society, including the way companies do business and the production processes of industrial plants. The technologies responsible for this change are manifold, but it is possible to bring them all back into two main areas, most responsible for the evolution of companies and industries. Cloud computing has profoundly changed the architecture of the IT infrastructures used by companies to manage one of their most precious assets: information. Features such as scalability, ubiquity, and on-demand services have convinced companies to leave their proprietary systems by outsourcing infrastructure to third parties. In this way, they can rely on services suited to their needs, without having to worry about maintenance or updating costs. Consequently, the IT infrastructure is no longer owned by the company, which loses direct control over the management of the hardware and software in use, including security systems. On the one hand, this brings enormous advantages, eliminating purchase costs, as well as increasing the reliability of the equipment. On the other hand, the company's data are hosted on third-party-owned systems, with obvious privacy and security issues. These problems were, at first, an obstacle that slowed the spread of the cloud model. Then, over the years, the advantages have prevailed, leading to the massive use of this technology. However, concerns about the outsourcing of data and its security have not subsided, also due to numerous security incidents over the years. The threat, therefore, remains an open problem, which could potentially cause major damage to the economy of the companies involved.

Automatic control systems have evolved enormously over the last two decades by taking advantage of technological progress in the field of information technology and automation. Today's industrial plants rely on several Industrial Control System (ICS)s, including Programmable Logic Controllers (PLC) devices, distributed control systems, Supervisory Control And Data Acquisition (SCADA) systems, and manufacturing execution systems. The production processes have evolved accordingly, becoming more advanced, reliable, and efficient. On the one hand, this innovation has brought great advantages, such as the automation of the production chains, which decreases personnel costs, boosts productivity, and consequently increases profits. On the other hand, smart production processes make the factories more dependent on technology, introducing new threats due to possible malfunctions, both malicious and unintentional. In fact, the complexity of the new generation production processes makes their manual management very difficult, if not impossible. Automation, therefore, becomes not only useful to obtain multiple advantages but essential for keeping the different production systems in operation. The advent of Internet of Things (IoT) has changed the way ICS systems are connected, improving their performance and allowing direct communication with the outside world. However, the innovation in the ICSs' network paradigm has introduced many difficulties in the management of security, dramatically increasing the virtual defense perimeter of the production plants.

These two technological advancements have modified the network infrastructures of the ICS used in production plants (in particular, in the critical infrastructures of every state), and ICT systems used by public and private companies. Unfortunately, in both cases, the respective security systems were not immediately adapted to the new environment, introducing significant security flaws. The resulting weaknesses can be exploited by several malicious actors, opening up new scenarios of cyber warfare that are potentially destructive for the well-being of a nation.

In this part, we discuss how the IT infrastructures in use by public or private companies, as well as the ICSs of critical infrastructures, can be directly attacked by malicious users to indirectly affect the country to which they reside, with potentially tremendous social and economic repercussions. The chapter on critical infrastructures analyzes the possible attacks against these important components of each state, identifying their causes, the countermeasures developed by the academic and industrial world, and the open problems. Furthermore, we investigate the possible consequences of such attacks, aimed at blocking such infrastructures, with potentially serious repercussions on the economy and health of the citizens of a state.

The chapter on companies, instead, analyzes how the ICT infrastructure used for the business processes of public or private companies can be attacked to undermine one of their most precious assets: information. The possible direct repercussions for the companies vary from the loss of trade secrets to economic losses so serious as to make the affected company go bankrupt. In these cases, the indirect consequences for the country to which they belong vary from the social results of closing a company with thousands of employees to the economic loss of companies owned by the state.

In both cases, the analysis of the attacks that took place in the real world helps to highlight the new tendency toward cyber warfare, now not only hypothesized but already underway in various world operating scenarios.

Chapter 5
Critical Infrastructure

Critical infrastructure represents an umbrella term used by governments to group all those resources that are essential for the economic, financial, and social system of a country. The Presidential Policy Directive 21 (PPD-21): Critical Infrastructure Security and Resilience, issued by the President of the United States in 2013, advances a national unity of effort to strengthen and maintain secure, functioning, and resilient critical infrastructure. PPD-21 identifies 16 critical infrastructure sectors: chemical sector; commercial facility sector; communication sector; critical manufacturing sector; dams sector; defense industrial base sector; emergency services sector; energy sector; financial service sector; food and agriculture sector; government facilities sector; health case and public health sector; information technology sector; nuclear reactors, materials, and waste sector; transportation system sector; and water and waste-water system sector [313].

The protection of these resources is crucial, because the destruction (or even the partial or momentary inability) could cause significant harm on the society or, worse, could jeopardize human lives. For example, in desert countries such as Qatar, Saudi Arabia, or the United Arab Emirates, attacking the critical infrastructures essential for the water supply (water desalinization plants) would be tantamount to leaving the entire population without drinking water for the entire duration of the fault. For these reasons, there is great concern among security and government officials about the vulnerabilities of critical infrastructure in their state. The possible threats to critical infrastructures' integrity and functioning are manifold. We can categorize them into three main classes.[1]

- **Natural.** Unpredictable natural disasters, such as earthquakes, floods, volcanic eruptions, hurricanes, and possibly others, can generate serious damage to critical

---

[1] https://www.securityinfowatch.com/access-identity/access-control/article/12427447/americas-critical-infrastructure-threats-vulnerabilities-and-solutions (Last checked August 2020).

infrastructures. Since such events are normally unpredictable, it is difficult to mitigate the problem. The only countermeasures are to locate infrastructure in areas not subject to such events and to use resilient construction techniques.

- **Human-related.** All man-made events, such as acts of terrorism (explosions, bombing), vandalism (rioting, theft), financial crimes, economic espionage, and possibly others.
- **Accidental or technical.** Events caused by technical errors, such as failures and accidents related to infrastructure and dangerous materials, failures of the power grid, failures of the safety systems, and a series of other catastrophes of omission and/or commission.

According to the Geneva Convention of 1949, It is prohibited to attack, destroy, remove, or render useless objects indispensable to the survival of the civilian population, such as foodstuffs, agricultural areas, crops, livestock, drinking water installations and supplies, and irrigation works, for the specific purpose of denying them for their sustenance value to the civilian population or to the adverse party, whatever the motive, whether in order to starve out the civilians, to cause them to move away, or for any other motive [314]. However, the threat of attacks against these infrastructures remains high, as well as the level of alert by security operators. The malicious actors possibly involved in attacks against critical infrastructures can be identified in six categories, listed below:

1. **Displeased or corrupted employees.** Disgruntled insiders, unqualified employees, and incompetent contractors create the opportunity for outsiders to infiltrate inside the protected environment of critical infrastructure. This category includes unethical employees involved in illegal activities, motivated mostly by earning extra money. They may also be driven by feelings like jealousy, rivalry, or revenge on their superiors or the institutions they work for.
2. **Individual hackers, small groups of hackers, and hacktivists.** People who use their skills, individually or in groups, to support a particular ideology. They could be driven by political views, cultural/religious beliefs, national pride, or even terrorist ideas.
3. **Competing companies.** Companies that work in the same sector that try to steal important information, such as valuable intellectual properties, in order to reuse them on the national/international market.
4. **Cybercriminal organizations.** Criminal organizations that conduct their illegal activities using IT systems. Their only motivation is to make an economic profit.
5. **Terrorists.** Terrorist actions usually arise from multiple causal factors, such as economic, political, religious, and sociological problems, among others.
6. **Foreign governments.** Foreign nations that, driven by different interests, attack the cyber-physical infrastructure of another country.

All these actors, regardless of motivation, have a potential advantage in attacking critical infrastructures. Their goals can be different, ranging from simple demonstration actions to attacks aimed at destroying. Criminal organizations, for example, driven by profit, could take control of a factory's IT system, partially or totally blocking its production. Then, they can request a ransom to return control to legitimate operators. The main purpose of the terrorists, instead, could be to destroy, disable, or exploit critical infrastructure to threaten national security, causing major casualties, weaken the economy, and reduce public morale and confidence in national institutions.

The list of cyber threats involving critical infrastructures grows exponentially with the increase in hacking-sensitive technologies used within them. The growth of the virtual perimeter attracts more and more malicious actors, whether they are individual, private, or state-sponsored groups. The external exposure of the IT systems used by critical infrastructures is the main threat, as it allows remote attacks carried out without having physical access to the equipment, usually very well protected.

The activities of a critical infrastructure are supported by particular IT systems called ICS. These systems are the result of hardware and software integration, capable of controlling and supporting various production activities. ICS technologies include, but are not limited to, SCADA systems, Distributed Control Systems (DCS)s, and PLCs. In several cases, ICS were put into operation decades ago, before the global spread of the Internet. At that time, cybersecurity was not considered of paramount importance, as communication networks were confined to restricted environments and only very few people had access to information. In addition, critical infrastructures were often closed systems, with no connection to the outside world. These types of systems, called air-gapped, make a remote cyberattack very difficult. To control an isolated system, in fact, it is necessary to have some kind of physical access to the target systems. However, the rapid diffusion of new communication technologies, such as IoT, radically changes this scenario. The convenience of features, like automation and remote control of the key equipment that operates in critical infrastructures, has prevailed over potential security problems, opening new opportunities for malicious actors. In this situation, a modern arms race has developed, with the aim of acquiring techniques, methodologies, and tools that can be used against the IT and ICS systems of rival nations. As a result, cybersecurity has acquired major strategic importance.

⌗ Definitions

Supervisory Control and Data Acquisition (SCADA) It is mainly a software toolkit for implementing ICS. These systems are normally used for remote monitoring and sending commands to valves and switches. For example, they can be found in water facilities and oil pipelines, where they monitor flow rates and pressures. Based on the data provided by these systems, computer programs or the operators of a central control center balance the flow of material using industrial control systems to activate valves and regulators. Normally SCADA systems are used as a means of

(continued)

entering data and exporting commands from a control center. These systems are vulnerable to implantation of faulty data and to remote access via external connections generally used for maintenance.

Distributed Control Systems (DCS) It is a process control system usually deployed in a single production complex. This system generally provides processed information to a control center or supports it in executing commands. A practical example could be identified inside a chemical facility. In this context, a DCS might simultaneously monitor the temperature of a series of reactors and control the rate at which reactants were mixed together. At the same time, it might perform real-time process optimization and reporting the progress of the reaction. An attack targeting DCS might interfere with ongoing production activities, causing extensive damages. However, due to its confined nature, it would be unlikely to affect more than a single infrastructure.

Programmable Logic Controllers (PLCs) They are devices used to automate monitoring and control of industrial plants and are generally used within a manufacturing facility. They tend to provide little external information and do the majority of their data processing internally. Programmable logic controllers can control as little as a single machine to as much as an entire manufacturing facility. An automated assembly line can be comprised of a series of PLCs, with each machine on the assembly line performing a distinct job. An attack targeting PLCs might cause significant turmoil at a single location, but the extent of the damage would depend on both the PLC's size and connectivity.

Air-Gapped System An air-gapped system is an IT system whose components are isolated from unsafe networks. As a result, these systems do not have direct Internet access, and they are not even connected to systems that have it. As a consequence, an air-gapped computer is also physically isolated, which means that data can only enter or leave it using physical media only (for example via USB or other removable media).

In this chapter, we will discuss possible attacks against critical infrastructure related to two major threats in particular: cyberwarfare exploiting vulnerabilities in IT and SCADA systems, especially malware-guided attacks, and a new cyber-physical threat from the sky: commercial drones.

5.1 Scenario: Cyberwarfare Targeting Critical Infrastructures

To better understand the threat of cyberwarfare against critical infrastructures, its different facets, and its potential consequences, it is necessary to know the modern architecture of these structures and the systems that govern them. The ICSs that support the operations of a critical infrastructure are composed of integrated hardware and software resources, interconnected with each other. These systems usually manage the production processes of essential services that underpin modern society and act as the backbone of every nation's economy, safety, and health. These facilities, among other things, produce and transport drinking water and electricity to citizens' homes, supply stores with primary goods, and offer means of transport and communication. To make an example, we can cite the production and distribution of essential goods such as drinking water and electricity, the management of airport facilities, critical manufacturing, and possibly others. Any malfunctioning of the ICSs that manage these infrastructures could lead to serious consequences ranging from slowing down production to a partial or total plant shutdown.

In the context of cyberwarfare, critical infrastructures are very sensitive targets because of the key role they play within a nation. For this reason, critical infrastructures are usually well defended, both physically and virtually, because they are expected to be among the first targets of a possible attack. In this context, the biggest concern is the intrusion, both physical and virtual, of malicious users aimed at interfering with normal operations or exfiltrating sensitive data. Before the spread of the Internet, the defense of critical infrastructures was mainly focused on the physical perimeter. Information systems were often not connected to the outside world. Consequently, the virtual perimeter was nonexistent or very small, which made the likelihood of suffering a cyberattack very low. The advent of new communication technologies has favored the emergence of new network paradigms, such as the Internet of Things, which have pushed the digitalization of production processes. This radical change has created a virtual perimeter that must be defended as, and more than, the physical one.

The defense of the physical perimeter is a need born together with critical infrastructures and is, therefore, a well-known and well-studied problem. On the contrary, the defense of the virtual perimeter is a relatively new need, exacerbated in the last decade following the advent of new communication technologies. The ICS infrastructures are usually composed of a large number of heterogeneous devices developed by different suppliers and often equipped with proprietary software. The lack of homogeneity and standardization considerably increases the costs of research, design, and implementation of cyber defense products and techniques. Furthermore, the privatization and market liberalization policies implemented worldwide in the last period have made the protection of critical infrastructures more difficult for the government. Taking the United States as a reference, the number of critical infrastructures owned and managed by the private sector is around 85%, according to a report edited by the Department of Homeland Security in 2009.[2] With the private sector so heavily involved, expensive security measures must inevitably run up against several economic considerations. In this scenario, security alone is never a decisive factor, since it must always be considered in relation to the available budget. This situation introduces two critical vulnerabilities: resource disparity and outsourcing complexity.

Cyber and physical security is an expensive task that requires the allocation of significant resources. Resource disparity between private companies of different sizes implies the possibility of coping with security payments in a different way. This could cause under-protection of critical infrastructures managed by small-medium companies, which will, therefore, be more exposed. Modern companies tend to focus on core business processes, outsourcing everything else to third-party organizations. For this reason, very often physical and cybersecurity are also outsourced, making optimized protection more complex and creating opportunities for malicious users.

The general architecture of the ICS systems, shown in Fig. 5.1, consists of several levels, listed below from the outermost to the innermost, representing the attack surface of a critical infrastructure:

- **External Systems.** This category contains all those systems that are not directly part of the ICS network but are used to interact with it. The corporate network is directly connected to Tier 2, while among the indirectly connected systems, it is worth to mention portable devices, such as USB storage, external users, and, more in general, the Internet.
- **TIER 2.** This level contains those systems which are directly part of the ICS network and are positioned in the outermost layer. Examples include all outward-facing applications that link resources or provide data to external users, such as information servers, historians, or generic web servers.
- **TIER 1.** This layer, also called the supervisory level, is the SCADA network layer. TIER 1 includes all the hardware and software components used to configure, monitor, and control the devices in TIER 0 while feeding data to the upper layers. Typical examples of systems belonging to TIER 1 include HMI, engineering workstations, and application servers.
- **TIER 0.** This category, also known as "production network layer," represents the innermost layer of the ICS architecture and the closest to the physical world. TIER 0 includes all the input/output end-devices, such as sensors, RTUs, and other physical devices that collect data, other systems that directly control physical equipment, such as PLCs, and general Wi-Fi and radio frequency networks.

Any device deployed in the three internal layers (i.e., TIER 0, 1, and 2), may become a potential target in case of attack. In case these devices were directly accessible from the outside, they would increase the attack surface exposed by the infrastructure to the outside world. As shown in Fig. 5.1, the propagation

---

[2]https://www.gao.gov/new.items/d09654r.pdf (Last checked August 2020).

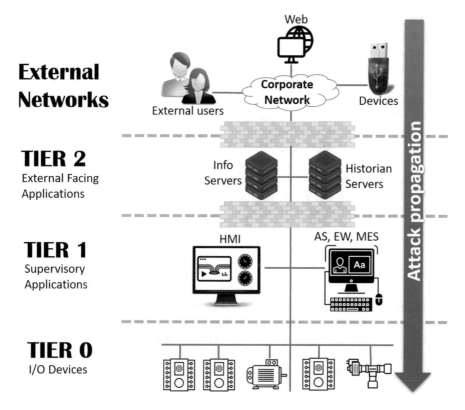

Fig. 5.1 Industrial control systems' common multitier security architecture

of a cyberattack in the ICS architecture occurs from top to bottom, i.e., from external systems to the TIER 0 devices. This is justified by the fact that, in the classic model, each device is reachable only from the layer immediately above. Consequently, the only devices directly accessible from the outside are those belonging to TIER 2. However, the attack surface has dramatically increased with the advent of new network paradigms, such as IoT and cloud computing, which have been integrated into industrial environments. In light of these new technologies, the general architecture of an ICS can be modified according to the specific use cases involved. In some scenarios, both TIER 1 and TIER 0 layers of the ICS architecture could be directly reachable from the Internet, introducing severe security threats. Any digital device operating within a critical infrastructure can be exploited by a mischievous user in different ways. While hardware devices can be physically destroyed, malicious programs can be created to alter the behavior of the software resources. Simple software errors or carefree third-party software executions can lead to external threats, causing the temporary (or definitive) malfunction of the control software, thus leading to the compromise of the protected critical resource. Even worse, instead of causing the control system to be altered or destroyed, an attacker could take control of it from the outside, deceiving security systems and tampering with the critical resource without triggering security alarms.

This scenario takes into account a critical infrastructure located within a country, which manages a critical resource. The critical infrastructure can be either a complex set of interconnected electrical components, as in the past, or a set of modern IoT communicating devices. In both cases, the critical infrastructure exposes interfaces on the web to receive commands remotely and to show the status of the managed resources. The exposure to the web is necessary, to reduce the amount of dedicated personnel and to real-time monitoring the status of the critical resource from centralized control centers. At the same time, however, exposure to the web could lead to an increase of the attack surface, opening the doors to different attacks such as malware-based attacks and attacks on the SCADA systems, a subset of the ICS widespread in critical infrastructures.

5.1.1 Threat: Malware

In recent years, several security incidents have demonstrated how concrete and potentially destructive the threat of an attack on critical infrastructure can be. Various types of malicious code have been used in these attacks, showing a trend toward the creation of specialized malware targeting ICSs, at least in the past decade. Looking at the examples of attacks that actually took place against critical infrastructures, we can identify two different cases:

- **Specialized malware.** A malware specialized in attacking a particular hard-ware/software infrastructure, generally a SCADA component, with the specific objective of interfering with its functionality. To design and implement this type of malware, the attacker needs extensive knowledge of the targeted systems. For this reason, this type of malware is usually developed by a highly specialized adversary with access to sensitive information. One of the most famous historical examples of this category of malware is *Stuxnet*, a malware which first appeared in 2010. The *Stuxnet* worm was designed to destroy the motors used in uranium enrichment centrifuges, causing them to spin out of control. Originally used to attack an Iranian nuclear plant, this malware has temporarily disabled around 1000 centrifuges.
- **Generic malware.** A malware designed to hit a generic platform, usually a particular operating system, on a large scale. A malware of this type is normally designed to target as many systems as possible, regardless of their owners and their use, to maximize the creator's profits. These types of malware could attack systems of critical infrastructures even unintentionally. An example of such malware is a ransomware called *WannaCry*, distributed on a large scale by an unidentified group of hackers in May 2017. Once a host is infected, *WannaCry* encrypts all the files inside and locks the system, showing a message with instructions for paying a ransom. Thanks to its ability to infect other hosts on the

same network, the spread was very fast and efficient, also affecting high-profile systems. Among them, the British national health system has recorded numerous infections which, among other things, have caused the partial blocking of several hospitals across the United Kingdom.

Several attack vectors contribute to the spread of malware within critical infrastructures, ranging from software vulnerabilities to human errors. The most common attack vectors for critical infrastructure fall into the following categories:

- **Unpatched vulnerabilities.** An attacker could gain unauthorized privileges by exploiting known vulnerabilities that have not been fixed by security administrators of critical infrastructures yet.
- **Zero-day vulnerabilities.** An attacker could exploit unknown vulnerabilities in both applications and operating systems to get unauthorized privileges, at least since reliable security patches are released.
- **Code injection.** When an application developer does not properly manage the handling of invalid or unexpected input, an attacker could take control of the software execution. In such cases, the introduction of malicious code into the vulnerable application may be possible. Such malicious code would be executed with the same privileges as the victim's application.
- **Social engineering.** A term that refers to all the techniques aimed at obtaining information from an individual and, more generally, to make a person do what he would not otherwise do.
- **Phishing.** Phishing is a particular social engineering technique that aims to obtain sensitive information, such as login credentials. Generally, the attacker impersonates an organization that the victim trusts, such as a bank or government institution, asking for personal data with the most varied reasons. Phishing is one of the most common attack vectors.
- **Misconfiguration.** When there are errors in the configuration of a device or software, such as enabled setup pages, an attacker can obtain information on hidden weaknesses or access systems without authorization.
- **Weak or stolen credential.** The use of weak passwords, i.e., easily guessable through brute force or dictionary attack, as well as the reuse of the same credentials on multiple systems, facilitates the entry and propagation of malware within a protected environment.

✎ Definitions

Attack Vector The method or process followed by an adversary to violate or infiltrate a network/system. Attack vectors allow malicious actors to exploit system vulnerabilities, including the human element.

Among the many countermeasures that can be used to mitigate the attack vectors discussed above, it is worth mentioning some common best practices, valid for any ICT system.

✎ Definitions

Malware The term malware, a contraction of the two words MALicious and softWARE, refers to any piece of software created to run in a system, without authorization, with the intent of stealing data, damaging the system, or generally causing any other harm.

In the literature, malware have been classified in several ways, the two most common are listed in the following:

1. By how the malware infects its victim:

   - **Virus.** A malicious piece of code, unable to work on its own, which must be inserted into a legitimate program. Once infected, the legitimate software is forced to behave maliciously and spread the virus on other software.
   - **Worm.** A standalone malicious code, which reproduces itself via the network.
   - **Trojan.** A malicious code inserted inside an apparently harmless program. Once the user execute such program, the malicious code will be activated, together with its harmful functions.

2. By its behavior on the infected host:

   - **Spyware.** A malware designed to remain silent on the infected computer for the sole purpose of collecting and exfiltrating information from a third party.
   - **Rootkit.** A collection of software used to obtain and maintain unauthorized access to a computer system. Also, this type of malware is able to mask its presence as well as the presence of other malware.
   - **Adware.** A malware that redirects the victim's browser to unwanted advertising or other potentially malicious web content.
   - **Ransomware.** A malware that encrypts all the files contained in the file on the infected host. The victim system is then blocked, displaying a screen with instructions for paying a ransom.
   - **Cryptojacking.** is a malware that uses the resources of the infected system to mine cryptocurrencies without the permission of the system owner.

Proper account management, for example, is certainly a good defense against the problem of weak or stolen credentials. Reducing or banning shared accounts and password reuse, as well as using advanced techniques such as two-factor authentication, would reduce the attacker's ability to propagate his malicious code within the target system. This simple countermeasure prevents attackers from violating multiple systems with a single stolen credential.

Very often, an attack starts with the exploitation of a known vulnerability, already fixed by the vendors but not yet applied in the system under attack. For this reason, the timely installation of security patches plays a fundamental role in reducing the probability of being attacked by exploiting unpatched vulnerabilities. Furthermore, vulnerability assessments and penetration tests must also be conducted regularly to test deployed defenses and identify any vulnerabilities due to both misconfigurations and zero-day vulnerabilities.

A simple best practice for mitigating the threat coming from social engineering techniques, such as phishing, consists of maintaining security awareness. Knowledgeable employees well trained in cybersecurity threats, in fact, would reduce the risk of opening security breaches due to the human factor, significantly limiting the probability of being attacked. Even if it is not possible to eliminate all possible attack vectors, strict compliance with these guidelines would significantly reduce the attack opportunities available to malicious actors, reinforcing the security perimeter.

In this section, we analyze the threat posed by malware to critical infrastructures. Starting from the most significant examples of attacks that took place in the past, we analyze the effectiveness of the countermeasures currently available to identify the weak points that still persist.

5.1.2   Attacks and Countermeasures

On Friday, May 12, 2017, the *WannaCry* ransomware was detected in several hospitals in the United Kingdom. Some time after, it exploded across the globe, spreading like wildfire, encrypting hundreds of thousands of computers distributed in more than 150 countries in a matter of hours (see Fig. 5.2). The attack affected a wide range of sectors, including health, government, oil and gas production, and telecommunications, in what was later recognized as the biggest ransomware campaign in the history of the Internet. The WannaCry ransomware sets foot on the infected computer in the form of a dropper, which includes the following components:

- An application that encrypts files (i.e., the encrypter)
- An application to decrypt files after a ransom has been paid (i.e., the decrypter)
- A zip file containing a copy of the Tor client
- Several individual files with (hard-coded) encryption keys and configuration information

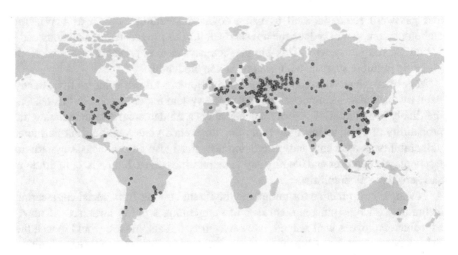

Fig. 5.2 The spread of the WannaCry malware across the globe in the early days of infection, according to @MalwareTechBlog

> ✂ **Definitions**
>
> **Dropper** A dropper is a vector used as a vehicle to introduce an application, called dropper payload and usually harmful, into another system. If the malicious application is contained in the dropper body in the form of a compressed file (e.g., to avoid being identified by antiviruses), the dropper is called single-stage. If the malicious payload is downloaded from the Internet after activation, the dropper is called two-stage.

The program code of WannaCry is not obfuscated and was relatively easy to analyze by security experts. Once the dropper runs on the victim computer, it extracts the malware components into its working directory. Then, it checks for other malicious programs and the existence of a particular hard-coded URL. If both checks fail, the malware starts the encrypter application. This software starts to encrypt all the files on the disk with common (hard-coded) extensions. Finally, the WannaCry encrypter launches the embedded decrypter, which displays two timers and instructions for sending the ransom. The instructions demand a payment of 300 US dollars worth of bitcoins to a specified (hard-coded) address. If the ransom is not paid before the first timer expires, the ransom price doubles. After the second timer expires, the malware states that the files will be unrecoverable. Since the malware uses the Microsoft Enhanced RSA and AES Cryptographic Provider libraries to perform the encryption, the encrypted files are unrecoverable without the decryption key (Fig. 5.2).[3]

---

[3]https://logrhythm.com/blog/a-technical-analysis-of-wannacry-ransomware/   (Last   checked August 2020).

According to a report by the Department of Health, the WannaCry campaign was devastating for the United Kingdom National Health Service (NHS). Several computers with strategic roles have been blocked by the malware in many hospitals, causing a total loss of about 92 million GBP. Staff from the affected hospitals were forced to return to pen and paper and use their cell phones after the attack hit key systems, including phones. Hospitals and medical clinics in several parts of England were forced to turn patients away and cancel appointments after the infection. People in the affected areas were advised to seek medical assistance only in case of emergency. The hack caused more than 19,000 appointments to be canceled, costing the NHS 20 million GBP between May 12 and May 19, and 72 million GBP in the subsequent cleanup and upgrades to its IT systems.[4] One of the most interesting aspects of WannaCry is the attack vector. In the first phase, it is often delivered via phishing, i.e., sending emails that induce the recipient to open attachments and release malware on their system. Hence, the worm component of the malware spread quickly through the victims' local network using unpatched vulnerabilities. The exploited weakness lies in the Windows implementation of the Server Message Block (SMB), a network protocol that provides shared access to files, printers, and serial ports between nodes on a network. The protocol version developed by Microsoft could be tricked by specifically crafted network packets into arbitrary code execution (vulnerability CVE-2017-0144). This vulnerability is believed to be discovered by the NSA which, instead of reporting it to the IT security community, developed an exploit called EternalBlue. Subsequently, a hacking group, known as the "Shadow Brokers," claimed to have stolen this exploit from the NSA and published an obfuscated version in April 2017. Microsoft discovered the vulnerability and released the corresponding patch a month earlier, but many systems have not been updated.

The rapid spread of WannaCry was stopped by chance by a young British security researcher, Marcus Hutchins, who discovered how the malware attempted to contact a particular URL in the early stages of the infection. Depending on the success of this connection, the malware decided whether to continue its malicious activity or to stop. Given that such a URL was a command and control server, Hutchins realized that the domain was free and decided to register it (for only 10.96 USD). Then, he redirected the traffic to a sinkhole controlled by his company to analyze network packets and produce statistics on the ongoing infection. Later, he realized that the newly registered URL was actually a malware kill switch. The spread of malware stopped suddenly as its new instances, once the domain registered by Hutchins was active, were deactivated without producing malicious effects.

The reason behind the choice of the WannaCry creators to develop such an easily identifiable kill switch is still a mystery. Some security experts speculated that the shutdown mechanism was designed to hinder malware analysis by security engineers. In fact, it is common practice to run malware in a "sandbox" once

---

[4]https://www.telegraph.co.uk/technology/2018/10/11/wannacry-cyber-attack-cost-nhs-92m-19000-appointments-cancelled/ (Last checked August 2020).

discovered. In these protected environments, generally, any URL or IP address will appear as reachable. Probably, by hard-coding an attempt to contact a meaningless URL that was not actually expected to exist, its creators hoped to ensure that the malware did not perform malicious actions while it was under observation.

At first, domain registration helped reduce, although not completely stop, the spread of the malware. This is due to the fact that in a network-restricted environment, with security devices like firewalls and network proxies, the connection was not successful even if the domain was regularly available online.

✂ Definitions

Sandbox A sandbox is a security mechanism used to run untrusted software, usually obtained from third parties, vendors, users, or websites, without risking damaging the host computer or operating system. A sandbox typically provides a tightly controlled set of resources for running the programs under consideration, such as storage space and memory. The access to the network, as well as the ability to inspect the host system, or read from input devices, is prohibited, severely limited, or simulated.

Sinkhole Sinkholing is a technique for manipulating data flow in a network; the network traffic is redirected from its intended destination to another server (the sinkhole). This technique can be used maliciously to drive legitimate traffic away from its destination. However, security professionals more commonly use sinkholing to redirect malicious traffic on a specific server. Once the suspected traffic is isolated in a sinkhole, it can no longer hurt its intended targets. Besides, the traffic can be analyzed to reveal the source of the attack as well as information about the techniques being employed.

In June 2017, ESET researchers discovered a malware, known as "Industroyer" or "Crash Override", that represents the biggest threat to critical infrastructure since Stuxnet. As its name may suggest, Industroyer was designed to disrupt critical industrial processes and is capable of doing significant harm to electric power systems. To make matters worse, there is the opportunity to easily make changes to the malware in order to target other types of critical infrastructures. The 2016 attack on Ukraine's power grid that deprived part of its capital, Kiev, of power for an hour was caused by a cyberattack. ESET researchers have suggested that the Win32/Industroyer malware would be capable of performing such an attack.[5] Industroyer is a particularly dangerous threat, since it can control electricity substation switches and circuit breakers directly. According to ESET, Industroyer leverages industrial communication protocols used worldwide in power supply infrastructures,

---

[5]https://www.welivesecurity.com/2017/06/12/industroyer-biggest-threat-industrial-control-systems-since-stuxnet/ (Last checked August 2020).

Table 5.1 Most popular malware used to attack critical infrastructure

	Major targeted nations	Start Date	Entry point	Duration of the attack	Known consequencies
Stuxnet	Iran Indonesia India	2010	Infected USBs	Unknown	Temporarily disable 1000 centrifuges used in uranium enrichment process
WannaCry	Over 150 countries	2017	Credential phishing	1 Week	Encrypt data and demand ransom payment
Havex	The United States Europe	2014	Cross-site scripting	Unknown	Information gathering and other malicious code injection
Industroyer	Ukraine	2016	Social Engineering— infected documents	Reconnaissance: several months before the attack Power outage: 1 h Damages: months after the attack	Energy blackout in part of the Ukrainian capital, affecting one-fifth of its electricity needs
Triton	Saudi Arabia	2017	Social Engineering	Unknown	Disable safety instrumented systems, potentially lead to a plant disaster

transportation control systems, and other critical infrastructure facilities (such as water and gas) [315]. Industroyer is described in detail in Sect. 5.1.4 since its main feature is to attack SCADA systems. The most important malware that have affected critical infrastructures are summarized in Table 5.1.

> ☛ **Resources**
>
> **WannaCry Analysis** An extensive analysis of the WannaCry ransomware, including its components and source code, infection and persistence techniques, and propagation mechanisms, can be found here [316].

Modern critical infrastructures are continually exposed to new threats due to the vulnerabilities and architectural weaknesses introduced by the extensive use of ICT solutions. Of particular significance are the vulnerabilities in the communication protocols used in SCADA systems that are commonly employed to control industrial processes. In [317], the authors investigated the impact of malware on SCADA systems, discussing the potential damaging effects. The authors recreated the physical environment of a power plant in a protected environment, considering its security policies, access policies, maintenance policies, and firewall rules. Later on, they used the source code of four known malware (i.e., Code Red, Nimda, Slammer, and Scalper) to infect the systems included in their test bed, to observe their effects on both ICT and SCADA systems. Results show how malware is capable of damaging the ICT systems that host SCADA servers. The effects observed include system reboots, malicious code propagation throughout the network infecting Windows PCs in the same subnet, and different activities that lead to Denial of Service (DoS) attacks.

Attacks on Modbus, a protocol designed to manage master-slave communications, are among the effects observed on SCADA systems. The main consequences are DoS attacks on system communications and attacks aimed at taking control of the end-devices in the targeted network, by exploiting the lack of authentication and integrity mechanisms in the Modbus protocol.

A similar study was also done in [318], where the authors implemented several attack scenarios within a protected environment. Their experimental test bed consists of a complex electromechanical system composed of several devices, used to physically emulate the different states and the thermodynamical processes of a real power plant. Considering the results obtained, the authors provided a series of countermeasures aimed at decreasing the intrinsic complexity of the ICS systems, which complicates the protection of critical infrastructures. Among the proposed methodologies, it is worth mentioning countermeasures based on standard communication protocols, such as TCP/IP, on SCADA protocols, such as DNP3, AGA 12, and Modbus, and several common security suggestions that regulate the interaction between ICT and SCADA systems.

An investigation into the effectiveness of existing control strategies for SCADA system malware has been provided in [319]. In particular, the authors analyzed the use of antivirus signatures and proposed a new control strategy, which combines the scanning of vulnerabilities with the implementation of security patches.

Several methods for assessing risks and vulnerabilities in ICS networks have been proposed in [320]. The authors first introduced basic information on industrial network protocols, their design, and their architecture. Then, they implemented security and access control mechanisms, as well as exceptions, anomalies, and threat detection methodologies. These contributions are very important to help security operators prepare against increasingly sophisticated ICS-targeted malware.

The aforementioned studies, along with many others in the literature, helped to raise the problem of malware attacks against ICS systems, also providing valuable information for the development of new, effective countermeasures.

In addition to ransomware, cryptojacking is another category of generic malware that is very dangerous for critical infrastructures. This type of malware is characterized by the use of the victim's computational power for mining activities. If installed on systems of critical infrastructures, they may no longer be able to perform their functions, causing risks of different types, depending on the criticality of the system concerned. Furthermore, this type of security incident could easily be perpetrated by insiders, attracted by easy profits, making it much more difficult to detect and block this harmful activity. Security incidents of this type have already occurred in very sensitive critical infrastructures, such as nuclear power plants,[6] research centers,[7] and even in the US federal reserve.[8] Since it is more prevalent as a browser-based threat, all existing countermeasures are mainly host-based, designed to protect ordinary users. Defending corporate networks and critical infrastructure from this threat, however, requires a different approach. In [321], for example, the authors profiled the network traffic generated by the mining software, managing to identify cryptojacking activities in a local network even if the malicious traffic is encrypted. The network-based approach makes the countermeasure suitable for the defense of corporate networks, as well as critical infrastructures, even if the attacker is an insider.

5.1.3 Threat: SCADA System Vulnerabilities

Many of today's ICSs derive from the application of IT methods into existing physical systems, often replacing or integrating physical control mechanisms. For example, the built-in digital controls replaced the analog mechanical controls in rotating machines and motors. Both the cost and the performance improvements have encouraged this evolution, resulting in the introduction of many of today's "smart" technologies such as smart grids, smart transportation, smart buildings, and smart manufacturing. While on the one hand, this evolution increases the connectivity and criticality of these systems, on the other hand, it creates a greater need for their adaptability, resilience, security, and protection. Engineering models are evolving to address these emerging properties including safety, protection, privacy, and interdependencies on the environmental impact. However, the full understanding of SCADA systems, their structure, as well as their functionality is fundamental for the management of their security. SCADA systems are essential components of the production processes used in several sectors, from the control of machinery in nuclear power plants to the management of traffic lights and cameras in cities. Since SCADA systems are involved in very critical processes, any kind of vulnerability, if exploited, could have serious repercussions not only within the critical infrastructures themselves but also across the whole region. The introduction of IT capabilities into physical systems involves a change in the structure and behavior of those systems, with implications for their security. These systems are constantly evolving, acquiring new functionalities in response to the new requirements of an increasingly connected world. In this section, we analyze the possible consequences of attacks against SCADA systems, discuss the state of

---

[6]https://www.bbc.com/news/world-europe-43003740 (Last checked August 2020).

[7]https://bitcoinmagazine.com/articles/government-bans-professor-mining-bitcoin-supercomputer-1402002877/ (Last checked August 2020).

[8]https://dealbreaker.com/2017/01/bitcoin-federal-reserve-scandal/ (Last checked August 2020).

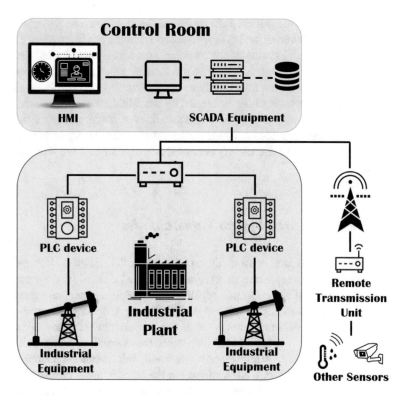

Fig. 5.3 SCADA systems components and common architecture

the art of existing countermeasures, and highlight the problems that are still open,
which would jeopardize the protection of critical infrastructures.

SCADA systems are a particular category of ICSs that provide specific
supervision-level control over industrial machinery and production processes that
cover a vast geographical area (such as electricity production and distribution
plants). The SCADA systems architecture, depicted in Fig. 5.3,[9] includes supervision and data acquisition systems and other devices that participate in the local
management of more specific sub-processes, such as PLC and Remote Transmission
Units (RTU). Both PLCs and RTUs have sensors and actuators that receive
commands and send information to other components of the SCADA system.
In particular, PLCs and RTUs are microcomputers that communicate with an array
of objects, such as factory machines, sensors, and other end-devices. From these
objects, they route the information to other computers equipped with supervisory
control and data acquisition software. This information supports supervisors in
making critical decisions based on real-time data. Administrators only need to

---

[9]https://www.trendmicro.com/vinfo/us/security/news/vulnerabilities-and-exploits/one-flaw-too-
many-vulnerabilities-in-scada-systems (Last checked August 2020).

examine Human Machine Interface (HMI), where the different functions and data elements of SCADA systems are presented for human review, interaction, and control. Thanks to their versatility and the critical role they play, SCADA systems are widespread in all types of industrial contexts and infrastructures.

Some of the sectors and infrastructures that use SCADA systems for the management and control of their processes are as follows:

- Energy production and distribution
- Oil and gas
- General manufacturing
- Food production
- Drinking water treatment plants
- Wastewater treatment and distribution
- Smart buildings
- Smart cities and transportation network

SCADA systems are crucial for industrial organizations since they help to maintain efficiency, process data for smarter decisions, and communicate system issues to help mitigate downtime. In particular, they allow organizations to:

- Control industrial processes locally or remotely in specialized control rooms.
- Monitor, gather, and process real-time data.
- Directly interact with devices such as sensors, valves, pumps, and motors.
- Record and display events through HMI software.

The current market of SCADA systems indicates that industries continue to appreciate the advantages that this technology offers to its production processes. However, the vulnerabilities they suffer from and the evolving threats affecting them pose a critical challenge for its users. These vulnerabilities could lead to potential financial losses in the case of private industries, as well as to possibly cascading effects down the supply chain. Furthermore, in the case of critical infrastructure, they can also easily translate into devastating effects for the population. The exposure to the network provides the attackers with a wide range of possibilities. When compromised, SCADA systems could be used by malicious users to gather a lot of information, such as the facility's layout, machinery details, critical safety thresholds, and possibly others.

A careful analysis of where vulnerabilities could be found in SCADA systems can help manufacturers and administrators understand how and where to apply mitigation against exploitation to promptly prevent and neutralize attacks. Unfortunately, SCADA systems control a large number of heterogeneous devices, sensors, and software that greatly increase the attack surface. The main classes of components where it is more likely to find vulnerabilities, and on which protection efforts must be concentrated, are the following:

- **HMI.** Human machine interfaces display data from various sensors and machines connected to a SCADA system to help administrators make and implement decisions using the same interface. Because of its capabilities and role in SCADA systems, HMIs can be a key target for potential malicious actors who aim to gain control over processes or steal critical information.

- **Mobile applications and web interfaces.** Following the spread of the IoT, several functions of the ICS systems, such as logging, monitoring, and even control functions, have been moved to the cloud. As a result, mobile applications and web interfaces have also become an integral part of SCADA systems. Mobile applications can be grouped into two classes: local applications, installed on devices directly connected to ICS devices in the field or process layers, and remote applications, which allow engineers to communicate with ICS servers using remote channels. These interfaces are subject to different types of attacks, including unauthorized physical or "virtual" access to the device data, compromised communication channel (Man-in-the-middle (MITM) attack), and compromised applications.

- **Communication protocols.** Communication protocols such as Modbus and Profinet help to manage and control the data flows generated by the various mechanisms supervised by SCADA systems. These protocols are generally dated, or, in some cases, they derive from updating old protocols. For this reason, there is a lack of security capabilities to defend against the new threats that endanger SCADA systems. Through vulnerabilities in communication protocols, malicious actors can damage ICS systems or lead to malfunctions of a SCADA component should they change the data sent by PLC and RTU or tamper with the firmware.

- **Other components.** There are countless technologies to make individual parts of SCADA systems stay connected, dynamic, and work in real time. Some of these components may be poorly equipped for threats currently faced by different sectors. These components are not necessarily used exclusively in SCADA systems but are fundamental for other technologies and systems. This large variety of systems and use cases makes very difficult the standardization of a defensive strategy, causing SCADA systems to be vulnerable to remote attacks.

➤ Resources

SCADA And Mobile Security In The Internet Of Things Era A thorough discussion of how the security landscape of SCADA systems has evolved in recent years, with an assessment of the security of SCADA systems and mobile applications in the Industrial Internet of Things (IIoT) era [322].

Previous attacks against critical infrastructures, described in Sect. 5.1.1, give us an idea of what are the possible impacts of attacks on SCADA systems. Potential damages could range from production delays, with possibly cascading effects along the supply chain, to damage to equipment and critical risks for human safety. These are devastating consequences for the organizations and governments that control critical infrastructures and consequently are a primary target for any cybercriminal groups. For this reason, the urgency to correct vulnerabilities in SCADA systems increases, to prevent future cyberattacks from being successful with similar, if not more serious, consequences than those that occurred in the past.

5.1.4 Attacks and Countermeasures

According to the Ukrainian President, Petro Poroshenko, several Ukrainian institutions have been subjected to about 6500 cyberattacks in the last 2 months of 2016. Part of the attacks targeted key elements of the government, such as the ministry of finance, the ministry of defense, and the state treasury that allocates money to other government institutions. In addition, a cyberattack also wiped out part of the Kiev's electricity grid, causing a blackout in part of the city.[10] According to the Ukrainian president, part of the incidents show that Russian security services were waging a cyberwar against the country, following the collapse of relations between the two nations due to Russia's annexation of Crimea in 2014. The attribution of a single incident, or an entire campaign of cyberattacks, to a specific entity is always difficult and controversial. However, whoever was responsible, this event has shown the tendency toward a cyberwar, proving its effectiveness and efficiency.

One of the most interesting things about the Ukrainian case is certainly the type of attack used to damage the national electricity grid. The Ukrainian power grid has undergone two different attacks, both malware enabled, directed to SCADA equipment. The first attack, which took place in December 2015, caused a power outage to around 225,000 customers, lasting up to 6 h. The second one, which took place in December 2016, is characterized by the use of much more sophisticated malware. Although different from each other, these two attacks marked a precedent that changed the international cyberwarfare scenario. In both of them, the attackers demonstrated the ability to plan, coordinate, and use malware for remote access and manipulation of particular SCADA systems, causing malicious changes to the distribution electricity infrastructure. Consequently, the implicit message behind these attacks has been far more worrying than the damage produced: attackers are now able and willing to invest time and resources to develop software specially designed to manipulate electricity network operations. For many years the possibility of attacking critical infrastructures, such as power grids, has been feared, and now Europe has direct experience. Given the particularity and their importance, the two attacks on the Ukrainian power grid are described in detail below.

December 2015: A Coordinated Attack on the Ukrainian Power Grid

On December 23, 2015, Kyivoblenergo, a Ukrainian electricity distribution company, reported a power outage to its customers. At around 3 pm, about 30 electrical substations were switched off for several hours, leaving around 80,000 users without

---

[10]https://www.reuters.com/article/us-ukraine-crisis-cyber-idUSKBN14I1QC (Last checked August 2020).

electricity. Subsequently, 3 other companies suffered the same attack, causing several other outages that left without power about 225,000 users, distributed across different areas of the country. A subsequent investigation, using information made available by interested power companies, researchers, and media, concluded that the power outages were the result of a coordinated cyberattack. Cybercriminals managed to remotely access the IT system of the distribution companies and their ICSs. Then, they manually changed the SCADA controllers' settings to disconnect several substations across the country. According to what emerged from the investigations, the cyberattacks were synchronized and coordinated, probably following a large reconnaissance phase of the victim networks, performed months before the main attack. According to the employees interviewed, the companies involved in the incident suffered the attacks within 30 min of each other. During the cyberattack, which affected several infrastructures at central and regional levels, malicious remote operations were conducted by multiple external humans to manipulate the state of circuit breakers. The attackers used remote administration tools already existing in the operating system and the ICSs client software, connected through Virtual Private Network (VPN) software. When the attack began, several workers noticed how their computer's cursor suddenly started moving on its own, running on the screen out of their control. Employees could only watch helplessly as the cursor intentionally moved over the buttons that control circuit breakers in a substation in the region, finally clicking to open the switches and take the substation offline. Even though they knew that such an action would have left an entire region without electricity, the workers had no way to prevent what happened or to restore proper operation. The system was not responding to their commands, logged them out of the control panel, and prevented them from logging in. The attackers continued to act undisturbed for several minutes, shutting down about 30 substations and disabling the backup power supplies for two of the three distribution centers in the region, leaving the operators themselves in the dark. The attackers proved to be skilled and stealthy. Their assault was carefully planned for many months, first making a reconnaissance to study the networks and discover credentials of the target systems and then launching a synchronized assault in a well-choreographed dance. The greatest ability shown by the attackers was not their skills or their choice of tools, but their capability of performing long-term reconnaissance operations necessary to learn the environment and perform a multistage, highly synchronized, and distributed attack. The attackers used a complex methodology, consisting of several technical components, listed below in chronological order of execution [323]:

- A phishing campaign aimed at targeting the attacked distribution companies
- The use of BlackEnergy 3 malware to gain access to the local network of attacked distribution companies
- Theft of the system's credentials of the impacted companies
- The use of VPNs to access the ICS network of the exposed companies
- The use of legitimate remote access tools, already installed inside the environment

- Compromise of serial-to-Ethernet communication devices at the firmware level using unpatched vulnerabilities
- The use of a modified malware, known as KillDisk, to clear the master boot record of the affected systems and delete some specific logs
- Denial of Service attack on the call centers of the companies involved, to delay the reporting of the energy blackout by customers

---

✏ Definitions

BlackEnergy BlackEnergy is a Trojan that is mainly used to compromise energy companies worldwide by attacking their ICS infrastructure. This malware is commonly delivered via phishing emails that include malicious Microsoft Office attachments and generally used as an initial access vector to acquire legitimate credentials, as well as for cyber recognition and installation of additional malware and backdoors.

KillDisk A family of malware used to sabotage computers by deleting and rewriting files, often associated with cyber espionage and cyber sabotage operations.

Power outages were caused by the manual use of ICS and SCADA systems and their software by the adversary. All other automatic tools and technologies, such as the BlackEnergy 3 and KillDisk malware, have been used to enable and support the attack, as well as to delay recovery efforts. The blackout did not last long. In all the affected areas, the electricity power was, in fact, restored in a period between 1 and 6 h. Despite this, 2 months after the accident, the control centers of the affected infrastructures still had not resumed full operation. This is because, as reported by Ukrainian and American investigative sources, the attackers have deleted or overwritten the firmware of several critical SCADA devices inside the affected substations. In this state, the tampered equipment had become useless and unresponsive to any remote control attempt by the operators. As a result, the electricity was restored, but the operators of the affected substations had to manually control the equipment for months.

December 2016: Win32/Industroyer: A Powerful Malware Against the Ukrainian Power Grid

In December 2016, Ukraine experienced a second attack on its electricity infrastructure. This time the target was an electrical transmission station located north of the city of Kiev, hit by new cyberattacks that left in the dark a part of the Ukrainian capital, equivalent to one-fifth of its electricity needs. The blackout lasted for about 1 h, causing several problems for the population. Security researchers did not take long to understand that this incident was also caused by a cyberattack, finding traces of what immediately seemed like a very powerful malware, called "Industroyer" or

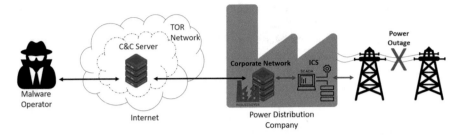

Fig. 5.4 Industroyer malware architecture

"Crash Override". It is not clear how the malware infected the victim's network yet. However, the attackers likely used phishing emails, the same technique employed in the 2015 attack. Unlike what happened in December 2015, however, the malware not only allowed the attackers to access the victim's systems but also directly caused the blackout, without any human interaction.

Industroyer is a highly sophisticated malware designed to interfere with the working processes of ICS systems using specific protocols that control the electrical equipment of substations. The developers of this malware have a thorough knowledge of these systems. In fact, it seems unlikely that malware of this type could be developed and tested without having available the specialized equipment used within the targeted industrial environment.

Industroyer's architecture is distributed on several levels, as shown in Fig. 5.4. Once it has infiltrated the network of the victim distribution company, it automatically maps the control systems and identifies the target equipment. The program also records network logs and sends information to its operators who, through a Command and Control (C&C) server, collect information about the target environment and decide where and when to hit.

The creators of the malware developed several payloads capable of directly interacting with different SCADA components active in the targeted substations, with support for several specific protocols, listed below:

- IEC 60870-5-101 (aka IEC 101)
- IEC 60870-5-104 (aka IEC 104)
- IEC 61850
- OLE for Process Control Data Access (OPC DA)

In addition, the malware authors developed a tool that exploits some vulnerabilities of a particular family of protection relays, the Siemens SIPROTEC range, implementing several attacks against them, such as Denial of Service (DoS).

The component of the malware, shown in Fig. 5.5, are described individually below.

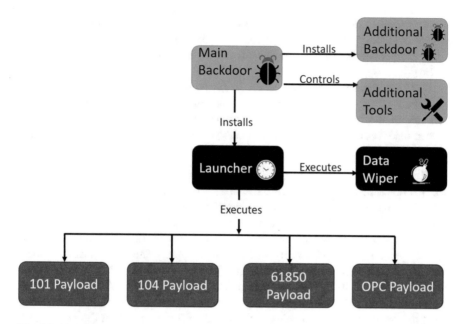

Fig. 5.5 Simplified scheme of industroyer components [324]

- *Main Backdoor.* The core component of Industroyer, used by the attackers to control all the other components of the malware. Once installed, this component communicates with a C&C server, sending the acquired data and receiving commands to be executed in the network under attack.
- *Additional Backdoor.* This component is a backup system that allows attackers to regain control of the compromised machine if the main backdoor is discovered and removed. This malicious application is a weaponized version of the Windows Notepad software. Once replaced with the malicious version, Windows Notepad works as expected, even if connected in the background with a C&C server, different than the one used by the main backdoor.
- *Launcher.* This element is an independent executable responsible for starting other components, such as payloads and data wiper applications.
- *101 payload component.* This component partially implements the protocol described in the IEC 101 standard, used for communications between ICS and RTU transmitted on a serial connection. Once launched, this payload terminates active connections between the victim host and the connected RTU devices. Then, it establishes a new connection to the RTU devices, maintaining their control and changing their state at will.
- *104 payload.* This payload has the same functions as payload 101, with the difference that it works using the IEC 104 standard, which is an extension of the IEC 101 protocol over TCP/IP networks.
- *61850 payload.* This component implements the IEC 61850 standard, used for multivendor communication between devices that perform protection, automa-

tion, measurement, monitoring, and control of electrical substation automation systems. Once executed, this payload tries to connect to known devices or tries to independently discover the devices available in the same subnet of the victim host.

- *OPC DA payload* This component implements the OLE for Process Control (OPC) protocol, which allows real-time data exchange between distributed components, based on a client-server model. As previous payloads, this software can discover compatible devices, establish a connection with them, and change their state.

The two attacks in Ukraine are the only confirmed cases of blackouts caused by a cyberattack in history. But while the first of those attacks received more public attention than what followed, some evidence about the malware used in the latter shows that it was much more than just a repetition. In December 2015, in fact, the attackers manually turned off the affected substations after illegally obtaining access to the systems of the electricity distribution company.The 2016 attack, instead, was carried out completely automatically. The used malware, Industroyer, has been programmed with the ability to communicate directly with SCADA components. This ability allowed Industroyer to send commands directly to the equipment, using the protocol employed to regulate the flows of electric current in the power grid. This means that malicious users are now able to attack an electrical distribution network faster, with little preparation and minimum human control.

> ⮞ **Resources**
>
> **Analysis of the Cyberattack on the Ukrainian Power Grid** A technical report that consolidates open-source information on the attack against the Ukrainian power grid in December 2015. The document clarifies important details surrounding the incident, offers important lessons learned, and recommends new strategies to help the ICS community avoid similar attacks [323].
>
> **Industroyer** A whitepaper released by security researchers at ESET with a detailed analysis of the malware known as Industroyer or Crash Override. The report includes a description of all the software components that compose the malware, including their goal and behavior [324].

A subsequent investigation showed that the attack that caused the blackout might have been just a dry run. From the evidence and testimonies collected, it appears that the attackers tested the most advanced sample of grid-sabotage malware ever detected. When it was discovered, Industroyer was only the second-ever known case of malware designed specifically to interact with SCADA systems and destroy their physical components. The only other malware known at the time capable of conducting such an attack, known as Stuxnet, was allegedly used to destroy centrifuges in an Iranian nuclear enrichment facility in 2009.

The two cyberattacks in Ukraine described above are the first publicly acknowledged incidents to result in power outages. Control systems in affected Ukraine power plants were surprisingly more secure than those operated by other nations. Indeed, their ICS networks were well segmented by the corporate networks using robust firewalls. But in the end, these security measures were not enough, paving the way for the attackers. For example, one of the safest authentication methodologies, the two-factor authentication, was not deployed for workers who remotely accessed the SCADA network at the time of the first attack. This neglect allowed attackers to easily hijack the credentials of legitimate employees, gaining crucial access to the systems that controlled critical end-devices, such as switches. A first stream of thought has speculated that these events are both of little relevance for concerns related to hacking electricity grids in the rest of the world, since the Ukraine case occurred under very particular technological and political conditions, difficult to apply elsewhere [325]. However, what happened in Ukraine holds many lessons for every critical infrastructure in the rest of the world. Researchers who studied Industroyer said this malware can automatize attacks on a state's electrical infrastructure to generate mass power outages. Its highly customizable nature, which includes interchangeable plug-in components, allows attackers to easily reuse its malicious code, adapt the malware to different infrastructures, and launch simultaneous attacks on multiple destinations. These capabilities suggest that Industroyer could cause much more serious disruptions than the Kiev blackout, with a much larger extension of the affected area, and significantly longer duration. Furthermore, the adaptability of the malware means that the tool potentially poses a threat to all the world's electricity networks, not just Ukraine's one, as claimed after the 2015 attack.

Furthermore, another consideration makes the threat observed in Ukraine extensible to the rest of the world. Both the cyberattacks of 2015 and 2016 impacted nationwide different portions of the Ukrainian electricity distribution network. This has led operators to switch from automatic control of the distribution network, governed by ICS systems, to a "manual mode." Indeed, the electricity companies involved in tech incident intervened by sending their technical staff to the disconnected substations. They manually close the switches to power the system and change the management mode from automatic to manual. The plan worked and all services were restored within 3–6 h. This operation allowed a quick resolution of the problem, bringing the electric current back to the homes of Ukrainian users after a few hours from the attack. However, the distribution network was managed without the aid of SCADA systems for the entire period of the infection, which lasted several months after the attacks, according to statements by the operators of the affected substations and local media. This scenario introduces several risk components that are impossible to ignore for any utility worldwide. First of all, the operation of a power grid without the advantages offered by ICS systems is very risky. Being a very complex system, both its monitoring and management operated by an automated control center are fundamental for the safety of the production and distribution processes of the electric current. Furthermore, utilities that depend heavily on this automation may not be able to restore large parts of their system, as happened in Ukraine. Generally, it is possible to lose the functionality of multiple SCADA devices for a considerable time without this resulting in outages, as happens, for example, during scheduled maintenance operations. However, such an event, when massive and unexpected, considerably exacerbates the risk of accidents. Without the advantage of SCADA systems, in fact, in the event of voltage overloads or other malfunctions, the system will continue to supply energy. This will potentially cause damages to infrastructure components, unless timely human intervention, which is, however, difficult to guarantee in any situation. It has been verified that the adversaries have developed knowledge and skills to create malware capable of taking over the ICT and ICS infrastructure of the targeted utilities, deploying a command and control server, and facilitating the planning of an attack by providing network access and necessary information. Besides, during the attack, some tools were used to delete system files and the firmware of some devices, in an attempt to deny the use of the SCADA system for recovery purposes to amplify the effects of the attack and possibly to delay the restoration. This procedure greatly complicates the full restore of ICSs, making attack mitigation very difficult. In these cases, in fact, if the attacked distribution infrastructures do not have manual backup functionalities, as often happens in different countries, it could be much harder for workers to restore power and outages could last much longer.

Academic research centers, after surveyed most important cybersecurity problems on SCADA systems, are focusing on forward-looking security solutions for these important control networks. In [326], the authors analyzed several cybersecurity incidents involving critical infrastructures and SCADA systems. They classified these incidents based on source sector, method of operations, impact, and target sector. Using this standardized taxonomy, is it possible to compare and counteract to current and future SCADA incidents? In [327], the authors surveyed ongoing research and provide a coherent overview of the threats, risks, and mitigation strategies in the area of SCADA security. The research done in this area looks more toward providing long-term solutions and applying both industry and academic work to the problem. As such, these institutes remain very connected and interact regularly with industry to make sure the research is gauged to provide a positive impact on the national infrastructure. Several open-source projects have been created for various efforts in the SCADA space as well, including items ranging from snort signatures to protocol-specific firewalls and encryption overlays. Some studies have been released in the attack vector space as well, such as SCADA protocol scanners, and information-gathering tools [328].

5.1.5   Open Issues and Future Directions

Ukraine's power grid attack demonstrated that malicious actors seem to have extensive knowledge about ICS hardware and protocols used in critical infrastructures. This knowledge could stem from employees involved in the development or management of ICS components. These highly skilled operators could transfer information to cybercriminals, or they could even actively participate in the design of malware. Alternatively, malicious actors could learn in the field the architecture of ICS components by gaining illicit access to corporate networks connected with them. Once done, attackers are free to explore systems and interact with ICS devices until the intrusion is discovered. This eventuality highlights the importance of discovering an attack as soon as possible, in order to minimize the time available for attackers to gather information about the system. According to Symantec researchers [329], zero-day attacks last on average more than 1 year before the vulnerability is discovered and corrected. During this time, cybercriminals are free to use the same vulnerability several times, on multiple systems, with low probabilities of being discovered. Since the possibility of being attacked and compromised cannot be excluded, a defense strategy must be developed to detect the attack as quickly as possible and, in the meantime, to prevent the attacker from doing any significant damage.

Cyber deception is one of the most promising technologies that aim to build such a defense methodology. The basic idea is to deploy traps or deception decoys along the virtual perimeter, designed to mimic the legitimate resources [330]. In this way, a possible attacker who obtains illegal access to the network will not be able to distinguish the real resources from the decoys, spending time to exfiltrate fake information or to compromise simulated devices. The feasibility of this defensive methodology has been investigated by several contributions in the literature, relating to multiple assets. In [331], for example, the authors proposed a system that protects devices connected to the network from malicious scans used by attackers to discover vulnerabilities. When a network scan is detected, the system responds with a mix of true and false information to confuse the attacker. If he believes that the answers are all true, he will be deceived. While if he realizes that some are false, he would have to spend time figuring out which ones are true. The same principle can be applied to other assets, such as digital documents. Indeed, the possibility to automatically create believable, hard-to-comprehend fake documents generated from real ones was demonstrated in [332]. The application of this methodology considerably improves cyber deception systems by creating fake documents that are credible and difficult to understand, to help defense mechanisms in misleading cyberattackers. Cyber deception techniques, although supported by several scientific studies, are still little used in production environments. However, this technology is among the most promising in the cyber defense landscape. For this reason, more research and development efforts are needed to enable and promote the use of these innovative techniques in real-world scenarios.

To mitigate the risk of ICS attacks, first, critical infrastructure administrators need to manage their system following the most simple and important best practices. Paul Edon, director at Tripwire, suggests that "security best practice includes selecting suitable frameworks such as NIST, ISO, CIS, ITIL to help direct, manage and drive security programs. It also means ensuring that the strategy includes all three pillars of security; People, Process, and Technology. Protection should apply at all levels; Perimeter, Network, and End Point. Finally, select the foundational controls that best suit your environment. There is a wealth of choice—Firewalls, IDS/IPS, Encryption, Dual Factor Authentication, System Integrity Monitoring,

Change Management, Off-line Backup, Vulnerability Management, and Configuration Management to name but a few".[11]

The examples described in Sect. 5.1.1 show that malware poses a real, pressing, and extremely dangerous threat to critical infrastructures. Whether specifically designed to attack a particular ICS or to accidentally attack critical infrastructures, any type of malware can generate severe consequences on public health, safety, and prosperity. The lessons learned from the attacks of recent years make us understand how the approach to the cyber defense of critical infrastructures is not fully adequate to the threat of malware. The main reason is the current defensive strategy that is not specifically designed for ICS but derives from the experience of protecting generic IT systems. On the one hand, this mitigates some common aspects shared between critical infrastructure and generic IT systems. However, on the other hand, it limits the countermeasures deployed, making them often inadequate for the protection of critical infrastructure. These observations reveal the need to adopt a holistic approach to information security that incorporates processes, technologies, and people. This new approach should be contextualized and used for the protection of all critical infrastructures, even those that are generally less protected, such as ships [333].

One of the key aspects of this new strategy should focus on understanding the differences between a generic IT system and an ICS. ICS technology is becoming increasingly accessible, with threat vectors now extending from centralized systems to individual atomic components, such as smart sensors. Designing the cyber defense strategy by having in mind a generic IT approach is no longer acceptable in this new reality. Operational constraints in industrial sectors such as energy, production, healthcare, and transportation require an approach to cybersecurity that safeguards ICS. The primary goal of IT systems is the management of data and its ability to flow freely and securely among users. IT systems and techniques exist in the virtual world, where data is stored, recovered, transmitted, and manipulated. A typical IT system is composed by many moving parts and gateways. This makes it highly vulnerable and liable to a large surface area for a wide array of ever-changing threats. Defending against attacks means safeguarding each level by identifying (and continuously correcting) the weak points to maintain the flow of data secure and consistent. ICS, on the contrary, belongs to the physical world. Its main goal is to guarantee the correct execution of all the actions undertaken during a production process. While IT must safeguard every level of the system, ICS aims to control physical systems that can be turned on or off, closed, or opened. ICS aims to guarantee the security and control of what were usually closed systems in the past. Everything in ICS is geared to physically move and control devices and processes to keep systems functioning as expected, with a primary focus on security and greater efficiency. With the advent of the IIoT and the integration of physical machines with sensors and software on the network, the dividing line between IT and ICS, well

---

[11]https://www.informationsecuritybuzz.com/expert-comments/industroyer-biggest-threat-critical-infrastructure-since-stuxnet-discovered/ (Last checked August 2020).

defined in the past, is moving. With the increase of objects connected to the Internet, there has been an increase in the number of potential targets for cybercriminals. Each connected device also represents a new gateway for private IT infrastructures that malicious actors are ready to exploit. Another important aspect is the placement of cybersecurity techniques in the software life cycle. In many cases, companies worry about the security of their software only after implementation. For a decrease in cyberattacks, it is essential to consider security threats during the initial design and development phase, rather than to integrate cyber resilience from the beginning of the life cycle.[12] This approach is fundamental in the development of information systems for critical infrastructures that use new technologies, such as edge and fog computing [334].

The WannaCry malware campaign that the world experienced in 2017 contains several lessons useful to understand how to avoid the repetition of such a dangerous event. Brad Smith, president of Microsoft, has identified several measures that, if implemented by public and private companies, could establish a protective barrier against cyberattacks. First of all, this attack demonstrated how cybersecurity has become a shared responsibility among tech companies, governments, and customers. The vulnerability exploited by attackers has persisted in several systems 2 months after the release of the security patch. This fact highlights how the basic rules of cybersecurity, like keeping computers updated, are not followed. However, the most important lesson is about the malicious code used as an attack vector. As confirmed by several sources, the exploit was stolen from a government agency and then used to start the attack. For this reason, Microsoft itself has asked for a world government's commitment to issue a digital version of the Geneva Convention that applies in cyberspace the same rules applied to weapons in the physical world. This convention should include a new requirement for governments to report vulnerabilities to vendors, rather than stockpile, sell, or exploit them.[13]

In order to plan an effective attack on SCADA systems, the malware developer should know at least the high-level details of the system architecture he wants to target and the protocols used. This knowledge, combined with the ability to send commands to end-devices, allows malware to take control of a SCADA system. According to [317], "generic" intrusion detection systems are not effective in protecting SCADA systems from unauthorized intrusions. This is because all commands sent by malware are legitimate commands. Consequently, one of the main future research directions is based on the design and development of intrusion detection systems that are aware of the SCADA protocols, traffic models, and operational context.

---

[12]https://iecetech.org/index.php/Technology-Focus/2019-02/Cyber-attacks-targeting-critical-infrastructure (Last checked August 2020).

[13]https://blogs.microsoft.com/on-the-issues/2017/05/14/need-urgent-collective-action-keep-people-safe-online-lessons-last-weeks-cyberattack/#sm.0000mpb068eggcqczh61fx32wtiui (Last checked August 2020).

5.2   Scenario: A New Cyber-Physical Threat from the Sky

As discussed in the previous sections, the defense strategy of a modern critical infrastructure takes into account both the physical and the cybernetic dimensions. The main goal is to avoid unauthorized intrusions, both in the real and virtual space. Unlike the virtual perimeter, which is a relatively new concept, the defense of the physical border of a state, as well as of its critical infrastructures, is a requirement that dates back to ancient times. In the absence of digital technologies, surveillance of the security perimeter was committed to lookouts posted in special watchtowers, serving 24 h a day. With the advent of technology, however, the surveillance of a perimeter is performed using cameras, sensors, and other digital alarm systems, often combined and automated.

The human component is still fundamental for the identification of a possible threat, but the support of IT systems has made the task easier and more accurate. Sophisticated equipment, such as high-definition cameras, radar, and sonar, allow the identification of unauthorized people or objects approaching the protected perimeter from anywhere: land, air, and sea. However, these countermeasures are geared toward identifying the classic threats affecting the infrastructure to be protected. The sensitivity of these devices allows the detection of medium/large objects, such as unauthorized people, vehicles (on land, air, and sea), and other fast objects (such as missiles and torpedoes). For example, the defense of an airport perimeter consists of several heterogeneous devices. First, its land border is closed by a fence, heavily guarded, and under constant surveillance. CCTV cameras monitor the perimeter to prevent unauthorized access of men and vehicles, possibly with the aid of motion sensors. Then, its airspace is monitored by several radars, capable of determining the distance and speed of approaching aircraft, even more than 100 km away. These defense systems are quite standard, and their technological evolution over time has affected their performance rather than the ability to identify new threats. The radar system, for example, detects the position of an aircraft by analyzing the signals that, previously emitted by a powerful antenna, have returned after being reflected by the target. This technology has evolved by increasing its coverage area, but its basic functioning, as well as the objects it can recognize, has remained the same. The slow evolution of the physical perimeter surveillance systems matched the static nature of the threats, which remained unchanged for a long time. In the IoT era, attention has shifted to cyber threats, which, on the contrary, are continuously evolving and characterized by an ever-increasing danger. The physical defense has therefore slowed down its evolution, becoming dangerously weak in some sectors.

In this section, we analyze how the advent of medium/small commercial drones brought a new threat to the physical security of critical infrastructures, for which defense systems are still not ready. Through the analysis of attacks that occurred in the real world, we highlight how the detection systems have been caught unprepared by this new threat. This resulted in the helplessness of security personnel during an attack, leaving the closure of critical infrastructure under attack as the only countermeasure to ward off possible harmful consequences.

5.2.1 Threat: Drones

The drone sector is a universe in constant evolution characterized by a continuous extension of use cases that advances hand in hand with technology. Throughout the years, the applications that these small aircraft find in the most disparate contexts are increasingly widespread. The range of activities related to drones is truly endless. For example, the use of drones in agriculture is very widespread, as well as for professional aerial shots that concern sectors of all kinds: from tourism to construction and from mining to aerial surveillance. The use of drones for environmental purposes is also frequent. In fact, the monitoring of geographical areas from the sky enables several activities, such as the detection of dangerous illegal landfills or the prevention of devastating forest fire outbreaks. The birth of the first drone is linked to the military world and dates back to the First World War, when the first prototypes of aircraft controlled via radio waves were developed.

> ✷ **Definitions**
>
> **Unmanned Vehicle** With Unmanned Vehicles (UV) we refer to a type of vehicle that is able to operate without a human pilot onboard. Most of these vehicles were developed in the military sector; however, there have been numerous developments for civil purposes available in the public markets. There are two major types of unmanned vehicles:
>
> - *Unmanned Underwater Vehicles:* UVs that are able to operate underwater without a human pilot onboard. There are two main categories of Unmanned Underwater Vehicles (UUV)s: Autonomous Underwater Vehicles (AUV)s, and Remotely Operated underwater Vehicles (ROV)s. The former is able to operate independently and can be thought of as a robot, and the latter, instead, is controlled remotely by a human operator.
> - *Unmanned Aerial Vehicles:* Unmanned Aerial Vehicles (UAV) are aircraft that are able to operate in airspace without a human pilot onboard. UAVs, together with a ground-based controller and a system of communication, compose the Unmanned Aircraft System (UAS). As UUVs, the UAVs can operate both under the remote control of a human operator and autonomously, by relying on an onboard computer.

From that moment on, the military world kept developing and using drones for war purposes, with research and development programs still in progress. Being a technology born within the military world, it took several years before the drones expanded their borders, also embracing civilian use. A driving force toward the success of these aircraft can be placed around the mid-2000s, with technological advancement that has increased reliability and lowered production costs.

The use of drones can be due to many different reasons: professional, commercial, security and defense purposes, or even for recreational uses. However, drones are increasingly used for illicit purposes, whether they are carried out with the will of the operator or as a consequence of the negligent use of the device. In fact, the advent of drones has introduced a whole new system of attacks aimed at mobile and nonmobile targets. In addition to the innocent fun related to making it fly to take breathtaking shots, there are some disturbing ways to use drones. Several news events, for example, have shown how significant the trouble created by the intrusion of a small drone in airport areas are and how they can harm air traffic, the safety of people, and also the economy of both the public and private sectors. It is therefore not difficult to imagine what the implications of a drone attack, carried out against the critical infrastructures of a nation, could be. Thanks to the technological advancement and miniaturization of drone components, they are a good way to perform an asymmetrical attack or complete stealth missions. With relatively low costs, it is possible to reach slightly high technical performances from devices so small that they can lift off almost anywhere. Furthermore, the use of inertial and odometric navigation systems, as well as the integration of new technologies such as 5G or artificial intelligence, increases the possible malicious applications of drones. Also, thanks to additive manufacturing, the drone can be highly customized to adapt to unconventional uses. In fact, an attacker could use a 3D printer to create components designed to maximize the negative effects of an attack.

✐ **Definitions**

Asymmetrical Attack The nature of modern conflicts has changed from traditional conflicts between states, often due to territorial expansion, to conflicts between states and non-state actors with a huge disparity of means and with purposes other than expanding their borders. Asymmetric warfare is an undeclared conflict, with a significant disparity in military or financial resources and the status of the two opponents. In these conflicts, the militarily and economically strongest contender is often at a disadvantage because he has to defend himself against an opponent that is difficult to identify. In this context, an asymmetric attack is therefore carried out by one of the two parties involved in an asymmetric war. A classic example is the 9/11 attack.

UVs can be categorized according to different aspects, such as their dimensions, capabilities, and costs. These categorizations allow different actors, such as developers and legislators, to understand the variety of existing devices and consequently calibrate national regulations, commercial products, and also defense strategies. In fact, classifying UV devices is essential for understanding the type of threat on which to customize the countermeasures of a sensible area. One of the most important categorizations of UV is based on the role played by a human operator during his mission:

Table 5.2 UAVs classification according to the US department of defense

Category	Size	Maximum gross takeoff weight	Normal operating altitude (ft)	Airspeed (knots)
Group 1	Small	0–20	<1200 (Above ground level)	<100
Group 2	Medium	21–55	<3500	<250
Group 3	Large	<1320	<18,000 (Mean sea level)	<250
Group 4	Large	<1320	<18,000 (mean sea level)	Any
Group 5	Largest	<1320	<18,000	Any

- **Human in the loop.** Remote-controlled systems that perform functions selected by a human operator in real time. These systems are generally controlled by radio frequencies, typically in the 2.4 and 5.8 GHz frequencies. This type of UV cannot perform any operation in real time without a command activated by the pilot.
- **Human on the loop.** Semiautonomous systems capable of selecting a target and attacking it independently. However, the activity as a whole remains constantly subordinated to the supervision of a human operator, who can intervene in each phase of the mission and decide whether to carry out the attack.
- **Human out of the loop.** Fully automated systems which, once activated, can select, engage, and attack targets without the further intervention of a human operator.

The US Department of Defense classifies UAVs into five categories, considering technical capabilities such as the maximum gross takeoff weight, the altitude, and the speed that a drone can reach, as showed in Table 5.2.

> **☛ Resources**
>
> **Other UAVs Classifications** Several UAV classification schemes have been proposed to help differentiate existing systems based on their operational characteristics and capabilities. A correct categorization is of fundamental importance for several reasons, including the development of adequate countermeasures, the design of standards, and commercial purposes. Furthermore, some of these categorizations are of regulatory importance since the metrics used by the legislator are often directly related to the risk of impact on the ground or of accidents in midair. This contribution provides several characteristic UAV classifications from a variety of sources, both civil and military cite [335].

A drone, in the hands of terrorists or malicious users, would make it easier to attack any target, causing massive damages. Strengthened by the fact that its limited size makes it extremely difficult to detect, the drone could be used for different purposes, involving both passive and active attacks:

- **Aerial surveillance.** A drone can easily be equipped with a high-definition camera, infrared sensors, thermal sensors, and any other device useful for aerial surveillance. With this type of equipment, a drone can be used for reconnaissance missions to acquire information on a future target, such as critical infrastructures. In this way, the attacker can accurately map the targeted site, identifying security systems in use such as alarm sensors and video surveillance. This will enable the identification of any weaknesses in the defense systems, crucial to elaborate a detailed attack plan.
- **Active Attacks.** A drone could also be used to actively attack a target by releasing objects or crashing on it. Low-cost drones easily available on the market, in fact, have a load capacity of several kilos, which can be used to carry explosives on and release them on the target. A drone could also carry other equipment to be used for malicious purposes. For example, a jammer could be carried by a drone near a critical infrastructure to disturb the wireless communication links used by workers, security personnel, and SCADA equipment. Another type of attack could be carried out using commercial drones capable of vaporizing substances in the air, typically used in agriculture, to spread chemical/bacteriological weapons in urban areas.

✐ Definitions

Jammer A Jammer is a sophisticated electronic device capable of producing and transmitting high-frequency signals that interfere with normal communications. These signals are set precisely in the frequencies used by a wide range of equipment, in order to occupy all the available bandwidth and prevent legitimate devices from sending or receiving data. A specially configured jammer can disturb any communication channel, such as GSM telephone transmissions, GPS, WIFI, satellite communications, and possibly others.

In the last decades, several episodes across the world have helped to raise awareness of the threat of UAVs against national institutions. A nonexhaustive list of the main demonstration actions carried out with the help of drones is shown below.

- **Germany.** In 2013, a drone controlled by an extremist political party managed to land near the German chancellor Angela Merkel, violating the security perimeter set by the authorities, during a sporting event in Dresden.

- **Japan.** In April 2015, a drone controlled by activists and carrying radioactive sand from the Fukushima nuclear power plant managed to land on the roof of the presidential palace in Tokyo, where the Japanese Prime Minister works.
- **USA.** In 2015, a small UAV have crashed into the White House lawn. This event, although it may seem of little importance, has demonstrated the difficulties of the Secret Services in protecting the White House from a new and unexpected type of threat.
- **Venezuela.** In 2018, two drones exploded near a military parade attended by Nicolas Maduro, the President of Venezuela.
- **Italy.** In July 2019, during a drone competition called "Drone Race," the drones in the race were subtracted from the control of their respective pilots remaining in flight without a guide for about 15 min. Thanks to the safety nets and the pilots' skills, there were no consequences for the health of the onlookers or the integrity of the drones involved.

In light of these and other incidents, it is not surprising that drones have been banned in several countries, such as Egypt, North Korea, and Iran, and limited in others, such as Russia, the United States and, Belgium. Features such as ease of use, availability on the market at low costs, and high performance make UVs a very dangerous weapon to use against critical infrastructures. In fact, these devices represent a new potentially destructive cyber-physical threat that cannot be underestimated. All types of attacks, both active and passive, which can be performed with the help of a drone are made even more dangerous by the physical characteristics of these devices. Thanks to their dimensions, often contained, and to their ability to fly at low altitude and in a relatively silent way, UVs are very difficult to detect and possibly neutralize. The perimeter defenses of critical infrastructures are normally calibrated on the profiles of typical objects that can intrude without authorization in protected areas. Some examples can be humans, identifiable with security cameras and alarm sensors, vehicles of any type, detectable with radar/sonar, missiles, and possibly others. The profile of a drone does not typically fall within these, making classic countermeasures almost useless. In fact, depending on the size, UVs have a very small radar trace, making their detection and tracking very difficult. Small drones that fly at low altitudes can travel completely unnoticed, be confused with birds, or be spotted late. Furthermore, once sighted, they are still difficult to neutralize using automatic systems.

The next section describes in detail the use of drones to attack the critical infrastructures of a country. We discuss several real cases of security incidents, such as the attack of armed drones at the Russian military base in Syria, and different episodes of UVs that flew over airports paralyzing air traffic for several hours.

5.2.2 Attacks and Countermeasures

In the last few years, several episodes have helped to raise awareness among the institutions of the threat of UAVs against critical infrastructures. In December 2014, France revealed that unauthorized and unidentified UAS had breached the restricted airspace over 13 of the country's 19 nuclear plants during the preceding 3 months. These UAS were described as highly sophisticated civilian devices, and the flights over nuclear facilities appeared to be coordinated, with most of the violations occurring at night. In light of the increasing security concerns in Europe following terrorist attacks in France and Belgium, there is concern over the possible motivations. There have been many notable incidents also in the United States. In early July 2016, the US Department of Energy revealed that its Savannah River Site, which processes and stores nuclear materials, had experienced eight unauthorized flyovers in the span of 2 weeks. There have been unauthorized flyovers of a US Navy nuclear submarine base, major sporting events, large public gatherings, and national monuments. UAVs have crashed into the White House lawn and the New York Capitol, and there has been widespread documentation that they are being used to deliver smuggled goods to prisons [336].

Although these incidents have demonstrated the real extent of the problem and the inability of current defense systems, there are no known consequences to people or things. Conversely, some attacks on critical infrastructures, carried out with the help of drones, have caused significant economic damage.

The first example took place in December 2018, when the air traffic at London Gatwick airport was interrupted due to the intrusion of an unspecified number of small UAVs, which entered the airport's security perimeter. Following the incident, the British authorities decided to block the airport's operations for security reasons. The blockade of air traffic lasted about 36 h, highlighting the substantial unpreparedness of the security systems of critical infrastructures to face this new type of threat. The incident was initially handled by the police force, which deployed several teams of specialized agents. After failing to locate and identify the aircraft, police forces called for army intervention. The military approach to the problem was immediately based on the physical shooting down of hostile aircraft, using specialized personnel, such as snipers. After a brief evaluation, however, the hypothesis of shooting down the aircraft was shelved. The collateral risks deriving from the use of firearms near the populated area located close to the airport were considered too high, as well as the possible fall of the drone, which could have also transported explosives. The intervention of the security forces ended the day after the beginning of the attack with the reopening of air traffic. However, still today, the UAVs, their pilots, and the reasons behind this malicious action have not been identified. Subsequent investigative activities have excluded that the air space violation was due to a simple human error, describing the incident as a deliberate act of disruption. The intrusions within Gatwick's airspace, which occurred several times over the same day, caused the paralysis of one of the most important airports in England for almost 2 days. There were over 800 flight cancellations, forcing more than 140,000 passengers to land, for an estimated total economic damage of around 25 million US dollars.

Three weeks later, in January 2019, the same type of attack occurred at Heathrow airport, following the same dynamic. After the sighting of an unidentified UAV, air traffic in the first airport of the United Kingdom was blocked for about an hour. In this circumstance, the British police used some of their own remotely piloted aircraft for reconnaissance and identification operations. However, this strategy only contributed to create further confusion, hindering the operations of mitigation of the attack. Also on this occasion, the investigative activities did not bring any results. The attackers have not been identified, and their motivations remain unknown.

The two incidents in England represent an important precedent, not only for the British authorities but for the whole world. The adjustment of public security systems to the continuous evolution of threats, both internal and external, represents an open problem for every nation. UAVs, especially those of group 1 (as defined in the table), are a very recent threat to critical infrastructures, and for this, there are no direct experiences. The attacks that took place in airports, therefore, represent an important case study, with fundamental lessons to be considered for the design and implementation of new generation cyber-physical defense systems. First of all, the simplicity with which the attacks were carried out, as well as the enormous damage suffered, highlighted the urgent need to develop legislation, both nationally and internationally, capable of regulating UVs and contrasting their illicit and malicious use. Furthermore, the uncoordinated and ineffective action of the police forces in handling the emergencies of Gatwick and Heathrow highlights the need to develop a specific contrasting strategy, which coordinates the work not only of the police but also of the private security systems of any critical infrastructure.

Since their introduction to the retail market, public opinion, as well as the research community, wondered about the actual danger of drones, opening the debate on what the threats and the benefits of this technology are. In [337], the author investigated drones' benefits, risks, and legal considerations. In [338], the authors, considering the significant number of non-military UAVs that can be purchased to operate in unregulated air space and the range of such devices test a specific UAV, the Parrot AR Drone version 2, and present a forensic analysis of tests used to deactivate or render the device inoperative. They found that these devices are open to attack, which means they could be controlled by a third party.

5.2.3   Open Issues and Future Directions

Most traditional radar cannot detect small, low-flying UAVs, so this trend is particularly troubling. The majority of previously discussed documented flyovers were only discovered because of human detection—often by vigilant security personnel with keen eyesight. There have been efforts to improve upon the available technology, and many companies are marketing drone detection security systems. However, even when they are detected, there are complications intercepting them and identifying the operators [336]. A possible solution is the design and implementation of anti-drone systems based on jamming technologies. However, such countermeasures may not always be efficient. In [339], for example, the authors used the signal emitted by a jammer as a navigation system for the drone under attack.

Recognizing and implementing security practices that meet states' regulatory requirements are key to successfully managing potential security incidents associated with UVs. Although no single solution will fully mitigate this risk, several measures can be taken to address UVs-related security challenges [340]:

- Research and implement legally approved counter-UV technology.
- Know the air domain around the facility and who has the authority to take action to enhance security.
- Update emergency/incident action plans to include UV security and response strategies.
- Build federal, state, and local partnerships for adaptation of best practices and information sharing.
- Sensitize citizens and institutions to the problem, inviting anyone to report potential UVs threats to local law enforcement agencies.

Chapter 6
Business Entities

If the economy is the backbone of a country, business entities define and affect its movements.

Those entities produce business that, with the provision of goods, services, and jobs, is confirmed as one of the key pillars of the nation. Business, among the other things, defines the direction in which the nation is moving toward the world economy. The technological progress of recent years led to an innovation race to which every company (corporation) that intended to grow or, actually, to survive has an obligation to participate. Participating, however, requires the company (corporation) to marry the digital transformation process.

> ✏ **Definitions**
>
> **Company** Legal entity formed by a group of individuals to engage in and operate a business—commercial or industrial—enterprise. A company may be organized in various ways for tax and financial liability purposes depending on the corporate law of its jurisdiction.[1]
>
> **Corporation** Legal entity that is separate and distinct from its owners. Corporations enjoy most of the rights and responsibilities that an individual possesses; that is, a corporation has the right to enter into contracts, loan and borrow money, sue and be sued, hire employees, own assets, and pay taxes.[2]

For the sake of simplicity, in the rest of the book, the umbrella term "company" will refer to companies, corporations, and other business entities.

---

[1] https://www.investopedia.com/terms/c/company.asp (Last checked August 2020).

[2] https://www.investopedia.com/terms/c/corporation.asp (Last checked August 2020).

© The Author(s), under exclusive license to
Springer Nature Switzerland AG 2021
R. Di Pietro et al., *New Dimensions of Information Warfare*, Advances in
Information Security 84, https://doi.org/10.1007/978-3-030-60618-3_6

> ✐ **Definitions**
>
> **Digital Transformation** Process of integrating digital technologies to create new (or modify existing) business processes, culture, and customer experiences to meet changing business and market requirements. In the digital age, this process is called digital transformation.[3]

While on the one hand, the digital transformation leads to increased transparency and easier collaboration processes for the company, on the other hand, it introduces new types of cybersecurity risks that cannot be addressed by relying on traditional, existing solutions. Confidential information, such as patents, productive processes, or knowledge about the most valuable assets, are now stored on (and accessible from) the Web and shared with the employees involved in the project, in many cases going out from any possible cybersecurity perimeter previously established.

How are the integrity, confidentiality, and availability of such information guaranteed? On which media are such information exchanged? In the event some third-party information exchange service is involved, how can the company trust it?

This chapter will analyze how information warfare could threaten a nation by jeopardizing specific type of residing companies that heavily contribute to its economic and intellectual wealth, including (i) nation's companies; (ii) companies that have a strong impact on a nation's GDP; (iii) companies that support nation's critical infrastructures; and (iv) companies that allow the nation to boast leadership in specific sectors.

Compromising such companies would have serious repercussions for the nation in which they operate, causing significant economic damage in some cases, jeopardizing the strategic plans of the nation in others. In the first scenario, we evaluate the risks faced by companies that do not manage properly their outgoing flow of information, while in the second scenario, we consider infrastructureless companies, showing how the migration on the cloud may open the door to unexpected threats.

6.1 Scenario 1: Unwary Company

The accurate management of outgoing information is crucial for companies, as it allows them to know the flow of information strangers would have access to from the outside. In the current era, where wealth mostly resides in data and information, providing potential adversaries with any free source of information may needlessly jeopardize the safety of the entire company. Information which at first glance may

---

[3]https://www.salesforce.com/eu/products/platform/what-is-digital-transformation/ (Last checked August 2020).

seem harmless may have fatal consequences for the company. To make an example, the disclosure of information about the employees of companies, such as their names and positions, although apparently harmless, may lead to targeted social engineering attacks, blackmail, and dozens more dangerous threats.

In this scenario, we will take into account a company that manages the flow of outgoing information unwisely. Those information are neither analyzed nor filtered, even if this would ensure less exposure to external hazards.

6.1.1 Threat: Information Gathering

In this threat, an adversary exploits information companies unwittingly make available, to achieve different goals, e.g., better identifying the attack surface of the company, obtaining detailed information about the strategic plans of the company, and possibly others.

To accurately describe the risks faced by any company that does not carefully manage its outgoing flow of information, the first step consists in identifying where the wealth of the company mainly resides. Companies may boast human capital, structural capital, relational capital, or a combination of them, eventually composing their intellectual capital, depicted in Fig. 6.1.

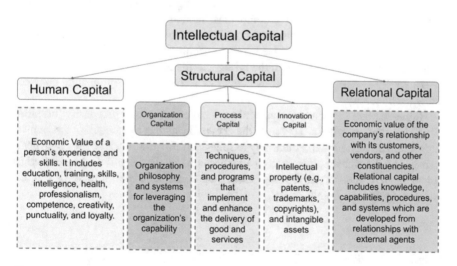

Fig. 6.1 Intellectual capital of a company

Human Capital-Based Companies

> In the long run, your human capital is your main base of competition. Your leading indicator
> of where you are going to be 20 years from now is how well you are doing in your education
> system.—Bill Gates

Human capital-based companies refer to those companies whose business and
economy heavily revolve around their human capital.

✐ Definitions

Human Capital Economic value of a person's experience and skills. This
term includes education, training, skills, intelligence, health, professionalism,
competence, creativity, and other values, such as punctuality and loyalty.

Human capital is strongly correlated to the economic growth of a company,
since expanding the skills and the knowledge of employees has visible effects on
the development of an economy. However, being inherent in people, human capital
cannot be owned by a company. Indeed, if the company has not made any effort to
allow the transfer of knowledge among employees or to effectively train the new
ones, as soon as they leave the company, the human capital will be lost as well.

Although any company substantially relies on human capital, many of them may
never afford to lose employees that are occupying strategic roles, crucial for the
company's business. Technology companies, such as Google, Facebook, Amazon,
and Microsoft, although having mind-boggling market capitalization, are among the
companies that make this list. Indeed, losing specific professional figures would lead
to irreparable damage, since both the hiring and the integration of new figures may
take a while. The frenetic pace to which today's companies are subjected does not
allow such "luxury."

Human capital in such companies plays a key role for their prosperity (or, more
often, for their survival). Thus, all the means available to safeguard the human
capital should be adopted. Potentially harmless information, such as the company's
staff list on the website, may lead to unexpected risks. For example, the competing
company may acquire all the key human resources with the promise of a more
important role (or a higher salary).

Relational Capital-Based Companies

Relational capital-based companies refer to those companies whose business and
economy heavily revolve around their relational capital.

> ✐ **Definitions**
>
> **Relational Capital** The economic value of the company's relationship with its customers, vendors, and other constituencies. Relational capital includes knowledge, capabilities, procedures, and systems, which are developed from relationships with external agents.[4]

Relational capital refers to the economy resulting from the relationship with all the players outside the company, such as vendors and customers. The supply chain of a company is an integral part of the relational capital.

> ✐ **Definitions**
>
> **Supply Chain** Network between a company and its suppliers to produce and distribute specific products to the final buyer. The network includes different activities, people, entities, information, and resources.[5]

The supply chain developed by a company is (at least) important as the company itself. Indeed, without a correct, resilient, and redundant supply chain, even the most promising business may fail. In the technological and information era, supply chains tend to be lightweight and optimized to meet the needs of efficiency and speed. However, these characteristics come at a cost that, most of the time, is paid by security. The interruption of the supply chain provokes delays in the best cases, while, in the worst cases, it may lead to significant (or worst, irreversible) damage to the company's business. Cyberattacks are a frequent cause of its interruption and are usually carried out by crafty attackers against the least defended links of the chain. Indeed, an adversary may exploit the apparently harmless information provided by the company to create a detailed map of the supply chain and put in place a specific attack to impair the weakest links. By compromising an essential element of the supply chain, the adversary would be able to reach the goal without attacking the target company directly.

This kind of attack is incredibly effective. While a company may rely on effective defenses, such as powerful security perimeters, to thwart any potential attacks, the security coverage it may provide to the supply chain is extremely low, due to its limited reach.

---

[4]https://en.wikipedia.org/wiki/Relational_capital (Last checked August 2020).

[5]https://investopedia.com/terms/s/supplychain.asp (Last checked August 2020).

Structural Capital-Based Companies

Structural capital-based companies refer to those companies whose business and economy heavily revolve around their structural capital.

> ✐ **Definitions**
>
> **Structural Capital** The economic value of the supportive infrastructures, processes, and databases of the organization that enables human capital to operate correctly. It includes capabilities, routines, methods, procedures, and methodologies embedded in the organization.[6]

Structural capital is an umbrella term that includes three sub-capitals: organization capital, process capital, and innovation capital. The organization capital refers to the culture of the company. The culture of a company, sometimes referred to as the personality of a company, defines the environment in which the employees work and a variety of other elements, such as the company mission, value, ethics, goals, and expectations.[7] In the long term, the organizational capital may be the capital that suffers the most from external attacks, especially the ones performed by powerful actors.

It is worth noting that the culture of a company is not, and cannot be, something written in stone. On the contrary, it is very fluid and dynamic, though sometimes it takes time to recognize that it has changed. A recent example is provided by Google which has deeply modified, if not abandoned, its once proverbial internal openness among Googlers. This change has been ignited by the internal resistance to allowing the pentagon to use advanced surveillance project.[8] The resistance of the Googlers was in contrast with the strategic views of the enterprise, and the change installed by the top management has been strong and radical, reaching its apex with the resignation[9] of the long-time human resources chief Eileen Naughton that incarnated the original "Don't Be Evil" motto. The very same clause has been removed from its code of conduct in 2018.[10] All elements clearly indicate an evident shift toward a more S&P500 standardized company culture. Efforts in the same direction, that is, decoupling the human capital of a company from influencing the direction of the company itself (decided by executives and boards),

---

[6]https://en.wikipedia.org/wiki/Structural_capital (Last checked August 2020).

[7]https://thebalancecareers.com/what-is-company-culture-2062000 (Last checked August 2020).

[8]https://nytimes.com/2018/04/04/technology/google-letter-ceo-pentagon-project.html   (Last checked August 2020).

[9]https://theverge.com/2020/2/10/21132366/google-eileen-naughton-culture-hr-people-operations-step-down (Last checked August 2020).

[10]https://gizmodo.com/google-removes-nearly-all-mentions-of-dont-be-evil-from-1826153393 (Last checked August 2020).

have been also implemented by Amazon.[11] These are two examples that show that Big Tech is leaving less and less space for shaping the company to their very same employees. While this is commonly accepted and time-tested for standard manufacturing companies, the long-term effect of this steering in direction in the highly creative job domain is still to see.

The culture of a company is vital, since it provides behavioral guidelines for every situation. There can be situations in which a company has difficulty understanding which is the best way to proceed, especially during emergencies. A possible answer may be found by relying on a principle which, in turn, follows the culture of the company. In short, the culture of a company can be seen as a compass which, in case there is the need to make decisions in the total absence of information, indicates a viable path, consistent with the policies and the principles of the company.

Endangering the culture of a company would have devastating repercussions on its image, from both the economic and the social perspectives.

The process capital refers to intangible assets that a company can boast of to improve its business processes. Examples of assets are the design of business processes, the information used by employees to conduct them, the technologies and the systems to automate them, the tools to complete them, and the data used to plan, execute, and optimize them.[12]

The innovation capital, instead, includes the intangible assets that allow a company to innovate. Examples of such assets are the brand, the competitive advantages, data that are used for the experiments, ideas, and, most importantly, the intellectual property (e.g., patents, trademarks, copyright).

Companies that owe their success to both their process capital and innovation capital must guard against disseminating information that can provide attackers with clues. The difficulty lies in reaching the perfect trade-off between transparency and security. On the one hand, the company which provides detailed information about its business and its processes appears to be more reliable; on the other hand, the more information is made available to the general public, the more likely it is that some malicious actor will find ways to compromise the company.

Adversaries

Adversaries, drawing on the information the company has made available online, have the opportunity to undertake several attacks, depending on their goals. In this context, an adversary may be modeled either as honest but curious or as malicious.

---

[11] https://vox.com/technology/2018/10/18/17989482/google-amazon-employee-ethics-contracts (Last checked August 2020).

[12] https://simplicable.com/en/process-capital (Last checked August 2020).

> ✒ **Definitions**
>
> **Honest But Curious Adversary** In our context, an honest but curious adversary is an individual that will attempt to learn all possible information of a company from the content the company has made available online.

An honest but curious adversary may be a team from a company that collects public information about a competing company for the purpose of initiating an "unfair" competition (e.g., if it is an online shop, specific prices may be tuned, to disadvantage the trading of the competing company) and taking customers away from it. Large companies have the opportunity to do so, considering their workforce and the economic resources available.

A malicious adversary refers to an actor who plans to endanger the company with all available means. A malicious adversary can be external to the company, e.g., a competitor or an individual who has interests in compromising the company, or internal, e.g., a disgruntled employee who wants to take revenge on his company or who has suffered blackmail.

Although the attacker's ultimate goal is to create inconvenience to the company, the attack can take place against several targets. The adversaries can compromise the confidentiality of the resources (e.g., by disseminating information that should remain secret), the integrity of the resources (e.g., by forging official information), and the availability of the resources (e.g., by either deleting information made available by the company or obscuring company services).

6.1.2   Attacks and Countermeasures

In the information age, the ever-increasing presence of technology and automation is putting a huge strain on the security (and the privacy) of both individuals and companies. The amount of information collected by the Web, sometimes automatically, is surprisingly rich, and a failure (or even just an oversight) to manage it may lead to tragic consequences.

Technological progress has led to the creation of several powerful tools, which allow to effectively aggregate data on the Web to obtain the most information about something/someone in the shortest possible time. Two of the most famous and used tools are Maltego and Shodan.

Maltego is a software used for OSINT and forensics. It allows to create virtual entities (e.g., people, domains, locations) and to analyze real-world relationships among them. The sources of such information include DNS records, whois records, search engines, online social networks, online APIs, and various metadata [341].

Shodan is the world's first search engine for Internet-connected devices. Specifically, Shodan is a search engine for service banners. Service banners are metadata that the server sends back to the client during any communication. These banners contain a lot of specific information, such as the software implemented to the server and the supported services [342].

These tools reduce both the complexity and the time required of searching for information on the boundless Web and can be extremely dangerous in the wrong hands. To make an example, by relying on Maltego, an attacker may easily obtain information about the employees of a company, usually considered the weakest ring in the cybersecurity chain. Once the information is recovered, employees may be blackmailed, threatened, or simply forced (or convinced, through social engineering techniques) to disclose confidential information to the detriment of the company in which they work. There are countless resources on the Web that serve as guides for waging attacks on this kind. Indeed, the easiest way to circumvent a security policy is to find users who do not follow it. In the article "Use Maltego to target company email addresses that may be vulnerable from third-party breaches,"[13] the author shows how straightforward it is to "locate breached accounts created using company mail addresses, potentially giving the attacker the opportunity to access the company account if the employee re-uses a compromised password" (who has no idea it has been compromised). In a similar article entitled "How to use Maltego to research & mine data like an analyst,"[14] the same author shows how to perform information-gathering tasks with the aforementioned, powerful tool. He relies on the free edition of Maltego and shows how to identify employees of "The Guardian" who had their accounts compromised in data breaches.

Shodan can be exploited to obtain detailed information about the devices of a target geographical location (e.g., a nation). To make a significant example, authors in [343] show how it is possible to easily perform a vulnerability scanning of IoT devices in the whole Jordan. The IoT devices, from the cybersecurity point of view, are unique in their kind. Indeed, on the one hand, their cost and resource constraint would make any security check excessively expensive; on the other hand, their availability always played a higher priority when compared with their security (privacy). Unfortunately, critical infrastructures all over the world heavily rely on IoT devices. Thus, performing targeted attacks on specific devices within specific critical infrastructure would jeopardize the critical infrastructure itself, with potential critical repercussions on the nation in which it resides. The authors identified two types of vulnerabilities of the IoT devices: (i) disregard security patches, i.e., even when a cybersecurity threat is found, the patch to resolve/mitigate it is not applied due to lack of time/will, and (ii) default username and password, i.e., the devices are often put into operation with the standard credentials, easily findable both in the product manual and on the Web.

In a similar study [344], the authors exploited Shodan to study the exposure of IoT devices in India. They focus on the Industrial Control Systems and highlight the risks to expose devices on the Web without even employing the simplest form of protection.

---

[13]https://null-byte.wonderhowto.com/how-to/use-maltego-target-company-email-addresses-may-be-vulnerable-from-third-party-breaches-0184453/ (Last checked August 2020).

[14]https://null-byte.wonderhowto.com/how-to/video-use-maltego-research-mine-data-like-analyst-0180985/ (Last checked August 2020).

Although the aforementioned information was already available on the Web, without an aggregator, their collection would have been extremely time-consuming and would have probably discouraged any attackers. Furthermore, it may be possible that some information is not indexed by the common search engines and cannot be easily retrieved manually.

Shodan and Maltego are just two of the many tools available. Other interesting projects have been listed in the resource box below.

📂 **Resources**

Other Interesting Projects

- **Google Dorks.**[15] Computer hacking techniques that exploit Google applications and services, such as Google search, to find security holes in the websites.
- **TheHarvester.**[16] Open-source tool to analyze a company's external threat landscape on the Internet. The tool allows to gather emails, subdomains, IPs, URLs, and names, by relying on 27 different public data sources, including LinkedIn, Google, and Twitter.
- **Recon-Ng.**[17] Open-source, modular framework that provides an intuitive environment to perform reconnaissance on a target.
- **SpiderFoot.**[18] Open-source automation tool that, with more than 170 modules, integrates results from every data source available and provides effective data analysis methods.
- **Creepy.**[19] Open-source geolocation intelligence tool that offers geolocation information gathered from social networking platforms.
- **Metagoofil.**[20] Open-source tool that allows extracting metadata of public documents (e.g., pdf, doc, ppt, xls) in target websites.
- **CheckUsernames.**[21] Website that allows checking for the presence of a particular username on more than 150 websites.
- **hunter.io.**[22] Website that allows finding names and email addresses found online of all the people working for a company.
- **Others.** The top 150 OSINT projects have been gathered here.[23]

---

[15] https://en.wikipedia.org/wiki/Google_hacking (Last checked August 2020).

[16] https://github.com/laramies/theHarvester (Last checked August 2020).

[17] https://github.com/lanmaster53/recon-ng (Last checked August 2020).

[18] https://spiderfoot.net/ (Last checked August 2020).

[19] https://geocreepy.com/ (Last checked August 2020).

[20] https://github.com/laramies/metagoofil (Last checked August 2020).

[21] https://checkusernames.com/ (Last checked August 2020).

[22] https://hunter.io/ (Last checked August 2020).

[23] https://awesomeopensource.com/projects/osint (Last checked August 2020).

It is worth to notice that all the tools making this list (and many others), although downright dangerous in the hands of any attackers, can be effectively used by defenders to analyze the current leakage of information, as well as the weak links in the chain, and take remedial actions, thus enhancing security. The company may put itself in the shoes of the attacker and try to discover to which information it would have access from outside. Information attackers would have access to include leaks coming from unexpected sources via unforeseen and not monitored communication channels, such as the impact that the company has on the online community (i.e., its sentiment) and the impact on the markets. More importantly, the company may get information that would allow assessing its exposed attack surface. After a careful identification and dedicated analysis, the company may implement and adopt new countermeasures to reduce the vulnerable surface and further improve its protection.

Usually, the defensive phase consists of three main steps:

1. **Hack yourself:** a company can start gathering information on itself by relying on Open-Source Intelligence techniques. The company may either hire an external team of experts, with the risk of disclosing information regarding its exposure to threats, or it can form an internal team in charge of carrying out such hack.
2. **Evaluate:** the information recovered is processed, analyzed, and evaluated, to assess to what extent it may represent a threat for the company.
3. **Control:** the sources of information that may lead to tedious consequences are evaluated, and their outgoing flows are filtered, to lower the risk of exposure to attacks. **Repeat Step 1.**

The three steps are repeated until the threats caused by the outgoing information are eliminated (or below a satisfactory threshold, chosen by the parties).

6.1.3   Open Issues and Future Directions

The disarming simplicity with which information is shared on the Web hides the resulting effects. Until the advent of today's technology, the damages were limited, due to the vastness of the Web and the difficulty of obtaining useful and detailed information in plausible times. Indeed, in the past, information was considered unknowingly safe due to the difficulty of finding them in the tangle of the Internet. However, the derived risks of sharing information became evident after the dissemination of tools that allow rapid aggregation and indexing of the material on the Web. The concepts of "security by obscurity" and "security by complexity" have become obsolete, and there is an obvious need to develop and implement more effective security solutions.

Risk Analysis

To develop an effective protection plan, every company has to carry out a risk analysis to identify the critical assets to protect and the adversaries that may potentially be interested in jeopardizing them.

> ✒ **Definitions**
>
> **Risk Analysis** Process of identifying critical assets and analyzing potential issues that may negatively impact key business initiatives or processes.[24]

The risk analysis is carried out by either internal or external teams that interact with the Chief Executive Officer of the company and other appointed internal members. The first step usually consists of identifying and prioritizing critical assets of the company and includes three phases:

- **Document analysis.** The risk analysis team obtains a set of documents from the company to identify its core businesses. Examples of these documents are the business continuity plan and any risk analysis report carried out in the past.
- **Critical asset identification.** The analysis of these documents allows to identify the critical assets of the company. An asset becomes critical for a company when a fail of a fraction of the asset affects the business of the company.
- **Continuous verification of critical assets.** The list of critical assets is continuously reviewed to assess their priority. It is worth noting that the ideal list of critical assets is extremely dynamic: it has to be continuously modified by adding or removing items according to changes in the threat landscape that, in order to ensure accurate and timely remedial actions, should always be monitored.

Although detailed guidelines are available, a unique procedure to identify and prioritize critical assets does not exist. Indeed, the resulting critical assets list and the prioritization of any item contained, besides varying due to several factors such as the type of the company, its location (i.e., the US branch of a company may have different critical assets than a European branch), the threat landscape, etc., also vary over time. The difficulty in drawing up an accurate list comes from the fact that a non-critical asset today may become critical tomorrow. Furthermore, the initial draft of the critical assets list is extremely biased with respect to the documents that have been received from the company. What if the previous risk analysis did not consider all critical assets? What if the previous risk analysis was correct but based on an incorrect business continuity plan?

The prioritization of the assets is an onerous task itself, prone to errors that are difficult to detect and to manage, and it represents only the first step of the procedure.

---

[24]https://searchsecurity.techtarget.com/definition/risk-analysis (Last checked August 2020).

Indeed, the threats, together with the vulnerabilities suffered from the critical assets and the countermeasures to develop, are still off the scene.

This makes it clear how the dynamic environment driven by new technologies makes it complex for companies to keep up. The risk analysis, in particular, would be a complex process even when the dust settles, and the changes information warfare is continuously bringing to the threat landscape only makes the situation worse. The creation of information warfare tools and techniques allowed assets that were not previously considered critical to becoming so, thus leading to the need to evaluate changes in the priority of the various assets over time.

Even if the information has always been around, scattered in the tangle of the Internet and available to everyone, the presence of algorithms that traverse them and effectively pull out data can jeopardize assets that were considered non-critical only because no such technology was available. Many times, indeed, an asset is considered to be critical for a company a posteriori, when the company has already lost business due to its compromise.

A case in point concerns the Cambridge Analytica data scandal that happened in early 2018. Cambridge Analytica gathered personal data of millions of Facebook users through an app originally created to build psychological profiles on users. The profiles of American voters have been sold to provide assistance and analytics to the political campaigns of some candidates. Although information was public and easy to obtain, the aggregation of them dramatically influenced American elections. To pay the price was also the reputation of Facebook social network, with Mark Zuckerberg, its Chief Executive Officer, forced to testify in front of Congress. After the data scandal, Facebook's share dropped by 19%, more than $119 billion has been wiped off Facebook's market value, and the company was fined $5 billion by the Federal Trade Commission.[25]

Defensive OSINT

As in the case of penetration testing (where companies hire professionals to attack the system to assess their security), companies may have the opportunity to hire OSINT professional to analyze the information they are exposing to the Web (i.e., to the whole world) and calculate an exposition value. Although in the literature OSINT techniques and their application have been widely analyzed [345–349], all the studies focus on the attacker's point of view. The branch that describes the most effective usage of OSINT techniques for defensive purposes is still missing, and, in the era of big data, it may open up a critical research topic.

---

[25] https://www.theguardian.com/technology/2018/jul/26/facebook-market-cap-falls-109bn-dollars-after-growth-shock (Last checked August 2020).

6.2   Scenario 2: Infrastructureless Company

The advent of the Internet is creating a data-driven world. Companies are racing to keep up with the shift to an economy that is increasingly digital. This new economy revolves around the adoption of new technologies, such as the IoT, artificial intelligence, and autonomous vehicles, all of them requiring pay-per-use, just-in-time, and on-demand features through performing infrastructures. To meet these needs, companies may rely on either in-house servers or cloud servers. The benefits of relying on the cloud are countless, including a reduction in IT costs, scalability, business continuity, collaboration efficiency, flexibility, mobility, elasticity, and access to automatic updates, to name a few. This has prompted most companies to opt for this alternative.

In this scenario we will consider a company that does not rely on in-house servers, thus voluntarily outsourcing its data, information, and services to the cloud. This company does not directly manage the security of the outsourcing material, thus ending up outsourcing security as well. Indeed, by relying on cloud servers, the information is likely to get out of the security perimeter built by the company that will no longer have control over them. Relying on cloud servers means embracing the cloud computing concept.

> ✐ **Definitions**
>
> **Cloud Computing** Cloud computing is a model for enabling ubiquitous, convenient, on-demand network access to a shared pool of configurable computing resources that can be rapidly provisioned and released with minimal management effort or service provider interaction. The computing resources term includes networks, servers, storage, applications, and services.[26]

The cloud model is composed of five main characteristics, three service models, and four deployment models that are briefly described in the following box.

> ✐ **Definitions**
>
> **Cloud Essential Characteristics**
>
> - *On-demand self-service.* A consumer may unilaterally provision computing capabilities as needed automatically.

(continued)

---

[26]https://nvlpubs.nist.gov/nistpubs/Legacy/SP/nistspecialpublication800-145.pdf (Last checked August 2020).

- *Broad network access.* Capabilities are available over the network and accessed through standard mechanisms that promote use by heterogeneous thin or thick client platforms.
- *Resource pooling.* The computing resources of the provider are pooled to serve multiple consumers using a multi-tenant model, with different physical (and virtual) resources dynamically assigned according to the demand of the consumer.
- *Rapid elasticity.* Capabilities are elastically provisioned and released to rapidly scale and accommodate the demand.
- *Measured service.* Cloud systems automatically control and optimize resource by relying on a metering capability at some level of abstraction according to the type of service.

Cloud Service Models (Depicted in Fig. 6.2)

- *Software as a Service (SaaS).* The consumer may use the provider's applications running on a cloud infrastructure.
- *Platform as a Service (PaaS).* The consumer may deploy onto the cloud infrastructure consumer-created or acquired applications.
- *Infrastructure as a Service (IaaS).* The consumer may deploy and run arbitrary software and has control over processing, networks, storage, and other computing resources.

Cloud Deployment Models

- *Private cloud.* The cloud infrastructure is provisioned exclusively for the usage of a single organization.
- *Community cloud.* The cloud infrastructure is provisioned exclusively for the usage of a specific community of consumers from organizations that have shared concerns.
- *Public cloud.* The cloud infrastructure is provisioned for open use by the general public.
- *Hybrid cloud.* The cloud infrastructure is a composition of two or more distinct cloud infrastructures described above.

In the cloud computing context, several security questions may arise. What would happen if the third-party service does not manage the security and privacy of data and information properly? Who should be responsible for the security and privacy of outsourced data and services?

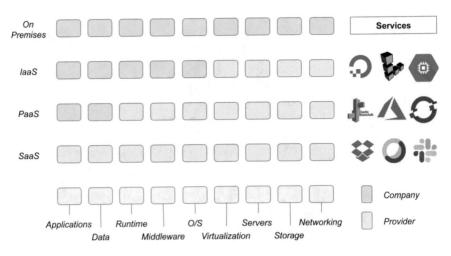

Fig. 6.2 Cloud service models

6.2.1 Threat: Outsourcing of Security

The threat relies on the disclosure of information about the company caused by the adoption of third-party services that are outside the company security perimeter.

Although companies are taking strong advantages of the cloud options available (i.e., 69% of enterprises are moving business-critical applications to the cloud[27]), the integrity and confidentiality of information always seem to be considered secondary aspects, of lesser importance than the service offered. Yet, should a data breach happen, the reputation of the business would be strongly affected. According to the Global Cloud Security Study carried out in 2019 by Thales,[28] 48% of all the corporate data is stored in the cloud (compared to 35% in 2016), but only 49% of organizations are encrypting sensitive data in the cloud. Furthermore, although 78% of the organizations recognize the importance of retaining ownership of the encryption keys, only 53% of the businesses that encrypt their data on the cloud are controlling the encryption keys. Another interesting Cloud Security Report by Crowd Research Partners confirms cloud security as a major concern for security professionals. The top three cloud security challenges, according to the experts, include protecting against data loss and leakage (67%), threats to data privacy (61%), and breaches of confidentiality (53%).[29]

This demand for cloud computing by companies has led to substantial investments by the big protagonists of this cloud revolution, to expand their data centers

---

[27] https://www.techrepublic.com/article/69-of-enterprises-moving-business-critical-applications-to-the-cloud/ (Last checked August 2020).

[28] https://cpl.thalesgroup.com/cloud-security-research (Last checked August 2020).

[29] https://crowdresearchpartners.com/portfolio/cloud-security-report/ (Last checked August 2020).

and provide additional services to more and more requesting entities. Indeed, the cloud computing market is predicted to grow globally at a 30% CAGR extending to $270 billion in 2020,[30] and in the past years, companies, such as Google, Facebook, Amazon, Alibaba, and Microsoft, led the market on Hyperscale data center investments in over 100 facilities with a power capacity of over 15MW.[31] Google, in particular, in its 2020 plan, announced to invest more than $10 billion in offices and data centers distributed in California, Colorado, Georgia, Massachusetts, Nebraska, New York, Ohio, Oklahoma, Pennsylvania, Texas, and Washington.[32]

Although the figures are mind-boggling and the adoption of cloud technologies by companies is increasingly widespread, several cybersecurity risks are not allowing adopters to sleep soundly. The major cybersecurity challenges in 2020 have been listed by Cloud Security Alliance in their website,[33] of which we report the top seven in the following:

1. **Data breaches.** Data breaches may have catastrophic consequences for a business and are considered the major cybersecurity threat in the cloud. Indeed, a data breach may have a strong impact on the reputation of the company, on its brand, as well as on the trust of customers, partners, or stakeholders, thus causing a decrease in the market value. Intellectual properties, such as patents, trade secrets, trademarks, and copyrights, may be lost and exploited by competitors. In an interesting research report commissioned by Egress and independently conducted by Opinion Matters, the authors highlighted worrying statistics: while 79% (61%) of IT leaders believe employees have put sensitive company data at risk accidentally (intentionally) in the last 12 months, 92% (91%) of the employees claim they haven't accidentally (intentionally) broken company policy when sharing information. This highlights the policy issues that may arise within a traditional company, which can only become larger and more dangerous in cloud environments. On the one hand, 60% of the IT leaders believe they will be victims of an accidental data breach in the next year; on the other hand, 55% of the employees that intentionally share data against company rules (thus potentially becoming the cause of these data breaches) claim that their organization did not provide them with the tools needed to share sensitive data securely.[34]

---

[30]https://financhill.com/blog/investing/7-challenges-businesses-face-moving-cloud (Last checked August 2020).

[31]https://www.globenewswire.com/news-release/2020/02/14/1985327/0/en/The-global-data-center-market-is-expected-to-grow-at-a-CAGR-of-over-2-during-the-period-2019-2025.html (Last checked August 2020).

[32]https://www.theverge.com/2020/2/26/21154358/google-10-billion-offices-data-centers-investment-sundar-pichai (Last checked August 2020).

[33]https://cloudsecurityalliance.org/blog/2020/02/18/cloud-security-challenges-in-2020/   (Last checked August 2020).

[34]https://scoop-cms.s3.amazonaws.com/566e8c75ca2f3a5d5d8b45ae/documents/egress-opinionmatters-insider-threat-research-report-a4-uk-digital.pdf (Last checked August 2020).

2. **Misconfiguration and inadequate change control.** The Alteryx's data breach is still vivid in anyone's mind and grants this threat a rightful place on the podium. A misconfigured Amazon Web Storage Service (S3) cloud storage bucket caused Alteryx, a marketing analytics firm, to accidentally made the personal information of 123 million American households public, including addresses, phone numbers, mortgage ownership, age, ethnicity, and personal interests, for a total of 248 fields per household.[35]

3. **Lack of cloud security architecture and strategy.** Although many companies are migrating portions of their IT infrastructure to public clouds, the process of implementing appropriate security architectures to protect from cyberattacks is still a mystery for many of them. It is still a common belief that data, process, and other assets of a company simply need to be transported to the cloud, along with the security mechanisms that were implemented within the company. The threat landscape, however, is completely different, and new threats, potentially coming from new and unthinkable sources, must be taken into account [350].

4. **Insufficient identity, credential, access, and key management.** Certain traditional IT security paradigms have to be rethought when approaching cloud technologies; the Identity and Access Management (IAM) is among them. The cloud owner has to deal with IAM without compromising the confidentiality and integrity of the hosted data.

5. **Account hijacking.** Account hijacking is defined as the process of stealing (or hijack) an account, thus impersonating the owner of the account on the platform to conduct unauthorized (often malicious) activities. Cloud account hijacking may be particularly calamitous since both the company's integrity and reputation can be compromised.

6. **Insider threat.** According to a Cloud Security Report conducted in 2018 by Netwrix, 58% of the companies attribute security breaches and incidents to insiders. The main causes of these incidents can be found in the negligence of the employees (64%), criminal insiders (23%), and credential theft (13%). Among the common scenarios, the Cloud Security Alliance report lists the misconfiguration of cloud servers, storing sensitive company's data and information on insecure personal devices and systems, and phishing emails.

7. **Insecure interfaces and APIs.** To interact with cloud computing technologies, cloud providers usually expose APIs to the customers. The security of these APIs, believe it or not, will directly affect the security of the cloud service they are allowing the interaction with. Access control mechanisms and strong authentication have to be put in place to protect the service against accidental (and more importantly malicious) attempts to circumvent the security policy, to avoid data breaches.

---

[35]https://www.latimes.com/business/technology/la-fi-tn-alteryx-data-breach-20171222-story.html (Last checked August 2020).

6.2.2   Attacks and Countermeasures

In this section, we first provide an overview of the concepts of trust and security perimeter, showing how they take on a different meaning following the transition to the cloud. Then, we describe the new attacks that can be carried out by dividing them into three categories, each representing a possible target:

- *Confidentiality.* How the concept of multitenancy is considered an outstanding feature for the cloud computing paradigm, but an extremely dangerous one when it comes to cybersecurity.
- *Integrity.* The ALCOA+ principle and the data integrity schemes are introduced, together with the features they need to have and the description of the most relevant studies in the literature.
- *Availability.* Both DoS and DDoS attacks are introduced, together with their types, interesting statistics, main motivations, and effective countermeasures.

Trust in the Cloud

The concept of trust has already been used in computer networks, distributed systems, and game theory, to name a few, and has different meanings depending on the application domain. In this section, we borrow the definition introduced by Huang et al. [351].

✐ Definitions

Trustor   Entity that trusts another entity.

Trustee   Entity who takes responsibility that may be trusted by the trustor.

Trust (For Cloud Computing)   Trust is a mental state comprising:

- expectancy: the trustor expects a specific behavior from the trustee
- belief: the trustor believes that the expected behavior occurs, based on the evidence of the trustee's competence, integrity, and goodwill
- willingness to take the risk: the trustor is willing to take the risk for that belief

---

The authors identified two types of trust, based on the expectancy of the trustor: the *trust in performance* and *the trust in belief. Trust in performance* is about what the trustee performs, while the *trust in belief* is about what the trustee believes. Differently from trust in belief, trust in performance is not transitive and can propagate through trust in belief.

While in traditional architectures trust may be "easily" enforced by relying on security policies, in cloud environments the complexity increases. Indeed, since the governance of data is outsourced to third-party entities, logically and, most of the time, even geographically far away from the owner's control, the trust depends on the deployment model (i.e., public, community, private, or hybrid cloud), but the control (and therefore, the security) of data and information is always in the hands of the infrastructure owners. These entities have the burden of enforcing security policies and implementing protection mechanisms to reduce the risks and minimize the threats.

Security Perimeter in the Cloud

The cloud environment completely revolutionized the perception of security perimeter [352].

> **⬚ Definitions**
>
> **Security Perimeter** Set of systems, technologies, and security policies that provides levels of protection on a conceptual borderline against remote malicious activities.

Traditionally, a security perimeter was maintained by relying on a physical entity built by piling up security modules to form an organization's cyber fortress. Additional pieces were added (or the current ones were updated) to keep up with changes in the dynamic threat landscape. Just as crown jewels were encircled with multiple layers of defense and castles were surrounded with moats, to protect the towers and keep the enemies away, nowadays, in traditional architectures, firewalls, antivirus, and other security mechanisms are put in place to protect the information inside the security perimeter and discourage any attacker. The more obstacles the defenders rely on, the more difficult they would make it for the attacker to overcome the fortifications.

However, with the wide adoption of cloud computing technologies, assets may continuously enter and leave the security perimeter, and any potential fortress would crumble. Valuable company's information is no longer sitting in a single place, thus making walls no longer enough.[36]

If we analyze the cloud technologies from a security point of view, i.e., from the security perimeter perspective, they appear decidedly outside the trust borderline. However, they allow implementing business processes and services essential for the companies. Given that placing a virtual security wall around a company became impossible because of the essential outsourced services, there is the need to

---

[36]https://symantec-enterprise-blogs.security.com/blogs/product-insights/cloud-security-era-vanishing-perimeter (Last checked August 2020).

accurately identify, authenticate, authorize, and monitor the actors that are accessing the critical assets of companies [352].

Confidentiality

The National Institute of Standard and Technology (NIST) defines the term confidentiality as "Preserving authorized restrictions on information access and disclosure, including means for protecting personal privacy and proprietary information."[37] The definition is the same when applied to cloud computing contexts, but the task of protecting data from unauthorized access becomes more difficult due to the dynamic nature of the environment. Indeed, in the cloud computing context, the increased number of parties, the increased numbers of points of access, and the dynamic security policies adopted by the cloud infrastructure owner make the confidentiality methods that were enforced in the company obsolete and not very effective. A company can either deal personally with the protection of the confidentiality of their data and information on the cloud, investing resources, or delegate control to the cloud, making data and information accessible to further actors.

Among the most feared enemies of data confidentiality, there is one of the most powerful architectures of the cloud computing who has strongly contributed to making it successful: multitenancy.

> ✏ **Definitions**
>
> **Multitenancy** Architecture in which a single instance of a software application operates in a shared environment and is used by multiple customers, called tenants.

The cloud infrastructure owners rely on the multitenancy architecture to make the most of the resources available. Tenants are virtually (i.e., the hardware is shared) isolated, and each software application is virtually partitioned to allow each tenant to work with a customized virtual application instance. However, as it often happens, if on the one hand sharing resources brings benefits from an economic and efficiency point of view, on the other hand, sharing resources is extremely dangerous when the confidentiality of data and information has to be preserved.

How can a company be sure that data and information have been kept confidential? How are the isolation and separation implemented for the tenant data? Do other tenants have the opportunity to access our data? Does the cloud infrastructure personnel have access to our data? Does the confidential data stored on a cloud

---

[37] https://csrc.nist.gov/glossary/term/confidentiality (Last checked August 2020).

remain confidential from third parties? In case there is an involuntary leakage of confidential data, what would be the countermeasures by the cloud?

The confidentiality of data, information, and services in cloud infrastructures is strongly correlated with user authentication. Indeed, access to resources such as documents, memory, databases, etc. should be strongly authenticated in order to avoid unauthorized parties to snoop around confidential resources [352].

Integrity

For the concept of integrity, we borrow again the definition of the National Institute of Standard and Technology (NIST). Integrity is defined as "Guarding against improper information or destruction, and includes ensuring information non-repudiation and authenticity."[38] Even in this case, the definition is the same when applied to cloud computing contexts, while the task of protecting the integrity of data is more challenging.

To ensure the integrity of data, the ALCOA principle may be taken into account. ALCOA, that is, the acronym of the adjectives Attributable, Legible, Contemporaneous, Original, and Accurate, can be seen as a framework (or a set of principles) to ensure integrity of data. In an extended version, ALCOA became ALCOA+, and added to the adjectives that made up the acronym were the terms Complete, Consistent, Enduring, and Available. The principles are detailed in the following:[39]

- **Attributable.** The data has to be traceable back to the individual who generated the information.
- **Legible.** The data has to be readable and permanent.
- **Contemporaneous.** The data related to results, measurements, etc. has to be recorded at the time the measurement is performed.
- **Accurate.** The data has to be truthful and representative of facts.
- **Complete.** The data has to contain all the information available until the moment it has been recorded. It has to be subject to audit trails to show that no information has been deleted or lost.
- **Consistent.** The data has to be coherent with the use companies make of it and with the specific characteristics they expect it to have.
- **Enduring.** The data has to be long-lasting and therefore properly preserved.
- **Available.** The data has to be accessible.

Outsourcing data to Cloud Service Providers introduces new, insidious challenges from the data integrity point of view. How can a company be sure that the Cloud Service Provider is actually storing their data without tampering with them? Over the years, many data integrity schemes have been proposed, to check

---

[38]https://csrc.nist.gov/glossary/term/integrity (Last checked August 2020).

[39]http://www.pharmtech.com/alcoa-and-data-integrity (Last checked August 2020).

the integrity of outsourced data and understand how reliable the Cloud Service Provider is.

Most of the data integrity schemes are probabilistic and involve three different entities: (i) the data owner, (ii) the Cloud Service Provider, and (iii) an auditor that has the burden of verifying the integrity of data. The latter can be either the data owner itself (private auditability) or a third-party auditor (public auditability). Data integrity schemes consist of two phases: a preprocessing phase and a verification phase, respectively. In the preprocessing phase, the data that has to be outsourced is preprocessed, and some additional metadata is generated. Both the data and the metadata will be used in the verification phase. The auditor sends a challenge to the Cloud Service Provider that relies on the data and the related metadata to generate the proof of possession. The auditor will be able to verify the proof to ensure that the integrity of the outsourced data is preserved.

In the following, some of the most important properties a data integrity scheme is preferable to possess are described [353].

- **Soundness.** A Cloud Service Provider should not be able to successfully perform a verification challenge without actually holding the original data. Although a malicious server may be able to corrupt the data (data integrity schemes are not tamper-resistant), once it did, it should not be able to pass the verification challenge (data integrity schemes are tamper-evident).
- **Remote verification.** Also known as blockless verification. Given the potential size of the file blocks to verify, a verifier should be able to perform verification without retrieving the file block from the remote server. The Cloud Service Provider should rely on the original file block to generate a (lightweight) proof of possession that will be then verified by the verifier.
- **Privacy preserving.** During the verification process, the verifier should not be able to obtain confidential information about the data. This property is critical when public auditability is performed (i.e., when the data owner delegates the responsibility of verifying the integrity of data to a third-party auditor).
- **Fairness.** A data integrity scheme should guarantee protection to honest Cloud Service Providers against dishonest users who intend to accuse the Cloud Service Provider unjustly for data manipulation/tampering that has never happened. Users may want to perform such an accusation to damage the reputation of the Cloud Service Provider or for other reasons.
- **Unrestricted challenge frequency.** Also known as unbounded queries. There should not be restrictions on the number of challenges made by an auditor to verify the integrity of the data. Being probabilistic, the verification of the integrity of outsourced data cannot be a one-shot activity. Furthermore, the data can be corrupted some time after the successful verification of integrity. For this reason, the client may want to execute the verification protocol after several time intervals.
- **Stateless verification.** Every verification challenge is independent of all the verification challenges performed in the past. This implies that neither the data

owner nor the Cloud Service Provider needs to store the results of the previous verification challenges.

- **Robustness.** Usually, deterministic data integrity schemes suffer from limitations due to the computational cost. This makes them unpractical when it comes to verifying the integrity of large datasets. Probabilistic approaches, instead, randomly choose samples of data to perform integrity verifications. Since relying on probabilistic approaches minor corruptions may go unnoticed, robustness is the property that enhances the soundness of data integrity by allowing to identify those tiny corruptions.
- **Data recovery.** Assessing the misbehavior of the Cloud Service Provider by identifying corruptions and tampering with data is important, but even more important is to recover the data in such cases. Not all data integrity schemes provide support for data recovery and the ones who did rely on error correcting codes (ECC) to perform the recovery.
- **Dynamic data handling.** Most of the data integrity schemes proposed in the literature allow to check for the integrity of the static data (i.e., backup of data or archives that do not support operations such as insertions, modifications, or deletions) and do not manage dynamic data. This is a heavy limitation since nowadays the outsourced data and services are mostly dynamic and subject to constant mutations to be reliable. This property allows to claiming that data integrity is preserved even after insertion, modification, or deletion operations.

➡ Resources

Some of the Data Integrity Schemes in the Literature

- [354]: **Provable data possession at untrusted stores.**
  The provable data possession model generates probabilistic proofs of possession by sampling random sets of blocks from the server, while the client maintains metadata to verify the proof. The amount of data transmitted during the challenge/response protocol is small to minimize network communication.
- [355]: **Scalable and efficient provable data possession.**
  The server is considered untrusted in terms of both security (e.g., it might maliciously erase data) and reliability (e.g., it might store data in offline storage devices). The provable data possession model implemented is based entirely on symmetric key cryptography and does not require any bulk encryption. Furthermore, the model proposed also considers dynamic data, with block modification, deletion, and append operation.
- [356]: **MR-PDP: multiple-replica provable data possession.**
  Many storage systems make use of replication to increase the availability of the data they store. However, no strong evidence of the existence of these replicas is given. MR-PDP model provides a client (that is promised

(continued)

to have t replicas per file) with a challenge-response mechanism that allows to check that (i) each unique replica t can be produced at the time of the challenge and (ii) the system uses t times the storage to store a single replica.

- [357]: **Proofs of storage from homomorphic identification protocols.** Framework for building public-key Homomorphic Linear Authenticator (HLA) from any identification protocol satisfying specific homomorphic properties. The authors show how to turn any public-key HLA into a publicly verifiable proof of storage with communication complexity independent of the length of the file and with an unbounded number of verification supported.

Availability

The National Institute of Standard and Technology (NIST) defines the term "availability" as "Ensuring timely and reliable access to and use of information."[40] Although the act of wondering whether data and services are available in a cloud context might seem an oxymoron (i.e., most of the companies migrate on the cloud to enjoy greater availability), several threats make the question sensible. Indeed, among the top vulnerabilities of cloud computing technology, the DoS attack deservedly appears.

> ✐ **Definitions**
>
> **Denial of Service** The prevention of authorized access to resources or the delaying of time-critical operations.[41]

The DoS takes the name DDoS when the incoming traffic flooding (overwhelming) the victim originates from many sources (e.g., botnets). The goal of the attacker is to jeopardize the availability of the service, preventing legitimate users (e.g., employees, customers, members, account holders) from accessing it. The three main types of DoS and DDoS attacks are described in the following box.

---

[40]https://csrc.nist.gov/glossary/term/availability (Last checked August 2020).

[41]https://csrc.nist.gov/glossary/term/DoS (Last checked August 2020).

> ✐ **Definitions**
>
> **Types of DoS and DDoS Attacks**
>
> 1. *Volume-based attacks.* The goal of the attacker is to saturate the bandwidth of the service with a high volume of packets or connections.
>
>   - Examples: UDP floods, ICMP floods.
>   - Measured in: Bits per second (Bps)
>
> 2. *Protocol attacks.* The goal of the attacker is to consume (and exhaust) actual resources as well as intermediate communication equipment, such as load balancers and firewalls.
>
>   - Examples: SYN floods, Ping of Death, Smurf DDoS.
>   - Measured in: Packets per second (Pps)
>
> 3. *Application layer attacks.* The goal of the attacker is to exploit vulnerabilities or issues of applications to jeopardize the availability of the service.
>
>   - Examples: low-and-slow attacks, GET/POST floods.
>   - Measured in: Requests per second (Rps)

Although the first DoS attack is dated back July 22, 1999, when a computer at the University of Minnesota suffered an attack from 114 computers guided from the Trin00 malicious script, DoS and DDoS have not gone out of fashion and continue to be one of the top threats worldwide. Their notoriety can be appreciated with some statistics:

- In the Annual Internet Report (2018–2023), Cisco claimed that the total number of DDoS attacks will double from 7.9 million in 2018 to 15.4 million by 2023.[42]
- DDoS attacks, being the dominant threat observed by the majority of service providers, can represent up to 25% of a country's total Internet traffic while they are occurring.[43]
- Kaspersky Lab, in 2019, warned about a DDoS storm at the gates, after an increase of 84% in just 3 months.[44]
- According to a report produced by MarketsandMarkets, the DDoS protection and mitigation market size is expected to grow from USD 2.4 billion in 2019 to USD

---

[42] https://www.cisco.com/c/en/us/solutions/collateral/executive-perspectives/annual-internet-report/white-paper-c11-741490.html (Last checked August 2020).

[43] https://cybersecurityventures.com/cybersecurity-almanac-2019/ (Last checked August 2020).

[44] https://usa.kaspersky.com/about/press-releases/2019_kaspersky-lab-finds-number-of-ddos-attacks-grows-after-long-period-of-decline (Last checked August 2020).

4.7 billion by 2024, at a compound annual growth rate (CAGR) of 14% during the forecast period.[45]

DoS and DDoS attacks may be carried out for a variety of reasons; some of the most frequent are listed and described below.[46]

- *Business feuds.* Companies may target competing companies to strategically knock them out during particular periods. E.g., e-commerce companies may compromise the availability of competitors' services over the Christmas period to increase their earnings.
- *Ideology.* Hacktivists (a portmanteau of the terms "hack" and "activists") rely on DoS and DDoS attacks to take down websites with which they ideologically disagree with. Among the attacks that have taken place in recent years, we may find Operation Tunisia, Operation Egypt, Operation Syria, Operation Russia, Operation HBGARY, Operation DarkNet, and many others.
- *Extortion.* Individuals and groups may rely on DoS or DDoS attacks to compromise the availability of the services and extort money from their target. Once a "ransom" is paid, the perpetrators will stop overwhelming the services. There have been episodes in which threatening companies to carry out DoS or DDoS attacks is enough to get money. In 2016, the Armada Collective group sent hundreds of threatening emails to businesses, asking to be paid between 10 and 50 Bitcoins (USD 4,600 to USD 23,000, at the time) as a "protection fee"; otherwise 1Tbps DDoS attacks would have happened. The group got USD 100,000 in total, yet none of the companies who declined to pay the protection fee were attacked.[47]
- *Boredom.* Cyber vandals, as well as would-be hacker "script-kiddies," may launch DoS or DDoS attacks when bored, looking for an adrenaline rush.
- *Cyberwarfare.* DoS or DDoS attacks may be authorized by governments to cripple opposition websites and enemy country's infrastructures.
- *Decoy.* DoS or DDoS attacks may be used to draw attention away from more delicate intrusion activities.

It is worth to notice that DoS and DDoS attacks may not be intentional. Indeed, there have been instances where services have suffered an abrupt termination without any malicious user around. Let us assume that a user/company hires a penetration testing team to assess the security of its services hosted to the cloud. The services in question may share the physical machine with other services offered by the same service provider to other users/companies. During the assessment, unwary penetration testers may unintentionally compromise the services of the wrong user/company causing, depending on the scenario, severe problems. Furthermore,

---

[45]https://www.marketsandmarkets.com/PressReleases/ddos-protection-mitigation.asp (Last checked August 2020).

[46]https://www.imperva.com/learn/application-security/ddos-attacks/ (Last checked August 2020).

[47]https://www.computerworld.com/article/3061813/empty-ddos-threats-deliver-100k-to-extortion-group.html (Last checked August 2020).

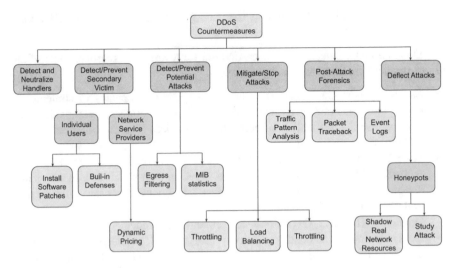

Fig. 6.3 DDoS countermeasures [358]

changes in infrastructure or cloud provider policies, as well as physical disruption, may cause the temporary interruption of services, often providential for companies.

When dealing with cloud computing technologies, a user/company should have the answer to the following questions: what if one of my critical systems/services go down? How much time does it take to recover data and to restore services from a DoS or DDoS event? Are my data and services replicated? Are the replicas protected? What does happen if the Cloud Service Provider I am entrusting go out of business?

Over the years, numerous solutions have been developed to prevent or, at least, mitigate both DoS and DDoS attacks. An effective taxonomy of the DDoS countermeasures has been provided by Specht et al. in [358], depicted in Fig. 6.3.

However, in general, the first step toward a comprehensive DoS and DDoS defense strategy should involve the development of an incident response plan. Being highly dependent on the infrastructure of the company's network, a detailed and accurate response plan may be instrumental in defending against this threat.

For any company, four key elements may be identified:

1. **identify the critical assets.** As for any risk analysis, the critical assets (e.g., assets that are vulnerable to either DoS or DDoS attacks) are identified;
2. **put in place protections.** Once the critical assets are known, effective defenses against DoS and DDoS attacks are put in place to provide protection;
3. **form a response team.** The defenses put in place may mitigate the attacks without actually eliminating them. A response team should be formed to ensure appropriate and organized reactions should any attack occur;
4. **develop communication strategies.** Since DoS and DDoS attacks can be carried out in a very short time with devastating results, team members should be

available, and effective communication strategies should be developed, to react immediately to the threat, thus limiting the disservice.

6.2.3   Open Issues and Future Directions

The open issues and future directions are collected and organized in the technical side and in the organizational side.

Technical Side

- **Rethinking the trade-offs.** Finding the ideal trade-off between accessibility, usability, and security is really far from being a trivial task for companies, and, unfortunately, security is always the term that has less weight on the equation. Every company should rely on interdisciplinary teams, composed of members of several departments, to think and agree on solutions that have been analyzed from all possible points of view. To make an example, UI designers should work together with security experts to study the experience of the user following the adoption of each new security measure. If the user does not understand how it works or if the measure requires too much effort on his part, he would stop using it, possibly creating damage to the company.
- **Protection of data at rest and in transit.** Data should be encrypted both when at rest and in transit, and the decryption keys should never be kept by the service provider. In addition to encryption, several best practices for robust data protection include the following: (i) rely on proactive security, rather than on reactive security; (ii) implement network security control, such as firewalls; (iii) create effective security policies; (iv) manage meticulously the access control to the data with strict permissions and log every access; and (v) keep the ability to restore backup in house, by duplicating data and services and protecting them appropriately.
- **Continuous authentication.** Continuous authentication is an authentication technology that allows real-time verifying users' identities. Usually, as soon as the user passes the login phase, he will be logged until the logout phase, without further verifications. With continuous authentication, the probability that individual users are who they claim to be is constantly measured, but several challenges arise. Who should manage and verify the authentication? The Cloud Service Provider? Could the management be moved on the Edge [359]? Could it be distributed?
- **OSINT teams.** Just as penetration testers are needed to assess the strength of the network and security mechanisms, a team of OSINT experts is needed to proactively assess the importance and dangers of publicly accessible company's information. Among the tasks of such a team, the analysis of social networks, hitherto dramatically neglected, is of fundamental importance for the company's

image. To make an example: what would happen if an employee posted very inappropriate material for the company on his social profiles? There would be the risk of negative press campaigns on the company that, if listed on the stock exchange, may lose millions even for false alarms. It may happen that the employee did not provide information about the company he works for in the social network he posts such content to. However, with the new powerful information warfare tools, all public information of an individual is aggregated almost instantly. The company should have effective means to understand whether it is relying on reliable people without limiting their freedom of speech. Many companies are relying on a background check of an individual before hiring her, but then no verification of compliance with the corporate values of the company is carried out.

Organizational Side

- **Rethinking the HR.** Brain-intensive companies, which are among the ones generating greater value nowadays, should rethink the human resource management. Given the importance of both their employees and the information of the company they have, they should adopt a proactive approach concerning employee retention. Understanding the needs of the employees, managing their professional growth, and providing them with constantly updated resources through training courses are just some of the actions that would allow the company to be able to rely on its employees by establishing a lasting professional relationship.
- **Rethinking the board.** There is the need to rethink the composition of the board and to start including cybersecurity, i.e., the Chief Information Security Officer (CISO) and the Chief Security Officer (CSO). The CISO is responsible for coordinating security initiatives concerning company programs and business objectives, ensuring that information assets and technologies are adequately protected. The CSO, instead, governs the technical processes to protect the key data for corporate competitiveness, being the executive responsible for the company's entire security posture. Including CSO and CISO to the board requires to have professional figures with valuable cybersecurity experience able to master the business-oriented language.
- **Rethinking the critical assets** Over the years, with the adoption of new technologies, critical assets are increasingly intangible. To make an example, the most critical asset of a bank nowadays is the credibility. The loss of credibility would result in the loss of trust by customers, who eventually will abandon the bank. The credibility, among other things, takes a long time to be built and a trifle to be demolished. There is the need to rethink the risk analysis, together with the identification and prioritization of the critical assets, to cope with a threat landscape that, with the adoption of new technologies, became inexorably more dynamic and unpredictable.

Bibliography

1. A. Halevy, P. Norvig, F. Pereira, The unreasonable effectiveness of data. IEEE Intell. Syst. **24**(2), 8–12 (2009)
2. R. Di Pietro, M. Caprolu, S. Raponi, Next generation information warfare: rationales, scenarios, threats, and open issues, in *Information Systems Security and Privacy—ICISSP 2019, Revised Selected Papers* (Springer, Berlin, 2019), pp. 24–47
3. How to escape your political bubble for a clearer view. https://www.nytimes.com/2017/03/03/arts/the-battle-over-your-political-bubble.html. (Last checked August 2020)
4. S. Cresci, A decade of social bot detection, *Communications of the ACM (Forthcoming)* (2020)
5. A. Marwick, R. Lewis, *Media Manipulation and Disinformation Online* (Data and Society Research Institute, New York 2017)
6. J. Yan, Bot, cyborg and automated turing test, in *The 2006 International Workshop on Security Protocols* (Springer, Berlin, 2006), pp. 190–197
7. Z. Chu, S. Gianvecchio, H. Wang, S. Jajodia, Detecting automation of twitter accounts: are you a human, bot, or cyborg? IEEE Trans. Dependable Secure Comput. **9**, 811–824 (2012)
8. E. Ferrara, The history of digital spam. Commun. ACM **62**(8), 82–91 (2019)
9. B. Waugh, M. Abdipanah, O. Hashemi, S.A. Rahman, D. M. Cook, The influence and deception of Twitter: the authenticity of the narrative and slacktivism in the Australian electoral process, in *The 14th Australian Information Warfare Conference (AIWC'13)* (2013)
10. J. Ratkiewicz, M.D. Conover, M. Meiss, B. Gonçalves, A. Flammini, F.M. Menczer, Detecting and tracking political abuse in social media, in *The Fifth International AAAI Conference on Weblogs and Social Media (ICWSM'11)* (AAAI, 2011)
11. G. Da San Martino, S. Cresci, A. Barrón-Cede no, S. Yu, R. Di Pietro, P. Nakov, A survey on computational propaganda detection, in *The 29th International Joint Conference on Artificial Intelligence (IJCAI'20)* (2020)
12. N. Persily, The 2016 US Election: can democracy survive the Internet? J. Democr. **28**(2), 63–76 (2017)
13. M. Mazza, S. Cresci, M. Avvenuti, W. Quattrociocchi, M. Tesconi, Rtbust: exploiting temporal patterns for botnet detection on twitter, in *The 11th International Conference on Web Science (WebSci'19)* (ACM, New York, 2019), pp. 183–192
14. A.M. Guess, M. Lerner, B. Lyons, J.M. Montgomery, B. Nyhan, J. Reifler, N. Sircar, A digital media literacy intervention increases discernment between mainstream and false news in the United States and India. Proc. Natl. Acad. Sci. **117**(27), 15536–15545 (2020)

© The Author(s), under exclusive license to
Springer Nature Switzerland AG 2021
R. Di Pietro et al., *New Dimensions of Information Warfare*, Advances in
Information Security 84, https://doi.org/10.1007/978-3-030-60618-3

15. D.K. Flaherty, The vaccine-autism connection: a public health crisis caused by unethical medical practices and fraudulent science. Ann. Pharmacother. **45**(10), 1302–1304 (2011)
16. C.A. Borella, D. Rossinelli, Fake news, immigration, and opinion polarization, in *SocioEconomic Challenges* (2017)
17. C. Garwood, *Flat Earth: The History of an Infamous Idea* (Pan Macmillan, 2008)
18. D.E. Allen, M. McAleer, Fake news and indifference to scientific fact: President Trump's confused tweets on global warming, climate change and weather. Scientometrics **117**(1), 625–629 (2018)
19. S. Van der Linden, A. Leiserowitz, S. Rosenthal, E. Maibach, Inoculating the public against misinformation about climate change. Global Chall. **1**(2), 1600008 (2017)
20. M. Gabielkov, A. Ramachandran, A. Chaintreau, A. Legout, Social clicks: what and who gets read on twitter? ACM SIGMETRICS Perform. Eval. Rev. **44**(1), 179–192 (2016)
21. R.M. Bond, C.J. Fariss, J.J. Jones, A.D. Kramer, C. Marlow, J.E. Settle, J.H. Fowler, A 61-million-person experiment in social influence and political mobilization. Nature **489**(7415), 295 (2012)
22. C.A. Bail, B. Guay, E. Maloney, A. Combs, D.S. Hillygus, F. Merhout, D. Freelon, A. Volfovsky, Assessing the Russian internet research agency's impact on the political attitudes and behaviors of American twitter users in late 2017. Proc. Natl. Acad. Sci. **117**(1), 243–250 (2020)
23. M. Rueda, 2012's biggest social media blunders in LatAm politics. https://abcnews.go.com/ABC_Univision/ABC_Univision/2012s-biggest-social-media-blunders-latin-american-politics/story?id=18063022. Last checked August 2020
24. T. Filer, R. Fredheim, Popular with the robots: accusation and automation in the argentine presidential elections, 2015. Int. J. Polit. Cult. Soc. **30**(3), 259–274 (2017)
25. T. Peel, The coalition's twitter fraud and deception. https://independentaustralia.net/politics/politics-display/the-coalitions-twitter-fraud-and-deception,5660. Last checked August 2020
26. E. Kusen, M. Strembeck, An analysis of the twitter discussion on the 2016 Austrian presidential elections (2017). arXiv preprint arXiv:1707.09939
27. H. Ellyatt, Us far-right activists, wikileaks and bots help amplify macron leaks. https://www.cnbc.com/2017/05/07/macron-email-leaks-far-right-wikileaks-twitter-bots.htm. Last checked August 2020.
28. R. Brandom, Emails leaked in 'massive hacking attack' on French presidential campaign. https://www.theverge.com/2017/5/5/15564532/macron-email-leak-russia-hacking-campaign-4chan. Last checked August 2020
29. S. Almasy, Emmanuel macron's French presidential campaign hacked. https://edition.cnn.com/2017/05/05/europe/france-election-macron-hack-allegation/index.html. Last checked August 2020
30. E. Ferrara, Disinformation and social bot operations in the run up to the 2017 French presidential election. First Monday **22**(8), 2017
31. C. Desigaud, P.N. Howard, S. Bradshaw, B. Kollanyi, G. Bolsover, Junk news and bots during the French presidential election: what are French voters sharing over twitter in round two? Tech. rep., COMPROP Data Memo, 2017
32. F. Brachten, S. Stieglitz, L. Hofeditz, K. Kloppenborg, A. Reimann, Strategies and influence of social bots in a 2017 German state election—a case study on twitter (2017). arXiv preprint arXiv:1710.07562
33. K. Kupferschmidt, Bot-hunters eye mischief in German election. Science **357**(6356), 1081–1082 (2017)
34. F. Morstatter, Y. Shao, A. Galstyan, S. Karunasekera, From alt-right to Alt-Rechts: twitter analysis of the 2017 German federal election, in *Companion Proceedings of the Web Conference 2018 (WWW Companion'18), (IW3C2, 2018)*, pp. 621–628
35. T.R. Keller, U. Klinger, Social bots in election campaigns: theoretical, empirical, and methodological implications. Polit. Commun. **36**(1), 171–189 (2019)

36. A. Applebaum, P. Pomerantsev, M. Smith, C. Colliver, 'make Germany great again': Kremlin, alt-right, and international influences in the 2017 German elections, in *London School of Economics* (2017)

37. A. Vogt, Hot or bot? Italian professor casts doubt on politician's twitter popularity. https://www.theguardian.com/world/2012/jul/22/bot-italian-politician-twitter-grillo. Last checked August 2020

38. N. Squires, Human or 'bot'? doubts over Italian comic Beppe Grillo's Twitter followers. https://www.telegraph.co.uk/technology/twitter/9421072/Human-or-bot-Doubts-over-Italian-comic-Beppe-Grillos-Twitter-followers.html. Last checked August 2020

39. C. Albanese, Now bots are trying to help populists win Italy's election. https://www.bloomberg.com/news/articles/2018-02-19/now-bots-are-trying-to-help-populists-win-italy-s-election. Last checked August 2020

40. DFRLab, #electionwatch: Italy's self-made bots. https://medium.com/dfrlab/electionwatch-italys-self-made-bots-200e2e268d0e. Last checked August 2020

41. TheLocal, Facebook shuts down more than 20 'fake news' pages in Italy. https://www.thelocal.it/20190513/facebook-shuts-down-more-than-20-fake-news-pages-in-italy. Last checked August 2020

42. S. Cresci, R. Di Pietro, M. Petrocchi, A. Spognardi, M. Tesconi, The paradigm-shift of social spambots: evidence, theories, and tools for the arms race, in *The 26th International Conference on World Wide Web Companion (WWW'17 Companion), IW3C2* (2017), pp. 963–972

43. M. Orcutt, Twitter mischief plagues Mexico's election. https://www.technologyreview.com/s/428286/twitter-mischief-plagues-mexicos-election/. Last checked August 2020

44. M. Glowacki, V. Narayanan, S. Maynard, G. Hirsch, B. Kollanyi, L. Neudert, V. Barash, et al., News and political information consumption in Mexico: mapping the 2018 Mexican presidential election on twitter and Facebook. The Computational Propaganda Project, 2018

45. J. Robertson, M. Riley, A. Willis, How to hack an election. https://www.bloomberg.com/features/2016-how-to-hack-an-election/. Last checked August 2020

46. E. Gallagher, Mexican botnet dirty wars: bots are waging a dirty war in Mexican social media. https://www.youtube.com/watch?v=I3D3iIZGSt8. Last checked August 2020

47. T. Guardian, 'i've had enough', says Mexican attorney general in missing students gaffe. https://www.theguardian.com/world/2014/nov/09/protests-flare-in-mexico-after-attorney-generals-enough-im-tired-remarks. Last checked August 2020

48. P. Suárez-Serrato, M.E. Roberts, C. Davis, F. Menczer, On the influence of social bots in online protests, in *Social Informatics* (Springer, Cham, 2016), pp. 269–278

49. M. Stella, E. Ferrara, M. De Domenico, Bots sustain and inflate striking opposition in online social systems (2018). arXiv preprint arXiv:1802.07292

50. D. Stukal, S. Sanovich, R. Bonneau, J.A. Tucker, Detecting bots on Russian political twitter. Big Data **5**(4), 310–324 (2017)

51. S. Zannettou, B. Bradlyn, E. De Cristofaro, G. Stringhini, J. Blackburn, Characterizing the use of images by state-sponsored troll accounts on Twitter (2019). arXiv preprint arXiv:1901.05997

52. S. Zannettou, T. Caulfield, W. Setzer, M. Sirivianos, G. Stringhini, J. Blackburn, Who let the trolls out? Towards understanding state-sponsored trolls, in *Proceedings of the 10th ACM Conference on Web Science* (ACM, New York, 2019), pp. 353–362

53. L.G. Stewart, A. Arif, K. Starbird, Examining trolls and polarization with a retweet network, in *Proceedings of the ACM WSDM, Workshop on Misinformation and Misbehavior Mining on the Web* (2018)

54. S. Shane, V. Goel, Fake Russian Facebook accounts bought $100,000 in political ads. https://www.nytimes.com/2017/09/06/technology/facebook-russian-political-ads.html. Last checked August 2020

55. R. Dutt, A. Deb, E. Ferrara, 'senator, we sell ads': analysis of the 2016 Russian Facebook ads campaign, in *International Conference on Intelligent Information Technologies* (Springer, Berlin, 2018), pp. 151–168

56. E. Poyrazlar, Turkey's leader bans his own twitter bot army. https://www.vocativ.com/world/turkey-world/turkeys-leader-nearly-banned-twitter-bot-army/. Last checked August 2020

57. S. Hegelich, D. Janetzko, Are social bots on twitter political actors? Empirical evidence from a Ukrainian social botnet, in *Proceedings of the Tenth International AAAI Conference on Web and Social Media (ICWSM 2016)* (2016), pp. 579–582

58. P.N. Howard, B. Kollanyi, Bots,#strongerin, and#brexit: computational propaganda during the UK-EU referendum. Available at SSRN 2798311 (2016)

59. M.T. Bastos, D. Mercea, The Brexit botnet and user-generated hyperpartisan news. Soc. Sci. Comput. Rev. **37**(1), 38–54 (2019)

60. C. Llewellyn, L. Cram, R.L. Hill, A. Favero, For whom the bell trolls: shifting troll behaviour in the twitter Brexit debate. J. Common Market Stud. **57**(5), 1148–1164 (2019)

61. H. Allcott, M. Gentzkow, Social media and fake news in the 2016 election. J. Econ. Perspect. **31**(2), 211–36 (2017)

62. A. Guess, B. Nyhan, J. Reifler, Selective exposure to misinformation: evidence from the consumption of fake news during the 2016 US presidential campaign. Eur. Res. Council **9**(3), 4 (2018)

63. A. Bessi and E. Ferrara, Social bots distort the 2016 US presidential election online discussion. First Monday **21**(11-7) (2016)

64. C. Shao, G.L. Ciampaglia, O. Varol, A. Flammini, F. Menczer, The spread of fake news by social bots. **96**, 104 (2017). arXiv preprint arXiv:1707.07592

65. W. Samuel, H. Phil, Bots unite to automate the presidential election. https://www.wired.com/2016/05/twitterbots-2/. Last checked August 2020

66. B. Ryan, Nearly half of Donald Trump's twitter followers are fake accounts and bots. https://www.newsweek.com/donald-trump-twitter-followers-fake-617873. Last checked August 2020

67. A. Fourney, M.Z. Racz, G. Ranade, M. Mobius, E. Horvitz, Geographic and temporal trends in fake news consumption during the 2016 US presidential election, in *Proceedings of the 2017 ACM on Conference on Information and Knowledge Management* (ACM, New York, 2017), pp. 2071–2074

68. E. Mustafaraj, P.T. Metaxas, From obscurity to prominence in minutes: political speech and real-time search (2010)

69. A. Badawy, E. Ferrara, K. Lerman, Analyzing the digital traces of political manipulation: the 2016 Russian interference twitter campaign, in *2018 IEEE/ACM International Conference on Advances in Social Networks Analysis and Mining (ASONAM)* (IEEE, Piscataway, 2018), pp. 258–265

70. A. Badawy, K. Lerman, E. Ferrara, Who falls for online political manipulation? in *Companion Proceedings of The 2019 World Wide Web Conference* (ACM, New York, 2019), pp. 162–168

71. M. Jensen, Russian trolls and fake news: information or identity logics? J. Int. Aff. **71**(1.5), 115–124 (2018)

72. M. Forelle, P. Howard, A. Monroy-Hernández, S. Savage, Political bots and the manipulation of public opinion in Venezuela (2015). arXiv preprint arXiv:1507.07109

73. S. Cresci, R. Di Pietro, M. Petrocchi, A. Spognardi, M. Tesconi, Fame for sale: efficient detection of fake twitter followers. Decis. Support Syst. **80**, 56–71 (2015)

74. S. Cresci, R. Di Pietro, M. Petrocchi, A. Spognardi, M. Tesconi, DNA-inspired online behavioral modeling and its application to spambot detection. IEEE Intell. Syst. **31**(5), 58–64 (2016)

75. S. Cresci, R. Di Pietro, M. Petrocchi, A. Spognardi, M. Tesconi, Social fingerprinting: detection of spambot groups through DNA-inspired behavioral modeling. IEEE Trans. Dependable Secure Comput. **15**(4), 561–576 (2017)

76. S. Cresci, R. Di Pietro, M. Petrocchi, A. Spognardi, M. Tesconi, Exploiting digital DNA for the analysis of similarities in twitter behaviours, in *2017 IEEE International Conference on Data Science and Advanced Analytics (DSAA)* (IEEE, Piscataway, 2017), pp. 686–695

77. S. Cresci, R. Di Pietro, M. Petrocchi, A. Spognardi, M. Tesconi, Emergent properties, models, and laws of behavioral similarities within groups of twitter users. Comput. Commun. **150**, 47–61 (2020)
78. A. Spangher, G. Ranade, B. Nushi, A. Fourney, E. Horvitz, Analysis of strategy and spread of Russia-sponsored content in the US in 2017 (2018). arXiv preprint arXiv:1810.10033
79. S. Zannettou, T. Caulfield, E. De Cristofaro, M. Sirivianos, G. Stringhini, J. Blackburn, Disinformation warfare: understanding state-sponsored trolls on twitter and their influence on the web, in *Companion Proceedings of the 2019 World Wide Web Conference* (ACM, New York, 2019), pp. 218–226
80. B.S. Bello, R. Heckel, Analyzing the behaviour of twitter bots in post Brexit politics
81. O. Solon, Facebook's fake news: Mark Zuckerberg rejects 'crazy idea' that it swayed voters. https://www.theguardian.com/technology/2016/nov/10/facebook-fake-news-us-election-mark-zuckerberg-donald-trump. Last checked August 2020
82. R. Max, Donald Trump won because of facebook. https://nymag.com/intelligencer/2016/11/donald-trump-won-because-of-facebook.html. Last checked August 2020
83. C. Dewey, Facebook fake-news writer: 'i think Donald Trump is in the white house because of me'. https://www.washingtonpost.com/news/the-intersect/wp/2016/11/17/facebook-fake-news-writer-i-think-donald-trump-is-in-the-white-house-because-of-me/. Last checked August 2020
84. N. Mele, D. Lazer, M. Baum, N. Grinberg, L. Friedland, K. Joseph, W. Hobbs, C. Mattsson, Combating fake news: an agenda for research and action (2017). *Di* https://www.hks.harvard.edu/publications/combating-fake-news-agenda-research-and-action (Retrieved October 17, 2018)
85. Z. Jin, J. Cao, Y. Zhang, J. Zhou, Q. Tian, Novel visual and statistical image features for microblogs news verification. IEEE Trans. Multimedia **19**(3), 598–608 (2016)
86. C. Castillo, M. Mendoza, B. Poblete, Information credibility on twitter, in *Proceedings of the 20th International Conference on World Wide Web* (2011), pp. 675–684
87. S. Vosoughi, M. Mohsenvand, D. Roy, Rumor gauge: predicting the veracity of rumors on twitter. ACM Trans. Knowl. Discov. Data **11**(4), 1–36 (2017)
88. N. Hassan, F. Arslan, C. Li, M. Tremayne, Toward automated fact-checking: detecting check-worthy factual claims by claimbuster, in *Proceedings of the 23rd ACM SIGKDD International Conference on Knowledge Discovery and Data Mining* (2017), pp. 1803–1812
89. G. Karadzhov, P. Nakov, L. Màrquez, A. Barrón-Cede no, I. Koychev, Fully automated fact checking using external sources (2017). arXiv preprint arXiv:1710.00341
90. K. Shu, A. Sliva, S. Wang, J. Tang, H. Liu, Fake news detection on social media: a data mining perspective. ACM SIGKDD Explorations Newsl. **19**(1), 22–36 (2017)
91. G. Pennycook, D.G. Rand, Fighting misinformation on social media using crowdsourced judgments of news source quality. Proc. Nat. Acad. Sci. **116**(7), 2521–2526 (2019)
92. M.R. Pinto, Y.O. de Lima, C.E. Barbosa, J.M. de Souza, Towards fact-checking through crowdsourcing, in *2019 IEEE 23rd International Conference on Computer Supported Cooperative Work in Design (CSCWD)* (IEEE, Piscataway, 2019), pp. 494–499
93. S.M. Mohammad, P. Sobhani, S. Kiritchenko, Stance and sentiment in tweets. ACM Trans. Internet Tech. **17**(3), 1–23 (2017)
94. Y. Yamaguchi, T. Takahashi, T. Amagasa, H. Kitagawa, Turank: twitter user ranking based on user-tweet graph analysis, in *Web Information Systems Engineering—WISE 2010*, ed. by L. Chen, P. Triantafillou, T. Suel (Springer, Berlin, 2010), pp. 240–253
95. B. Rath, W. Gao, J. Ma, J. Srivastava, From retweet to believability: utilizing trust to identify rumor spreaders on twitter, in *Proceedings of the 2017 IEEE/ACM International Conference on Advances in Social Networks Analysis and Mining 2017* (2017), pp. 179–186
96. J. Zhang, J. Tang, J. Li, Expert finding in a social network, in *International Conference on Database Systems for Advanced Applications* (Springer, Berlin, 2007), pp. 1066–1069
97. A. Bozzon, M. Brambilla, S. Ceri, M. Silvestri, G. Vesci, Choosing the right crowd: expert finding in social networks, in *Proceedings of the 16th International Conference on Extending Database Technology* (2013), pp. 637–648

98. R.M. Tripathy, A. Bagchi, S. Mehta, A study of rumor control strategies on social networks, in *Proceedings of the 19th ACM International Conference on Information and Knowledge Management* (2010), pp. 1817–1820

99. N.P. Nguyen, G. Yan, M.T. Thai, S. Eidenbenz, Containment of misinformation spread in online social networks, in *Proceedings of the Fourth Annual ACM Web Science Conference* (2012), pp. 213–222

100. T. Mitra, E. Gilbert, Credbank: a large-scale social media corpus with associated credibility annotations, in *Ninth International AAAI Conference on Web and Social Media* (2015)

101. W.Y. Wang, "liar, liar pants on fire": a new benchmark dataset for fake news detection (2017). arXiv preprint arXiv:1705.00648

102. E. Tacchini, G. Ballarin, M.L. Della Vedova, S. Moret, L. de Alfaro, Some like it hoax: automated fake news detection in social networks (2017). arXiv preprint arXiv:1704.07506

103. G.C. Santia, J.R. Williams, Buzzface: a news veracity dataset with Facebook user commentary and egos, in *Twelfth International AAAI Conference on Web and Social Media* (2018)

104. J. Golbeck, M. Mauriello, B. Auxier, K.H. Bhanushali, C. Bonk, M.A. Bouzaghrane, C. Buntain, R. Chanduka, P. Cheakalos, J.B. Everett, et al., Fake news vs satire: a dataset and analysis, in *Proceedings of the 10th ACM Conference on Web Science* (ACM, New York, 2018), pp. 17–21

105. K. Shu, D. Mahudeswaran, S. Wang, D. Lee, H. Liu, Fakenewsnet: a data repository with news content, social context and spatialtemporal information for studying fake news on social media (2018). arXiv preprint arXiv:1809.01286

106. A. Pathak, R. Srihari, BREAKING! presenting fake news corpus for automated fact checking, in *Proceedings of the 57th Annual Meeting of the Association for Computational Linguistics: Student Research Workshop* (Florence, Italy) (Association for Computational Linguistics, Stroudsburg, 2019), pp. 357–362

107. F.K.A. Salem, R. Al Feel, S. Elbassuoni, M. Jaber, M. Farah, Fakes: a fake news dataset around the Syrian war, in *Proceedings of the International AAAI Conference on Web and Social Media*, vol. 13 (2019), pp. 573–582

108. F. Torabi Asr, M. Taboada, Big data and quality data for fake news and misinformation detection. Big Data Soc. **6**(1) (2019). https://doi.org/10.1177/2053951719843310

109. N. Abokhodair, D. Yoo, D.W. McDonald, Dissecting a social botnet: growth, content and influence in twitter, in *Proceedings of the 18th ACM Conference on Computer Supported Cooperative Work and Social Computing* (ACM, New York, 2015), pp. 839–851

110. O. Varol, E. Ferrara, C.A. Davis, F. Menczer, A. Flammini, Online human-bot interactions: detection, estimation, and characterization, in *Eleventh International AAAI Conference on Web and Social Media* (2017)

111. R.J. Oentaryo, A. Murdopo, P.K. Prasetyo, E.-P. Lim, On profiling bots in social media, in *International Conference on Social Informatics* (Springer, Berlin, 2016), pp. 92–109

112. N. Agarwal, S. Jabin, S.Z. Hussain, et al., Analyzing real and fake users in Facebook network based on emotions, in *2019 11th International Conference on Communication Systems and Networks (COMSNETS)* (IEEE, Piscataway, 2019), pp. 110–117

113. R. Plutchik, Emotions: a general psychoevolutionary theory. Approaches Emotion **1984**, 197–219 (1984)

114. J. Echeverrìa, E. De Cristofaro, N. Kourtellis, I. Leontiadis, G. Stringhini, S. Zhou, Lobo: evaluation of generalization deficiencies in twitter bot classifiers, in *The 34th Annual Computer Security Applications Conference (ACSAC'18)* (ACM, 2018), pp. 137–146

115. N. Chavoshi, H. Hamooni, A. Mueen, Identifying correlated bots in twitter, in *International Conference on Social Informatics* (Springer, Berlin, 2016), pp. 14–21

116. A. Anwar, U. Yaqub, Bot detection in twitter landscape using unsupervised learning, in *The 21st Annual International Conference on Digital Government Research* (2020), pp. 329–330

117. C.A. Davis, O. Varol, E. Ferrara, A. Flammini, F. Menczer, Botornot: a system to evaluate social bots, in *Proceedings of the 25th International Conference Companion on World Wide Web, IW3C2* (2016), pp. 273–274

118. N. Chavoshi, H. Hamooni, A. Mueen, On-demand bot detection and archival system, in *Proceedings of the 26th International Conference on World Wide Web Companion, IW3C2* (2017), pp. 183–187
119. V. Subrahmanian, A. Azaria, S. Durst, V. Kagan, A. Galstyan, K. Lerman, L. Zhu, E. Ferrara, A. Flammini, F. Menczer, The DARPA twitter bot challenge. Computer **49**(6), 38–46 (2016)
120. F. Rangel, P. Rosso, Overview of the 7th author profiling task at PAN 2019: bots and gender profiling in twitter, in *Proceedings of the CEUR Workshop, Lugano, Switzerland* (2019), pp. 1–36
121. DFRLab, #botspot: twelve ways to spot a bot. https://medium.com/dfrlab/botspot-twelve-ways-to-spot-a-bot-aedc7d9c110c. Last checked August 2020
122. M. Conti, R. Poovendran, M. Secchiero, Fakebook: detecting fake profiles in on-line social networks, in *Proceedings of the 2012 International Conference on Advances in Social Networks Analysis and Mining (ASONAM 2012)* (IEEE Computer Society, Washington, 2012), pp. 1071–1078
123. Q. Cao, M. Sirivianos, X. Yang, T. Pregueiro, Aiding the detection of fake accounts in large scale social online services, in *Proceedings of the Ninth USENIX conference on Networked Systems Design and Implementation* (USENIX Association, Berkeley, 2012), p. 15
124. M. La Morgia, A. Mei, S. Raponi, J. Stefa, Time-zone geolocation of crowds in the dark web," in *2018 IEEE 38th International Conference on Distributed Computing Systems (ICDCS)* (IEEE, Piscataway, 2018), pp. 445–455
125. M. La Morgia, A. Mei, E. Nemmi, S. Raponi, J. Stefa, Nationality and geolocation-based profiling in the dark (web). IEEE Trans. Serv. Comput. (2019)
126. S. Gurajala, J.S. White, B. Hudson, J.N. Matthews, Fake twitter accounts: profile characteristics obtained using an activity-based pattern detection approach, in *Proceedings of the 2015 International Conference on Social Media and Society* (ACM, New York, 2015), p. 9
127. D. Ramalingam, V. Chinnaiah, Fake profile detection techniques in large-scale online social networks: a comprehensive review. Comput. Electr. Eng. **65**, 165–177 (2018)
128. S. Adikari, K. Dutta, Identifying fake profiles in linkedin, in *PACIS* (2014), p. 278
129. J. Haikarainen, Astroturfing as a global phenomenon (2014)
130. F.B. Keller, D. Schoch, S. Stier, J. Yang, Political astroturfing on twitter: how to coordinate a disinformation campaign. Polit. Commun. **37**(2), 256–280 (2020)
131. J. Zhang, D. Carpenter, M. Ko, Online astroturfing: a theoretical perspective (2013)
132. T. Chen, N.H. Alallaq, W. Niu, Y. Wang, X. Bai, J. Liu, Y. Xiang, T. Wu, J. Liu, A hidden astroturfing detection approach base on emotion analysis, in *International Conference on Knowledge Science, Engineering and Management* (Springer, Berlin, 2017), pp. 55–66
133. S. Mahbub, E. Pardede, A. Kayes, W. Rahayu, Controlling astroturfing on the internet: a survey on detection techniques and research challenges. Int. J. Web Grid Serv. **15**(2), 139–158 (2019)
134. A.H. Wang, Detecting spam bots in online social networking sites: a machine learning approach, in *IFIP Annual Conference on Data and Applications Security and Privacy* (Springer, Berlin, 2010), pp. 335–342
135. G. Stringhini, C. Kruegel, G. Vigna, Detecting spammers on social networks, in *Proceedings of the 26th Annual Computer Security Applications Conference* (ACM, New York, 2010), pp. 1–9
136. M. Singh, D. Bansal, S. Sofat, Who is who on twitter–spammer, fake or compromised account? A tool to reveal true identity in real-time. Cybern. Syst. **49**(1), 1–25 (2018)
137. Z. Miller, B. Dickinson, W. Deitrick, W. Hu, A.H. Wang, Twitter spammer detection using data stream clustering. Inf. Sci. **260**, 64–73 (2014)
138. C. Yang, R. C. Harkreader, G. Gu, Die free or live hard? Empirical evaluation and new design for fighting evolving twitter spammers, in *International Workshop on Recent Advances in Intrusion Detection* (Springer, Berlin, 2011), pp. 318–337
139. C. Grier, K. Thomas, V. Paxson, M. Zhang, @ spam: the underground on 140 characters or less, in *Proceedings of the 17th ACM conference on Computer and Communications Security* (ACM, Berlin, 2010), pp. 27–37

140. K. Thomas, C. Grier, D. Song, V. Paxson, Suspended accounts in retrospect: an analysis of twitter spam, in *Proceedings of the 2011 ACM SIGCOMM Conference on Internet Measurement Conference* (ACM, New York, 2011), pp. 243–258

141. A. Caspi, P. Gorsky, Online deception: prevalence, motivation, and emotion. CyberPsychol. Behav. **9**(1), 54–59 (2006)

142. Z. Bu, Z. Xia, J. Wang, A sock puppet detection algorithm on virtual spaces. Knowl.-Based Syst. **37**, 366–377 (2013)

143. D. Liu, Q. Wu, W. Han, B. Zhou, Sockpuppet gang detection on social media sites. Front. Comput. Sci. **10**(1), 124–135 (2016)

144. S. Kumar, J. Cheng, J. Leskovec, V. Subrahmanian, An army of me: sockpuppets in online discussion communities, in *Proceedings of the 26th International Conference on World Wide Web*, IW3C2 (2017), pp. 857–866

145. T. Solorio, R. Hasan, M. Mizan, A case study of sockpuppet detection in wikipedia, in *Proceedings of the Workshop on Language Analysis in Social Media* (2013), pp. 59–68

146. M. Tsikerdekis, S. Zeadally, Multiple account identity deception detection in social media using nonverbal behavior. IEEE Trans. Inf. Forensics Secur. **9**(8), 1311–1321 (2014)

147. B. Stone, M. Richtel, The hand that controls the sock puppet could get slapped. N.Y. Times (2007)

148. R.M. Milner, Media lingua franca: fixity, novelty, and vernacular creativity in internet memes. AoIR Sel. Pap. Internet Res. **3** (2013)

149. L. Shifman, *Memes in Digital Culture* (MIT Press, Cambridge, 2014)

150. J. Leskovec, L. Backstrom, J. Kleinberg, Meme-tracking and the dynamics of the news cycle, in *Proceedings of the 15th ACM SIGKDD International Conference on Knowledge Discovery and Data Mining* (ACM, New York, 2009), pp. 497–506

151. J. Ratkiewicz, M. Conover, M. Meiss, B. Gonçalves, S. Patil, A. Flammini, F. Menczer, Truthy: mapping the spread of astroturf in microblog streams, in *The 20th International Conference Companion on World Wide Web (WWW'11)* (ACM, New York, 2011), pp. 249–252

152. C. Bauckhage, Insights into internet memes, in *Fifth International AAAI Conference on Weblogs and Social Media* (2011)

153. C. W. Seah, H. L. Chieu, K. M. A. Chai, L.-N. Teow, L. W. Yeong, Troll detection by domain-adapting sentiment analysis, in *2015 18th International Conference on Information Fusion (Fusion)* (IEEE, Piscataway, 2015), pp. 792–799

154. P. Fornacciari, M. Mordonini, A. Poggi, L. Sani, M. Tomaiuolo, A holistic system for troll detection on twitter. Comput. Hum. Behav. **89**, 258–268 (2018)

155. F.J. Ortega, J.A. Troyano, F.L. Cruz, C.G. Vallejo, F. EnríQuez, Propagation of trust and distrust for the detection of trolls in a social network. Comput. Netw. **56**(12), 2884–2895 (2012)

156. E. Cambria, P. Chandra, A. Sharma, A. Hussain, Do not feel the trolls, in *ISWC, Shanghai* (2010)

157. P. Galán-García, J.G.D.L. Puerta, C.L. Gómez, I. Santos, P.G. Bringas, Supervised machine learning for the detection of troll profiles in twitter social network: application to a real case of cyberbullying. Logic J. IGPL **24**(1), 42–53 (2016)

158. J. Im, E. Chandrasekharan, J. Sargent, P. Lighthammer, T. Denby, A. Bhargava, L. Hemphill, D. Jurgens, E. Gilbert, Still out there: modeling and identifying Russian troll accounts on twitter (2019). arXiv preprint arXiv:1901.11162

159. D. Kim, T. Graham, Z. Wan, M.-A. Rizoiu, Analysing user identity via time-sensitive semantic edit distance (t-SED): a case study of Russian trolls on twitter. J. Commer. Soc. Sci. **2**(2), 331–351 (2019)

160. T. Mihaylov, G. Georgiev, P. Nakov, Finding opinion manipulation trolls in news community forums, in *Proceedings of the Nineteenth Conference on Computational Natural Language Learning* (2015), pp. 310–314

161. T. Mihaylov, P. Nakov, Hunting for troll comments in news community forums, in *Proceedings of the 54th Annual Meeting of the Association for Computational Linguistics (Volume 2: Short Papers)* (2016), pp. 399–405

162. S. Cresci, M. Petrocchi, A. Spognardi, S. Tognazzi, From reaction to proaction: unexplored ways to the detection of evolving spambots, in *Companion Proceedings of the Web Conference 2018 (WWW'18)* (2018), pp. 1469–1470

163. D. Boneh, A.J. Grotto, P. McDaniel, N. Papernot, How relevant is the turing test in the age of sophisbots? IEEE Secur. Priv. **17**(6), 64–71 (2019)

164. S. Raponi, I. Ali, G. Oligeri, Sound of guns: digital forensics of gun audio samples meets artificial intelligence (2020). arXiv preprint arXiv:2004.07948

165. Y. Li, M.-C. Chang, S. Lyu, In ictu oculi: exposing ai generated fake face videos by detecting eye blinking (2018). arXiv preprint arXiv:1806.02877

166. A. Rössler, D. Cozzolino, L. Verdoliva, C. Riess, J. Thies, M. Nießner, Faceforensics: a large-scale video dataset for forgery detection in human faces (2018). arXiv preprint arXiv:1803.09179

167. S. Nakamoto, Bitcoin: a peer-to-peer electronic cash system, tech. rep., Manubot, 2019

168. U. W. Chohan, State-sponsored cryptocurrencies: the diverse motivations (2020)

169. D. Kushner, Sony vs. the hackers. IEEE Spectr. **48**, 16 (2011)

170. K. Michaelis, C. Meyer, J. Schwenk, Randomly failed! the state of randomness in current java implementations, in *Topics in Cryptology—CT-RSA 2013*, ed. by E. Dawson (Springer, Berlin, 2013), pp. 129–144

171. B.B. Brumley, N. Tuveri, Remote timing attacks are still practical, in *European Symposium on Research in Computer Security* (Springer, Berlin, 2011), pp. 355–371

172. H.C. Van Tilborg, S. Jajodia, *Encyclopedia of Cryptography and Security* (Springer, Berlin, 2014)

173. F. Chabaud, A. Joux, Differential collisions in SHA-0, in *Annual International Cryptology Conference* (Springer, Berlin, 1998), pp. 56–71

174. H. Dobbertin, Cryptanalysis of MD4, in *International Workshop on Fast Software Encryption* (Springer, Berlin, 1996), pp. 53–69

175. H. Dobbertin, Cryptanalysis of MD5 compress (may 1996), in *Rump Session of Eurocrypt*, vol. 96 (1996)

176. H. Dobbertin, The status of MD5 after a recent attack, in *Crypto-Bytes the Technical Newsletter of RSA Laboratories, a Division of RSA Data Security, Inc.*, vol. 2(2) (1996)

177. H. Dobbertin, Ripemd with two-round compress function is not collision-free. J. Cryptol. **10**(1), 51–69 (1997)

178. H. Handschuh, L.R. Knudsen, M.J. Robshaw, Analysis of SHA-1 in encryption mode, in *Cryptographers' Track at the RSA Conference* (Springer, Berlin, 2001), pp. 70–83

179. B. Preneel, R. Govaerts, J. Vandewalle, Differential cryptanalysis of hash functions based on block ciphers, in *Proceedings of the First ACM Conference on Computer and Communications Security* (ACM, 1993), pp. 183–188

180. M.-J.O. Saarinen, Cryptanalysis of block ciphers based on SHA-1 and MD5, in *International Workshop on Fast Software Encryption* (Springer, Berlin, 2003), pp. 36–44

181. C. Meadows, The NRL protocol analyzer: an overview. J. Log. Program. **26**(2), 113–131 (1996)

182. R. Kemmerer, C. Meadows, J. Millen, Three systems for cryptographic protocol analysis. J. Cryptol. **7**(2), 79–130 (1994)

183. C. Meadows, Open issues in formal methods for cryptographic protocol analysis, in *Proceedings DARPA Information Survivability Conference and Exposition. DISCEX'00*, vol. 1 (2000), pp. 237–250

184. P. W. Shor, Algorithms for quantum computation: discrete logarithms and factoring, in *Proceedings of the 35th Annual Symposium on Foundations of Computer Science, 1994* (IEEE, 1994), pp. 124–134

185. The threat quantum computers pose to modern security. https://www.scmagazineuk.com/the-threat-quantum-computers-pose-to-modern-security/article/709472/. Last checked August 2020
186. V. Mavroeidis, K. Vishi, M.D. Zych, A. Jøsang, The impact of quantum computing on present cryptography. Int. J. Adv. Comput. Sci. Appl. **9**(3) (2018)
187. I. M. Ali, M. Caprolu, R. Di Pietro, Foundations, properties, and security applications of puzzles: a survey. ACM Comput. Surv. (2020)
188. F. Arute, K. Arya, R. Babbush, D. Bacon, J.C. Bardin, R. Barends, R. Biswas, S. Boixo, F.G. Brandao, D.A. Buell, et al., Quantum supremacy using a programmable superconducting processor. Nature **574**(7779), 505–510 (2019)
189. A. Davenport, S. Shetty, X. Liang, Attack surface analysis of permissioned blockchain platforms for smart cities, in *2018 IEEE International Smart Cities Conference (ISC2)* (2018), pp. 1–6
190. S. Dey, Securing majority-attack in blockchain using machine learning and algorithmic game theory: a proof of work, in *2018 Tenth Computer Science and Electronic Engineering (CEEC)* (2018), pp. 7–10
191. C. Bendiksen, S. Gibbons, The bitcoin mining network—trends, composition, average creation cost, electricity consumption and sources, in *CoinShares Research, Whitepaper* (2019)
192. M. Apostolaki, A. Zohar, L. Vanbever, Hijacking bitcoin: routing attacks on cryptocurrencies, in *2017 IEEE Symposium on Security and Privacy (SP)* (IEEE, Piscataway, 2017), pp. 375–392
193. M. Apostolaki, M. Gian, M. Jan, V. Laurent, Sabre: protecting bitcoin against routing attacks, in *NDSS* (2019), pp. 1–15
194. A. Boldyreva, R. Lychev, Provable security of S-BGP and other path vector protocols: model, analysis and extensions, in *Proceedings of the 2012 ACM conference on Computer and communications Security* (ACM, New York, 2012), pp. 541–552
195. P. Gill, M. Schapira, S. Goldberg, Let the market drive deployment: a strategy for transitioning to bgp security. ACM SIGCOMM Comput. Commun. Rev. **41**, 14–25 (2011)
196. Y.-C. Hu, A. Perrig, M. Sirbu, SPV: secure path vector routing for securing BGP. ACM SIGCOMM Comput. Commun. Rev. **34**(4), 179–192 (2004)
197. P.C. van Oorschot, T. Wan, E. Kranakis, On interdomain routing security and pretty secure BGP (PSBGP). ACM Trans. Inf. Syst. Secur. **10**(3), 11 (2007)
198. E. Heilman, A. Kendler, A. Zohar, S. Goldberg, Eclipse attacks on bitcoin's peer-to-peer network, in *USENIX Security Symposium* (2015), pp. 129–144
199. A. Gervais, G. Karame, S. Capkun, V. Capkun, Is bitcoin a decentralized currency? IEEE Secur. Priv. **12**(3), 54–60 (2014)
200. X. Shi, Y. Xiang, Z. Wang, X. Yin, J. Wu, Detecting prefix hijackings in the internet with argus, in *Proceedings of the 2012 Internet Measurement Conference* (ACM, New York, 2012), pp. 15–28
201. Z. Zhang, Y. Zhang, Y. C. Hu, Z. M. Mao, Practical defenses against BGP prefix hijacking, in *Proceedings of the 2007 ACM CoNEXT Conference* (ACM, New York, 2007), p. 3
202. Z. Zhang, Y. Zhang, Y.C. Hu, Z. M. Mao, R. Bush, iSPY: detecting IP prefix hijacking on my own. IEEE/ACM Trans. Netw. **18**(6), 1815–1828 (2010)
203. E. Piscini, S.J.L. Rosenberg, State-sponsored cryptocurrency: adapting the best of bitcoin's innovation to the payments ecosystem (report)
204. P. Schueffel, Taming the beast: a scientific definition of fintech. J. Innov. Manag. **4**(4), 32–54 (2016)
205. K. Leong, A. Sung, Fintech (financial technology): what is it and how to use technologies to create business value in fintech way? Int. J. Innov. Manag. Technol. **9**(2), 74–78 (2018)
206. R. Guidotti, A. Monreale, S. Ruggieri, F. Turini, F. Giannotti, D. Pedreschi, A survey of methods for explaining black box models. ACM Comput. Surv. **51**(5), 1–42 (2018)
207. A. W. Lo, Moore's law vs. Murphy's law in the financial system: who's winning? J. Invest. Manag. **15**(1), 17–38 (2017)

208. R.T. Thakor, R.C. Merton, Trust in lending, tech. rep., National Bureau of Economic Research, 2018
209. K. Gai, M. Qiu, X. Sun, A survey on fintech. J. Netw. Comput. Appl. **103**, 262–273 (2018)
210. S.R. Das, The future of fintech. Financ. Manag. **48**(4), 981–1007 (2019)
211. A. Zaborovskaya, V. Zaborovskiy, K. Pletnev, Possibilities of preventing manipulative transactions on the stock market in the conditions of new industrialization, in *The Second International Scientific Conference on New Industrialization: Global, National, Regional Dimension (SICNI 2018)* (Atlantis Press, 2019)
212. S. Cresci, F. Lillo, D. Regoli, S. Tardelli, M. Tesconi, Cashtag piggybacking: uncovering spam and bot activity in stock microblogs on twitter. ACM Trans. Web **13**(2), 1–27 (2019)
213. A.K. Nassirtoussi, S. Aghabozorgi, T.Y. Wah, D.C.L. Ngo, Text mining for market prediction: a systematic review. Expert Syst. Appl. **41**(16), 7653–7670 (2014)
214. H.S. Moat, C. Curme, A. Avakian, D.Y. Kenett, H.E. Stanley, T. Preis, Quantifying wikipedia usage patterns before stock market moves. Sci. Rep. **3**, 1801 (2013)
215. T. Preis, H.S. Moat, H.E. Stanley, Quantifying trading behavior in financial markets using Google trends. Sci. Rep. **3**, 1684 (2013)
216. R. H. Gálvez, A. Gravano, Assessing the usefulness of online message board mining in automatic stock prediction systems. J. Comput. Sci. **19**, 43–56 (2017)
217. R.P. Schumaker, H. Chen, Textual analysis of stock market prediction using breaking financial news: the AZFin text system. ACM Trans. Inf. Syst. **27**(2), 1–19 (2009)
218. A. Atkins, M. Niranjan, E. Gerding, Financial news predicts stock market volatility better than close price. J. Financ. Data Sci. **4**(2), 120–137 (2018)
219. X. Ding, Y. Zhang, T. Liu, J. Duan, Deep learning for event-driven stock prediction, in *The 24th International Joint Conference on Artificial Intelligence (IJCAI'15)* (2015)
220. R. Luss, A. d'Aspremont, Predicting abnormal returns from news using text classification. Quant. Finan. **15**(6), 999–1012 (2015)
221. J. Bollen, H. Mao, X. Zeng, Twitter mood predicts the stock market. J. Comput. Sci. **2**(1), 1–8 (2011)
222. V. Voukelatou, L. Gabrielli, I. Miliou, S. Cresci, R. Sharma, M. Tesconi, L. Pappalardo, Measuring objective and subjective well-being: dimensions and data sources. Int. J. Data Sci. Anal. (2020)
223. A. Bujari, M. Furini, N. Laina, On using cashtags to predict companies stock trends, in *Proceedings of the 14th IEEE Annual Consumer Communications and Networking Conference (CCNC'17)* (IEEE, Piscataway, 2017), pp. 25–28
224. N. Rajesh, L. Gandy, CashTagNN: using sentiment of tweets with CashTags to predict stock market prices, in *Proceedings of the 11th International Conference on Intelligent Systems: Theories and Applications (SITA'16)* (IEEE, Piscataway, 2016), pp. 1–4
225. Y. Mao, W. Wei, B. Wang, B. Liu, Correlating S&P 500 stocks with Twitter data, in *Proceedings of the First International Workshop on Hot Topics on Interdisciplinary Social Networks Research (SIGKDD'12 Workshops)* (ACM, New York, 2012), pp. 69–72
226. E.J. Ruiz, V. Hristidis, C. Castillo, A. Gionis, A. Jaimes, Correlating financial time series with micro-blogging activity, in *Proceedings of the Fifth International Conference on Web Search and Data Mining (WSDM'12)* (ACM, New York, 2012), pp. 513–522
227. L. Cazzoli, R. Sharma, M. Treccani, F. Lillo, A large scale study to understand the relation between Twitter and financial market, in *Proceedings of the Third European Network Intelligence Conference (ENIC'16)* (IEEE, Piscataway, 2016), pp. 98–105
228. M. Kharratzadeh, M. Coates, Weblog analysis for predicting correlations in stock price evolutions, in *Proceedings of the Sixth International Conference on Web and Social Media (ICWSM'12)* (AAAI, 2012)
229. Y. Wei, P. Yildirim, C. Van den Bulte, C. Dellarocas, Credit scoring with social network data. Market. Sci. **35**(2), 234–258 (2016)
230. T. Berg, V. Burg, A. Gombović, M. Puri, On the rise of fintechs: credit scoring using digital footprints. Rev. Financ. Stud. (2019)

231. M. Lin, N.R. Prabhala, S. Viswanathan, Judging borrowers by the company they keep: friendship networks and information asymmetry in online peer-to-peer lending. Manag. Sci. **59**(1), 17–35 (2013)

232. S. Cresci, F. Lillo, D. Regoli, S. Tardelli, M. Tesconi, $FAKE: evidence of spam and bot activity in stock microblogs on Twitter, in *The 12th International AAAI Conference on Web and Social Media (ICWSM'18)* (AAAI, 2018), pp. 580–583

233. S. Tardelli, M. Avvenuti, M. Tesconi, S. Cresci, Characterizing social bots spreading financial disinformation, in *The 20th International Conference on Social Computing and Social Media (SCSM'20)* (2020)

234. M.J. Aitken, F. Harris, S. Ji, Trade-based manipulation and market efficiency: a cross-market comparison, in *The 22nd Australasian Finance and Banking Conference* (2009), p. 18

235. R.K. Aggarwal, G. Wu, Stock market manipulations. J. Bus. **79**(4), 1915–1953 (2006)

236. J.-P. Rodrigue, *The Geography of Transport Systems* (Taylor & Francis, London, 2016)

237. L. Nizzoli, S. Tardelli, M. Avvenuti, S. Cresci, M. Tesconi, E. Ferrara, Charting the landscape of online cryptocurrency manipulation. IEEE Access (2020)

238. M. Glenski, E. Saldanha, S. Volkova, Characterizing speed and scale of cryptocurrency discussion spread on reddit, in *The 28th International Conference on World Wide Web (WWW'19)* (2019), pp. 560–570

239. J. Xu, B. Livshits, The anatomy of a cryptocurrency pump-and-dump scheme, in *The 28th USENIX Security Symposium (SEC'19)* (2019), pp. 1609–1625

240. A. Feder, N. Gandal, J. Hamrick, T. Moore, A. Mukherjee, F. Rouhi, M. Vasek, The economics of cryptocurrency pump and dump schemes. Discussion Papers 13404, C.E.P.R., 2018

241. M. Mirtaheri, S. Abu-El-Haija, F. Morstatter, G.V. Steeg, A. Galstyan, Identifying and analyzing cryptocurrency manipulations in social media (2019). arXiv preprint arXiv:1902.03110

242. J. Kamps, B. Kleinberg, To the moon: defining and detecting cryptocurrency pump-and-dumps. Crime Sci. **7**(1), 18 (2018)

243. M. Vasek, T. Moore, Analyzing the bitcoin Ponzi scheme ecosystem, in *The 23rd International Conference on Financial Cryptography and Data Security (FC'19)* (2019), pp. 101–112

244. M. Bartoletti, B. Pes, S. Serusi, Data mining for detecting bitcoin ponzi schemes, in *The First Crypto Valley Conference on Blockchain Technology (CVCBT'18)* (IEEE, Piscataway, 2018), pp. 75–84

245. I. Goodfellow, P. McDaniel, N. Papernot, Making machine learning robust against adversarial inputs. Commun. ACM **61**(7), 56–66 (2018)

246. V. Duddu, A survey of adversarial machine learning in cyber warfare. Def. Sci. J. **68**(4), 356 (2018)

247. A. Chakraborty, M. Alam, V. Dey, A. Chattopadhyay, D. Mukhopadhyay, Adversarial attacks and defences: a survey (2018). arXiv preprint arXiv:1810.00069

248. I.J. Goodfellow, J. Shlens, C. Szegedy, Explaining and harnessing adversarial examples (2014). arXiv preprint arXiv:1412.6572

249. H. Hosseini, Y. Chen, S. Kannan, B. Zhang, R. Poovendran, Blocking transferability of adversarial examples in black-box learning systems (2017). arXiv preprint arXiv:1703.04318

250. I. Goodfellow, J. Pouget-Abadie, M. Mirza, B. Xu, D. Warde-Farley, S. Ozair, A. Courville, Y. Bengio, Generative adversarial nets, in *Advances in Neural Information Processing Systems (NeurIPS'14)* (2014), pp. 2672–2680

251. N. Akhtar, A. Mian, Threat of adversarial attacks on deep learning in computer vision: a survey. IEEE Access **6**, 14410–14430 (2018)

252. N. Carlini, D. Wagner, Audio adversarial examples: targeted attacks on speech-to-text, in *The 2018 IEEE Security and Privacy Workshops (SPW'18)* (IEEE, Piscataway, 2018), pp. 1–7

253. W.E. Zhang, Q.Z. Sheng, A. Alhazmi, C. Li, Adversarial attacks on deep-learning models in natural language processing: a survey. ACM Trans. Intell. Syst. Technol. **11**(3), 1–41 (2020)

254. S. Cresci, M. Petrocchi, A. Spognardi, S. Tognazzi, Better safe than sorry: an adversarial approach to improve social bot detection, in *The 11th ACM Conference on Web Science (WebSci'19)* (2019), pp. 47–56

255. S. Cresci, M. Petrocchi, A. Spognardi, S. Tognazzi, On the capability of evolved spambots to evade detection via genetic engineering. Online Soc. Netw. Media **9**, 1–16 (2019)
256. B. Wu, L. Liu, Y. Yang, K. Zheng, X. Wang, Using improved conditional generative adversarial networks to detect social bots on twitter. IEEE Access **8**, 36664–36680 (2020)
257. R. Zellers, A. Holtzman, H. Rashkin, Y. Bisk, A. Farhadi, F. Roesner, Y. Choi, Defending against neural fake news, in *The 33rd Conference on Neural Information Processing Systems (NeurIPS'19)* (2019), pp. 9051–9062
258. X. Zhou, Z. Pan, G. Hu, S. Tang, C. Zhao, Stock market prediction on high-frequency data using generative adversarial nets. Math. Prob. Eng. **2018**, 4907423 (2018)
259. K. Zhang, G. Zhong, J. Dong, S. Wang, Y. Wang, Stock market prediction based on generative adversarial network. Proc. Comput. Sci. **147**, 400–406 (2019)
260. F. Feng, H. Chen, X. He, J. Ding, M. Sun, T.-S. Chua, Enhancing stock movement prediction with adversarial training, in *The 28th International Joint Conference on Artificial Intelligence (IJCAI'19)* (AAAI Press, 2019), pp. 5843–5849
261. S. Takahashi, Y. Chen, K. Tanaka-Ishii, Modeling financial time-series with generative adversarial networks. Phys. A Stat. Mech. Appl. **527**, 121261 (2019)
262. G.K. Palshikar, M.M. Apte, Collusion set detection using graph clustering. Data Min. Knowl. Disc. **16**(2), 135–164 (2008)
263. M.N. Islam, S.R. Haque, K.M. Alam, M. Tarikuzzaman, An approach to improve collusion set detection using mcl algorithm, in *The 12th International Conference on Computers and Information Technology* (IEEE, Piscataway, 2009), pp. 237–242
264. M. Franke, B. Hoser, J. Schröder, On the analysis of irregular stock market trading behavior, in *Data Analysis, Machine Learning and Applications* (Springer, 2008), pp. 355–362
265. J. Wang, S. Zhou, J. Guan, Detecting potential collusive cliques in futures markets based on trading behaviors from real data. Neurocomputing **92**, 44–53 (2012), pp. 355–362
266. D. Harmon, M. Lagi, M.A. de Aguiar, D.D. Chinellato, D. Braha, I.R. Epstein, Y. Bar-Yam, Anticipating economic market crises using measures of collective panic. PLoS One **10**(7), e0131871 (2015)
267. E. Monaco, What fintech can learn from high-frequency trading: economic consequences, open issues and future of corporate disclosure, in *Disrupting Finance* (Springer, 2019), pp. 51–70
268. M. Lewis, *Flash Boys* (W.W. Norton & Company, New York, 2014)
269. G.F. Thompson, Time, trading and algorithms in financial sector security. New Polit. Econ. **22**(1), 1–11 (2017)
270. T. Hendershott, R. Riordan, Algorithmic trading and the market for liquidity. J. Finan. Quant. Anal. **48**(4), 1001–1024 (2013)
271. J. Hasbrouck, G. Saar, Low-latency trading. J. Financ. Mark. **16**(4), 646–679 (2013)
272. A.J. Menkveld, High frequency trading and the new market makers. J. Financ. Mark. **16**(4), 712–740 (2013)
273. S. Chesterman, 'move fast and break things': law, technology, and the problem of speed. NUS Law Working Paper (2020)
274. M. Bellia, K. Christensen, A. Kolokolov, L. Pelizzon, R. Renò, High-frequency trading during flash crashes: walk of fame or hall of shame? SAFE Working Paper (2020)
275. D. Sornette, S. von der Becke, Crashes and high frequency trading: an evaluation of risks posed by high-speed algorithmic trading, in *The Future of Computer Trading in Financial Markets* (2011)
276. S. Galeshchuk, Technological bias at the exchange rate market. Intell. Syst. Account. Finan. Manag. **24**(2–3), 80–86 (2017)
277. A. W. Lo, The adaptive markets hypothesis. J. Portf. Manag. **30**(5), 15–29 (2004)
278. M. Davis, A. Kumiega, B. Van Vliet, Ethics, finance, and automation: a preliminary survey of problems in high frequency trading. Sci. Eng. Ethics **19**(3), 851–874 (2013)
279. M. Baron, J. Brogaard, B. Hagströmer, A. Kirilenko, Risk and return in high-frequency trading. J. Financ. Quant. Anal. **54**(3), 993–1024 (2019)

280. O. Linton, S. Mahmoodzadeh, Implications of high-frequency trading for security markets. Ann. Rev. Econ. **10**, 237–259 (2018)
281. E. Budish, P. Cramton, J. Shim, The high-frequency trading arms race: frequent batch auctions as a market design response. Q. J. Econ. **130**(4), 1547–1621 (2015)
282. J. Grahl, P. Lysandrou, The European Commission's proposal for a financial transactions tax: a critical assessment. J. Common Market Stud. **52**(2), 234–249 (2014)
283. W.L. Currie, J.J. Seddon, The regulatory, technology and market 'dark arts trilogy'of high frequency trading: a research agenda. J. Inf. Technol. **32**(2), 111–126 (2017)
284. E. Hu, D. Murphy, Vestigial tails: floor brokers at the close in modern electronic markets. Available at SSRN (2020)
285. A. Neyret, Stock market cybercrime, tech. rep., Autorité des Marchés Financiers (AMF), 2020
286. A. Abhishta, R. Joosten, S. Dragomiretskiy, L.J. Nieuwenhuis, Impact of successful ddos attacks on a major crypto-currency exchange, in *The 27th Euromicro International Conference on Parallel, Distributed and Network-Based Processing (PDP'19)* (IEEE, Piscataway, 2019), pp. 379–384
287. A. Feder, N. Gandal, J. Hamrick, T. Moore, The impact of DDoS and other security shocks on Bitcoin currency exchanges: evidence from Mt. Gox. J. Cybersecur. **3**(2), 137–144 (2017)
288. B. Johnson, A. Laszka, J. Grossklags, M. Vasek, T. Moore, Game-theoretic analysis of DDoS attacks against bitcoin mining pools, in *The International Conference on Financial Cryptography and Data Security* (Springer, Berlin, 2014), pp. 72–86
289. M. Vasek, M. Thornton, T. Moore, Empirical analysis of denial-of-service attacks in the bitcoin ecosystem, in *The International Conference on Financial Cryptography and Data Security* (Springer, Berlin, 2014), pp. 57–71
290. T. Peng, C. Leckie, K. Ramamohanarao, Survey of network-based defense mechanisms countering the DoS and DDoS problems. ACM Comput. Surv **39**(1), 3-es (2007)
291. S.T. Zargar, J. Joshi, D. Tipper, A survey of defense mechanisms against distributed denial of service (DDoS) flooding attacks. IEEE Commun. Surv. Tutorials **15**(4), 2046–2069 (2013)
292. F. Caccioli, P. Barucca, T. Kobayashi, Network models of financial systemic risk: a review. J. Comput. Soc. Sci. **1**(1), 81–114 (2018)
293. A.G. Haldane, R. M. May, Systemic risk in banking ecosystems. Nature **469**(7330), 351–355 (2011)
294. D. Bisias, M. Flood, A. W. Lo, S. Valavanis, A survey of systemic risk analytics. Annu. Rev. Financ. Econ. **4**(1), 255–296 (2012)
295. L. Alessi, C. Detken, Quasi real time early warning indicators for costly asset price boom/bust cycles: a role for global liquidity. Eur. J. Polit. Econ. **27**(3), 520–533 (2011)
296. C. Borio, Implementing a macroprudential framework: blending boldness and realism. Capital. Soc. **6**(1) (2011)
297. K. Giesecke, B. Kim, Risk analysis of collateralized debt obligations. Oper. Res. **59**(1), 32–49 (2011)
298. D. Duffie, Systemic risk exposures: a 10-by-10-by-10 approach, in *Risk topography: Systemic Risk and Macro Modeling* (University of Chicago Press, Chicago, 2013), pp. 47–56
299. V.V. Acharya, L.H. Pedersen, T. Philippon, M. Richardson, Measuring systemic risk. Rev. Financ. Stud. **30**(1), 2–47 (2017)
300. T. Adrian, H.S. Shin, Liquidity and leverage. J. Financ. Intermed. **19**(3), 418–437 (2010)
301. M. Brunnermeier, A. Krishnamurthy, *Risk Topography: Systemic Risk and Macro Modeling* (University of Chicago Press, Chicago, 2014)
302. S. Battiston, M. Puliga, R. Kaushik, P. Tasca, G. Caldarelli, Debtrank: too central to fail? Financial networks, the fed and systemic risk. Sci. Rep. **2**, 541 (2012)
303. D. Burdick, M. Hernández, H. Ho, G. Koutrika, R. Krishnamurthy, L. Popa, I.R. Stanoi, S. Vaithyanathan, S. Das, Extracting, linking and integrating data from public sources: a financial case study. IEEE Data Eng. Bull. 60 (2011)
304. S. Vitali, J.B. Glattfelder, S. Battiston, The network of global corporate control. PLoS One **6**(10), e25995 (2011)

305. X. Huang, I. Vodenska, S. Havlin, H.E. Stanley, Cascading failures in bi-partite graphs: model for systemic risk propagation. Sci. Rep. **3**, 1219 (2013)
306. M. Bardoscia, F. Caccioli, J.I. Perotti, G. Vivaldo, G. Caldarelli, Distress propagation in complex networks: the case of non-linear debtrank. PLoS One **11**(10), e0163825 (2016)
307. S. M. Krause, H. Štefančić, V. Zlatić, G. Caldarelli, Controlling systemic risk-network structures that minimize it and node properties to calculate it (2019). arXiv preprint arXiv:1902.08483
308. D. Delpini, S. Battiston, G. Caldarelli, M. Riccaboni, Systemic risk from investment similarities. PLoS One **14**(5), e0217141 (2019)
309. P. Mazzarisi, F. Lillo, S. Marmi, When panic makes you blind: a chaotic route to systemic risk. J. Econ. Dyn. Control **100**, 176–199 (2019)
310. F. Corsi, F. Lillo, D. Pirino, L. Trapin, Measuring the propagation of financial distress with granger-causality tail risk networks. J. Financ. Stab. **38**, 18–36 (2018)
311. M. Bailey, R. Cao, T. Kuchler, J. Stroebel, The economic effects of social networks: evidence from the housing market. J. Polit. Econ. **126**(6), 2224–2276 (2018)
312. P. Gai, S. Kapadia, Networks and systemic risk in the financial system. Oxf. Rev. Econ. Policy **35**(4), 586–613 (2019)
313. Presidential policy directive—critical infrastructure security and resilience. https://obamawhitehouse.archives.gov/the-press-office/2013/02/12/presidential-policy-directive-critical-infrastructure-security-and-resil. Last checked August 2020
314. A. Roberts, R. Guelff, *Documents on the Laws of War* (Oxford University Press, Oxford, 2000)
315. N. Ismail, New malware represents biggest threat to critical infrastructure (2017). https://www.information-age.com/new-malware-represents-biggest-threat-critical-infrastructure-123466733/. Last checked August 2020
316. M. Akbanov, V.G. Vassilakis, M.D. Logothetis, Wannacry ransomware: analysis of infection, persistence, recovery prevention and propagation mechanisms. Res. J. Telecommun. Inf. Technol. (2019)
317. I.N. Fovino, A. Carcano, M. Masera, A. Trombetta, An experimental investigation of malware attacks on SCADA systems. Int. J. Crit. Infrastruct. Prot. **2**(4), 139–145 (2009)
318. I.N. Fovino, M. Masera, L. Guidi, G. Carpi, An experimental platform for assessing SCADA vulnerabilities and countermeasures in power plants, in *Third International Conference on Human System Interaction* (2010), pp. 679–686
319. A. Falaye, O. Osho, M. Emehian, S. Ale, Dynamics of SCADA system malware: impacts on smart grid electricity networks and countermeasures, in *International Conference on Information and Communication Technology and Application. ICTA* 1st edn. (Nigeria, 2016)
320. E.D. Knapp, J.T. Langill, *Industrial Network Security: Securing Critical Infrastructure Networks for Smart Grid, SCADA, and Other Industrial Control Systems* (Syngress, Rockland, 2014)
321. M. Caprolu, S. Raponi, G. Oligeri, R. D. Pietro, Cryptomining makes noise: a machine learning approach for cryptojacking detection (2019)
322. A. Bolshev, I. Yushkevich, SCADA and mobile security in the internet of things era. EMBEDI, IOActive, Whitepaper (2017)
323. L. Robert, A. Michael, C. Tim, Analysis of the cyber attack on the Ukrainian power grid. E-ISAC and SANS Whitepaper (2016)
324. A. Cherepanov, Win32/industroyer: a new threat for industrial control systems. ESET Whitepaper (2017)
325. I. Overland, The geopolitics of renewable energy: debunking four emerging myths. Energy Res. Soc. Sci. **49**, 36–40 (2019)
326. B. Miller, D. Rowe, A survey SCADA of and critical infrastructure incidents, in *Proceedings of the 1st Annual Conference on Research in Information Technology, RIIT '12* (ACM, New York, 2012), pp. 51–56
327. A. Nicholson, S. Webber, S. Dyer, T. Patel, H. Janicke, SCADA security in the light of cyber-warfare. Comput. Secur. **31**(4), 418–436 (2012)

328. T. Yardley, SCADA: issues, vulnerabilities and future directions.; login:: the magazine of USENIX SAGE **33**(6), 14–20 (2008)
329. L. Bilge, T. Dumitraş, Before we knew it: an empirical study of zero-day attacks in the real world, in *Proceedings of the 2012 ACM Conference on Computer and Communications Security, CCS '12* (Association for Computing Machinery, New York, 2012), pp. 833–844
330. S. Jajodia, V. Subrahmanian, V. Swarup, C. Wang, *Cyber Deception*, vol. 6 (Springer, Berlin, 2016)
331. S. Jajodia, N. Park, F. Pierazzi, A. Pugliese, E. Serra, G.I. Simari, V.S. Subrahmanian, A probabilistic logic of cyber deception. IEEE Trans. Inf. Forensics Secur. **12**(11), 2532–2544 (2017)
332. P. Karuna, H. Purohit, S. Jajodia, R. Ganesan, and O. Uzuner, Fake document generation for cyber deception by manipulating text comprehensibility. IEEE Syst. J. 1–11 (2020)
333. M. Caprolu, R.D. Pietro, S. Raponi, S. Sciancalepore, P. Tedeschi, Vessels cybersecurity: issues, challenges, and the road ahead. IEEE Commun. Mag. **58**(6), 90–96 (2020)
334. P. Tedeschi, S. Sciancalepore, Edge and fog computing in critical infrastructures: analysis, security threats, and research challenges, in *2019 IEEE European Symposium on Security and Privacy Workshops (EuroS&PW)* (IEEE, 2019), pp. 1–10
335. K. Dalamagkidis, Classification of UAVs, in *Handbook of Unmanned Aerial Vehicles* (2015), pp. 83–91
336. A.E. Dan Shea, B. Husch, Drones and critical infrastructure (2016)
337. K.W. Smith, Drone technology: benefits, risks, and legal considerations. Seattle J. Envtl. L. **5**, i (2015)
338. M. Peacock, M.N. Johnstone, Towards detection and control of civilian unmanned aerial vehicles (2013)
339. P. Tedeschi, G. Oligeri, R. Di Pietro, Leveraging jamming to help drones complete their mission. IEEE Access **8**, 5049–5064 (2019)
340. U.H. Security, Unmanned aircraft systems (UAS)—critical infrastructure. https://www.dhs.gov/uas-ci. Last checked August 2020
341. Maltego ce., https://www.paterva.com/web7/buy/maltego-clients/maltego-ce.php. Last checked August 2020
342. Shodan: the world's first search engine for internet-connected devices. https://www.shodan.io/. Last checked August 2020
343. H. Al-Alami, A. Hadi, H. Al-Bahadili, Vulnerability scanning of IoT devices in Jordan using shodan, in *2017 2nd International Conference on the Applications of Information Technology in Developing Renewable Energy Processes and Systems (IT-DREPS)* (IEEE, Piscataway, 2017), pp. 1–6
344. N. Zaidi, H. Kaushik, D. Bablani, R. Bansal, P. Kumar, A study of exposure of IoT devices in India: using shodan search engine, in *Information Systems Design and Intelligent Applications* (Springer, Berlin, 2018), pp. 1044–1053
345. M. Glassman, M.J. Kang, Intelligence in the internet age: the emergence and evolution of open source intelligence (OSINT). Comput. Hum. Behav. **28**(2), 673–682 (2012)
346. R.D. Steele, Open source intelligence, in *Handbook of Intelligence Studies* (2007), pp. 129–147,
347. C. Best, Challenges in open source intelligence, in *Intelligence and Security Informatics Conference (EISIC), 2011 European* (IEEE, Piscataway, 2011), pp. 58–62
348. S.C. Mercado, Sailing the sea of OSINT in the information age, in *Secret Intell. Reader* (2009), p. 78
349. R.A. Best Jr., A. Cumming, *Open Source Intelligence (OSINT): Issues for Congress* (2007)
350. M. Caprolu, R. Di Pietro, F. Lombardi, S. Raponi, Edge computing perspectives: architectures, technologies, and open security issues, in *2019 IEEE International Conference on Edge Computing (EDGE)* (IEEE, Piscataway, 2019), pp. 116–123
351. J. Huang, D.M. Nicol, Trust mechanisms for cloud computing. J. Cloud Comput. Adv. Syst. Appl. **2**(1), 9 (2013)

352. D. Zissis, D. Lekkas, Addressing cloud computing security issues. Futur. Gener. Comput. Syst. **28**(3), 583–592 (2012)
353. F. Zafar, A. Khan, S.U.R. Malik, M. Ahmed, A. Anjum, M.I. Khan, N. Javed, M. Alam, F. Jamil, A survey of cloud computing data integrity schemes: design challenges, taxonomy and future trends. Comput. Secur. **65**, 29–49 (2017)
354. G. Ateniese, R. Burns, R. Curtmola, J. Herring, L. Kissner, Z. Peterson, D. Song, Provable data possession at untrusted stores, in *Proceedings of the 14th ACM conference on Computer and communications Security* (2007), pp. 598–609
355. G. Ateniese, R. Di Pietro, L.V. Mancini, G. Tsudik, Scalable and efficient provable data possession, in *Proceedings of the Fourth International Conference on Security and Privacy in Communication Netowrks* (2008), pp. 1–10
356. R. Curtmola, O. Khan, R. Burns, G. Ateniese, MR-PDP: multiple-replica provable data possession, in *2008 the 28th International Conference on Distributed Computing Systems* (IEEE, Piscataway, 2008), pp. 411–420
357. G. Ateniese, S. Kamara, J. Katz, Proofs of storage from homomorphic identification protocols, in *International Conference on the Theory and Application of Cryptology and Information Security* (Springer, Berlin, 2009), pp. 319–333
358. S. Specht, R. Lee, Taxonomies of distributed denial of service networks, attacks, tools and countermeasures, in *CEL2003-03, Princeton University, Princeton, NJ, USA* (2003) l
359. S. Raponi, M. Caprolu, R. Di Pietro, Intrusion detection at the network edge: solutions, limitations, and future directions, in *International Conference on Edge Computing* (Springer, 2019), pp. 59–75

Glossary

AI	Artificial Intelligence
AML	Anti-Money Laundering
AS	Autonomous System
AT	Automatic Trading
AUV	Autonomous Underwater Vehicles
BGP	Border Gateway Protocol
C&C	Command and Control
CA	Corporations Act
CDOs	Collateralized Debt Obligations
CISO	Chief Information Security Officer
CSO	Chief Security Officer
DCS	Distributed Control Systems
DDoS	Distributed Denial of Service
DJIA	Dow Jones Industrial Average
DMZ	Demilitarized Zone
DoS	Denial of Service
ECC	Elliptic Curve Cryptography
ETFs	Exchange-Traded Funds
FINRA	Financial Industry Regulatory Authority
GAN	Generative Adversarial Network
GFC	Global Financial Crisis
HFT	High-Frequency Trading
HKEx	Hong Kong Stock Exchange
HMI	Human Machine Interface
ICS	Industrial Control System
ICT	Information and Communication Technologies
IIoT	Industrial Internet of Things
IOSCO	International Securities Commission Association
IoT	Internet of Things

© The Author(s), under exclusive license to
Springer Nature Switzerland AG 2021
R. Di Pietro et al., *New Dimensions of Information Warfare*, Advances in
Information Security 84, https://doi.org/10.1007/978-3-030-60618-3

ISP	Internet Service Providers
IT	Information Technologies
KYC	Know Your Customer
MAD	Market Abuse Directive
MFA	Multifactor Authentication
MITM	Man-in-the-middle
ML	Machine Learning
NHS	National Health Service
NLP	Natural Language Processing
NSE	National Stock Exchange of India
NYSE	New York Stock Exchange
OPC	OLE for Process Control
OPSEC	Operational security
OSINT	Open Source INTelligence
OSN	Online Social Network
P2P	Peer to Peer
P&D	Pump-and-dump
PCA	Principal Component Analysis
PLC	Programmable Logic Controllers
PoW	Proof of Work
PPD-21	Presidential Policy Directive 21
PSYOPS	Psychological Operations
RDP	Remote Desktop Protocol
ROV	Remotely Operated underwater Vehicles
RTU	Remote Transmission Units
S&P	Standard & Poor's
SCADA	Supervisory Control And Data Acquisition
SEA	Securities and Exchange Act
SMB	Server Message Block
SVM	Support Vector Machine
UAS	Unmanned Aircraft System
UAV	Unmanned Aerial Vehicles
UUV	Unmanned Underwater Vehicles
UV	Unmanned Vehicles
VPN	Virtual Private Network

Index

Printed in the United States
by Baker & Taylor Publisher Services